Introduction to
United States International Taxation

Introduction to

United States

International Taxation

by

Paul R. McDaniel   *and*   **Hugh J. Ault**
Professor of Law   *Professor of Law*
New York University
  School of Law   *Boston College Law School*
New York, New York   *Newton, Massachusetts*

Fourth revised edition

The Hague • London • Boston

Published by Kluwer Law International,
P.O. Box 85889, 2508 CN The Hague, The Netherlands.

Sold and distributed in the U.S.A. and Canada
by Kluwer Law International,
675 Massachusetts Avenue, Cambridge, MA 02139, U.S.A.

In all other countries, sold and distributed
by Kluwer Law International,
P.O. Box 85889, 2508 CN The Hague, The Netherlands.

Library of Congress Cataloging-in-Publication Data on File

ISBN 9041106197
ISBN 904110626X (Student Edition)

Preface

The 1998 edition of Introduction to United States International Taxation, as did its predecessor editions, presents the basic principles and rules of the United States international tax system in a relatively brief and manageable form. We would emphasize the word "Introduction" in the title. The book is not intended to serve as an exhaustive treatise that discusses in depth the wealth of technical detail involved in applying US tax rules in an international context. Instead, the purpose is to provide an overview of the principles adopted by the US in taxing US or foreign individuals and corporations as they invest, work, or carry on a trade or business in the US or abroad.

The book seeks to provide a structural framework within which a US tax problem can be placed. As a general matter, tax practitioners outside the US whose clients have activities in the US will rely on their US tax advisors for technical advice on the US tax aspects of their clients' transactions. However, the book is intended to enable the foreign tax advisor to place the material he receives from his US counterpart in the overall structure of the US international tax system and thus be in a position better to evaluate the advice received and to relate it to his own tax system.

We have also found that the book has proven useful to professors and students both within and outside the US who desire to obtain a grasp of the fundamentals of US international tax principles and rules. The book can serve as a text or supplement to courses that deal in whole or in part with the US tax system.

In line with these objectives, we have included references to the Internal Revenue Code provisions under discussion and to the more important Treasury Regulations that are issued interpreting the statutory rules. In addition, we have also included significant administrative announcements of the Internal Revenue Service (Revenue Rulings and Revenue Procedures) as well as references to illustrative principal cases that have arisen. We realize that our readers abroad may not have access to the reference materials cited in the footnotes, although technology rapidly is rendering this assumption obsolete. Accordingly, we have attempted to insure that the text discussion of a provision is self-contained so that the reader will be able to obtain a general understanding of the matter under discussion without resort to the footnote references. On the other hand, we did feel it important to provide sufficient reference materials so that the tax practitioner, professor or student would have a starting point to examine in greater technical detail the explanation offered in the text.

The statutory references throughout the book are to the Internal Revenue Code of 1986, as amended, and are given without further explanation as, for example, "Section 954". References to particular revenue legislation are made by the year of enactment and typically do not include the full name of the legislation. Thus, for example, the Tax Reform Act of 1986 is referred to as the "1986 Act" and the Taxpayer Relief Act of 1997 as the "1997 Act." The rapid acceleration of tax legislative change in the US during the 1980's and 1990's has required the use of numerous and highly important transition rules. As a general matter, transition rules are not discussed. Regulations issued by the Treasury Department in final form are cited, for example, "Treas. Reg. Sec. 1.954-1." Temporary Treasury Regulations, which are binding on taxpayers and tax administrators while in force, are cited, for example, "Temp. Treas. Reg. Sec. 1.263A-1T". Proposed Regulations, which may not be relied upon until made final, are cited, for example, "Prop. Treas. Reg. Sec. 1.904-1". Citations to the Internal Revenue Code and to the Treasury Regulations issued thereunder are current as of 1 December 1997.

We are indebted to Charles Rhett Shaver for research and editorial assistance and to Allan MacDonald for aid in preparing the manuscript for printing.

Hugh J. Ault   Paul R. McDaniel

Table of Contents

CHAPTER 9 – SPECIAL TREATMENT OF FOREIGN INCOME

Chapter 1
Introduction

This book is intended to provide an introduction to the application of the US income and wealth transfer tax systems to taxpayers investing or transacting business in the US and other countries. The bulk of the materials deals with the income tax since this is the tax that affects most directly the day-to-day conduct of business and investment affairs by individuals and corporations. The wealth transfer tax system is dealt with in less detail, both because within the US context it is a less fully developed tax than the income tax and because it is more limited in its application to international transactions. Other US taxes such as the social security tax, the unemployment tax, various excise taxes, tariff duties and State taxes are not considered in this book although, of course, it is possible for a particular taxpayer engaged in international transactions to encounter these taxes.

A grasp of the basic structure of the US income tax system as it is applied in its purely domestic context is essential to an understanding of the US international income tax system. These basic rules are always applied to US citizens and corporations in their international transactions and to foreign individuals or corporations engaged in a trade or business or investing in the US. Accordingly, Chapter 2 provides an overview of the US income tax system, briefly describing the corporation income tax, the individual income tax, the tax treatment of partnerships, trusts and estates and accounting aspects of the US income tax. The purpose of the general description is to provide a structural framework against which the international tax rules may be considered. Where particular provisions have special significance in the international context, they are only cursorily considered in Chapter 2, with more detailed analysis deferred until subsequent chapters. This approach is adopted, for example, in the case of the provisions dealing with the various forms of tax-free corporate reorganizations (considered in Chapter 7).

The basic jurisdictional principles adopted by the US with respect to application of its income tax to international investment and business transactions are considered in Chapters 3 and 4. These provisions are fundamental and cut across all the situations dealt with in subsequent chapters. That is, the basic provisions governing jurisdiction and the source of income are applied alike to

US taxpayers investing, working, or carrying on a trade or business abroad and to foreign individuals and corporations investing, earning income, or carrying on a trade or business in the US.

Chapter 5 then turns to the specific application of the income tax to foreign corporations and nonresident alien individuals. The material in this chapter examines the US rules for taxing foreign corporations, foreign partnerships, foreign trusts and nonresident aliens on their business and investment income derived from US sources. Procedural aspects in the application of the tax are also considered.

The basic mechanism adopted by the US to alleviate international double taxation on foreign source income derived by US persons is the foreign tax credit. The credit is discussed in detail in Chapter 6.

Historically, one of the most controversial aspects of the US international tax structure has been the income tax treatment of foreign corporations controlled by the US shareholders. These provisions are contained in "subpart F" of the Internal Revenue Code. The operation of subpart F and the role it plays in the overall US international income tax structure are discussed in Chapter 7, along with other provisions applicable to controlled foreign corporations, foreign investment companies and foreign trusts.

The general intercompany pricing rules of section 482 and special transfer pricing rules applicable to particular transactions, which are of importance to multinational corporations, are discussed in Chapter 8.

Special rules intended to provide incentives for increased US exports are considered in Chapter 9, including those dealing with the foreign sales corporation (FSC) and the taxation of income earned abroad by US individuals.

The US has adopted a comprehensive set of rules for the treatment of transactions involving currencies other than the US dollar. Those provisions are taken up in Chapter 10.

Chapter 11 then turns to a consideration of the income tax treaties entered into by the United States to resolve on a bilateral basis aspects of the application of the tax systems of the treaty countries to particular transactions, types of income and categories of taxpayers. The basic approach of the US in its income tax treaties is considered. Particular emphasis is placed on typical treaty provisions, especially those contained in the US Model Treaty, that deal with the matters considered in Chapters 3 through 10 and on the scope of and limitations on treaty benefits. The purpose of this discussion is to examine those situations in which US income tax treaty provisions modify the basic rules discussed in the preceding chapters.

Chapter 12 deals with the US wealth transfer tax system. As in the case of the income tax, a very general description is provided of the US wealth transfer tax system. The jurisdictional bases of the tax are considered. Then the three separate transfer taxes — estate tax, gift tax, and generation-skipping tax — are examined in their application to transfers of property owned abroad by US citizens and property owned in the US by nonresident alien individuals. Estate and gift tax treaties entered into by the US are also discussed, again with the focus centering on the situations in which the treaty provisions modify the otherwise applicable wealth transfer tax rules.

Chapter 2
The US income tax system: general description

2.1 Introduction

2.1.1 SCOPE

Sections 2.2 and 2.4 to 2.6 of this Chapter outline basic principles of the US income tax system as it applies to corporations, partnerships, trusts and certain hybrid entities. An important initial determination is the proper classification for income tax purposes of a particular entity. Under US rules, an entity may be classified as a corporate entity for substantive law purposes but the owners may elect to have it treated as a partnership for US income tax purposes. In addition, once entity classification has been resolved, it is also necessary to determine whether, under US rules, the entity will be classified as domestic or foreign.

Section 2.3 of this Chapter discusses the US tax system as it applies to individuals. For individuals, of course, the only classification issue is domestic (US citizen or resident) versus foreign (nonresident aliens).

The domestic versus foreign classification tests for individuals and entities are considered at relevant points in subsequent chapters. The discussion in 2.1.2 focuses on the rules used by the US to classify an entity, whether domestic or foreign, as a corporation, partnership or trust.

2.1.2 CLASSIFICATION ISSUES

The US corporate income tax applies to an entity, either foreign or domestic, that is a "corporation" as determined under Treasury Regulations issued in 1996 (the so-called "check-the-box" regulations).[1]

---

1. Treas. Reg. Sec. 301.7701-2(b). Prior to 1996, the Regulations used a six-part test to determine whether an entity should be classified as an association taxable as a corporation, a partnership or a trust: (1) the existence of associates; (2) an object to carry on a business for profit; (3) continuity of life; (4) centralization of management; (5) limited liability; and (6) free transferability of interests. An entity was classified as a corporation if it had three or more of characteristics (3)-(6) and a partnership if it had two or less. For a discussion of these tests, see the Third Edition of this book at pages 5-6.

Under the Regulations, certain entities are always classified as corporations. In the domestic context these include, among others, entities incorporated under state corporate law and insurance companies.[2] In the foreign context, the Regulations first list entities organized under the laws of various countries which always will be classified as corporations, e.g., an *Aktiengesellschaft* in Germany and a *Société Anonyme* in France.[3].

Next, if an entity is not classified as a corporation under the above rules, its owner(s) may elect to have the entity classified and hence taxed either as a corporation, a partnership or a division (branch) depending on whether there are two or more owners or only one.[4] In the default of an election, a US entity (other than one always classified as a corporation) with two or more owners is classified as a partnership. Hence, the owner(s) of an entity need make an election only if they desire to have it taxed as a corporation.[5] A foreign entity, other than one that is always classified as a corporation under the above rules, is classified as a partnership if it has two or more owners and at least one of them does not have limited liability or as a corporation if all of its owners have limited liability.[6] Again, then, owners of a foreign entity need make an election only if they desire a classification other than that provided by the default rules, e.g., if the entity is classified as a corporation but the owner(s) desires to have it classified as a partnership or branch. In the international context, one result of the elective regime is likely to be an increased number of situations in which the US classifies an entity as a partnership or branch and another country classifies it as a corporation, or vice versa, so-called hybrid entities. The treaty aspects of hybrid entities are discussed at 11.4.1.2.

2.2 The corporation income tax

2.2.1 TAX RATES

Corporations are subject to graduated tax rates on the first $100,000 of taxable income: fifteen per cent on the first $50,000 of taxable income, and 34 percent on the next $25,000. A 35 per cent rate is imposed on taxable income in excess

---

2. Treas. Reg. Sec. 301.7701-2(b)(1)-(7).
3. The entire list is set forth in Treas. Reg. Sec. 301.7701-2(b)(8)(i). A foreign entity that properly was classified as a partnership prior to May 8, 1996 continues to be classified as such if the requirements of Treas. Reg. Sec. 301.7701-2(d) are met.
4. Treas. Reg. Sec. 301.7701-2(c).
5. Treas. Reg. Sec. 301.7701-3(a),(b)(1).
6. Treas. Reg. Sec. 301.7701-3(b)(2). The determination whether an owner has limited liability is made by reference to the law of the country under which the entity is organized.

of $100,000.[7] The two lower rates are phased-out beginning at $100,000 of taxable income so that corporations with taxable income in excess of $18,333,333 are taxed at a flat 35 per cent rate on all taxable income

2.2.2 THE TAX BASE

The corporate tax rates are applied to *taxable income*. The starting point in computing taxable income is *gross income* (gross receipts minus the cost of goods sold). In general, no distinction is made between sources or categories of income. From this figure are subtracted the allowable *deductions*. The difference is taxable income.[8]

2.2.2.1 *Gross income*

Most receipts constitute gross income to a corporation. The notable exceptions are interest from state and local bonds, life insurance proceeds, contributions to the capital of the corporation, cancellation of indebtedness income under certain circumstances and gifts or bequests.[9]

2.2.2.2 *Deductible expenditures*

The deductions allowed in arriving at taxable income fall into two broad classifications:
1. those deductions that constitute costs of producing income for the year in question, with accounting and economic principles providing the norms for determining the proper amount;
2. special deductions that are permitted to be taken in amounts in excess of those otherwise allowable for the year under the principles developed in classification one above.
In the first classification, the principal deductions are for the ordinary and necessary expenses incurred in a trade or business (wages, overhead, advertising, etc.), contributions to employee retirement plans, interest incurred for trade or business, taxes and depreciation (declining balance method for machinery and

---

7. Sec. 11.
8. Sec. 61, 63(a).
9. In the case of non-shareholder contributions to capital, the corporation must, as the corollary to nonrecognition of income, reduce its tax basis (see note 14) in corporation assets. Sec. 362(c). As to shareholder non-cash contributions to capital, the corporation takes as its basis the basis of the property (other than cash) in the hands of the contributor. Sec. 362. Income from the cancellation of debt is exempt only if the taxpayer is in a bankruptcy proceeding or is insolvent. Sec. 108(a). The exemption is coupled with a reduction in specified tax attributes such as net operating loss carryovers and basis. Sec. 108(b).

equipment; straight-line method for improved real estate).[10] Losses on business assets are deductible when the asset is disposed of or becomes totally worthless.[11] Similar rules apply to bad debts.[12] In the case of inventory a loss may be deducted for a decline in value.[13] Capital expenditures — outlays the benefits of which extend beyond the year the costs are incurred or which create a new asset — must be added to the cost basis[14] of the asset to which they relate and recovered over the prescribed period for the asset either through annual depreciation (or amortization) deductions or, in the case of certain nondepreciable assets, upon ultimate sale of the asset (through decreased taxable gain or increased deductible loss).[15]

In the second classification are a large number of provisions that permit certain capital expenditures to be recovered for tax purposes more rapidly than would be allowed under the principles applicable to items in classification one. The total amount deductible is not changed; but the timing of the deductions is altered. Various techniques are employed to accelerate the deductions.

In some cases, the entire capital cost may be deducted in the year paid or incurred. Principal examples of such items are intangible drilling and development costs incurred by companies involved in oil and gas drilling and development; research and development expenditures; circulation costs incurred by newspapers or other periodicals; certain expenditures to remove architectural barriers to the handicapped and the elderly; and costs incurred to abate or control toxic substances which have contaminated sites determined to be environmentally hazardous.[16]

In other situations, capital expenditures are permitted to be amortized and deducted over an arbitrary period — usually five years — even though the useful life of the asset to which the expenditure relates is longer (or indeterminate). Examples of costs that qualify for special five-year amortization include those for start-up of a new trade or business, organization of a corporation or partnership, and constructing pollution control facilities.[17] The costs of purchased intangible assets such as goodwill may be amortized over a fifteen-year period.[18]

---

10. *See* in general Sec. 162-168, 401-415.
11. Sec. 165.
12. Sec. 166. In some cases, a deduction for partial worthlessness is allowed.
13. Treas. Reg. Sec. 1.471-4.
14. "Cost basis", as the name implies, is the original cost of the asset. Sec. 1012. This figure is adjusted for various items during the time the asset is held, e.g. the cost basis is reduced by depreciation or increased by capital improvements. Sec. 1016. The "adjusted basis" thus is a kind of running balance of the tax attributes of an asset.
15. Sec. 263(a). Sec. 263A provides detailed rules for the capitalization of costs, including interest expenses, to self-produced or constructed assets and inventory.
16. *See,* respectively, Sec. 263(c), 174, 173, 190, and 198.
17. *See,* respectively, Sec. 195, 248, 709, and 169.
18. Sec. 197.

Other techniques adopted by the US to permit more rapid recovery of asset costs than would be available under normal depreciation rules are to provide accelerated rates of depreciation for certain assets or to provide time periods over which depreciation may be taken which are shorter than the economic useful life of the property. Thus, tangible personal property, i.e. machinery, equipment, etc. is depreciated at a rate not in excess of 200 per cent of the rate that would have been used had the depreciation deduction been computed under the straight-line method.[19] Some acceleration of depreciation deductions for commercial real estate and residential rental property is provided by permitting the costs of such property to be depreciated over 39 and 27.5 years, respectively, rather than over the useful life of the property. Shorter depreciation time periods are also provided for tangible personal property.[20]

Another important deduction concerns intercorporate dividends. Dividends received by a corporation on stock of another corporation are includible in income. A deduction is then granted to the payee corporation equal to 70 per cent of the dividend received if the payee corporation owns less than 20 per cent of the stock of the payor corporation, 80 per cent of the dividend received if the payee corporation owns twenty per cent or more of the payor corporation, and 100 per cent of the dividend received if the payor and payee corporations are members of an affiliated group, i.e. subject to 80 per cent common control.[21]

2.2.2.3   Expenditures not deductible

A few expenditures are disallowed as deductions. In some cases, a deduction is not permitted because the expenditure incurred often may constitute a disguised dividend. Principal examples include amounts paid as "excessive compensation"; premiums for life insurance on the life of any officer or shareholder of the corporation if the corporation is the beneficiary under the policy; certain travel and entertainment costs; nonemployee corporate gifts in excess of $25 per donee; and fifty per cent of certain costs involving meals or entertainment.[22] In addition, losses incurred in sales or exchanges between related taxpayers, such as a corporation and a shareholder owning 50 per cent or more of the stock of the corporation (or between two corporations owned by such a shareholder), are not deductible.[23]

Deductions are also disallowed where the expenditures constitute a cost of producing tax-exempt income (including interest incurred to purchase or carry

---

19. Sec. 168(a) and (b).
20. Sec. 168(c)(1).
21. Sec. 243(a) and (b)(2)(A).
22. *See,* respectively, Sec. 162(a)(1), 264 and 274(n).
23. Sec. 267.

tax-exempt state and local bonds).[24] In this category too may be placed the limitation on the deductibility of interest incurred in making certain acquisitions of the stock or assets of another corporation (dividends from the acquired corporation being in general nontaxable).[25]

In other instances, deductions are disallowed for nontax policy reasons. Examples include the limitation on deductible charitable contributions to ten per cent of taxable income; limitations imposed on costs of lobbying; the denial of deduction for "golden parachute" payments made to executives and other costs of a target corporation in corporate takeover situations; and the denial of a deduction for executive compensation in excess of $1 million per year.[26]

2.2.2.4 *Special limitations on tax shelter losses and interest deductions*

Limitations are imposed on the deductibility of losses from activities in which the taxpayer is a passive investor. These rules are intended to limit the benefits of "tax shelter" transactions. Although the rules apply to closely held corporations and personal service corporations, their primary impact is on individuals and they are discussed at 2.3.2.5.3. Numerous and stringent limitations also are imposed on the deductibility of interest expense. Again, individual taxpayers are primarily affected and the rules are considered at 2.3.2.5.2.

2.2.2.5 *Net operating loss carryforward and carryback*

If the corporation's deductions for the year exceed its income, the resulting "net operating loss" can be carried back against the income of the preceding two years and, if not exhausted by the carryback, carried forward for twenty years.[27] Special carryback and carryover periods are provided for specific categories of losses.[28]

2.2.3 CAPITAL GAINS AND LOSSES

Unlike individuals, sales or exchanges of "capital assets" by corporations do not qualify for a special tax rate. Capital gains realized by corporations are subject to the general 35 per cent rate. Capital gain or loss classification can be im-

---

24. Sec. 265.
25. Sec. 279. The acquisition must involve convertible securities.
26. *See,* respectively, Sec. 170(b)(2), 162(e), 280G, 162(m).
27. Sec. 172(b)(1)(A) and (B).
28. For example, at the taxpayer's election, product liability losses may be carried back for a ten-year period and casualty losses are carried back for a three-year period in lieu of the normal carryback period described in the text. Sec. 172(b)(1)(C), (F).

portant for purposes of recovering basis in certain taxable transactions and for imposing limitations on the deductibility of capital losses. Thus, capital losses may be deducted only against capital gains. If capital losses exceed capital gains, in general the excess can be carried back three years and forward five years.[29]

"Capital assets" include tangible and intangible assets owned by a corporation other than (1) inventory, (2) property held primarily for sale to customers in the ordinary course of business, (3) copyrights, and (4) accounts receivable.[30]

Depreciable property is not a capital asset under the basic definition. Section 1231, however, provides that if the total transactions for the year concerning such property result in a net gain, that gain is treated as a capital gain. If a net loss is produced, an ordinary loss deduction results.

However, gain that would otherwise qualify as capital gain under Section 1231 may be treated as ordinary income if one of the various "recapture" provisions is applicable. Thus, under Section 1245, the gain on the sale of depreciable personal property (e.g. machinery and equipment) is taxed as ordinary income to the extent of depreciation previously taken with respect to the property. That is, despite Section 1231, the prior depreciation deductions are recognized as ordinary income upon sale at a gain (because the sale at a gain has demonstrated that the taxpayer's prior depreciation deductions exceeded economic depreciation). Similar recapture rules apply to gain on the sale of certain depreciable real estate placed in service before 1987, oil and gas interests as to which the deduction for intangible drilling and development costs has been taken, and farm land with respect to which certain special deductions or exclusions have been claimed.[31] Given that no preferential tax rate is provided for capital gains realized by corporations, the only significance of the recapture provisions is that capital losses cannot be deducted against recapture income and, in some cases, characterization of gain as recapture income can accelerate the timing of gain recognition.

Certain sales or exchanges of capital assets are tax-free. For example, no tax is imposed on gain realized on exchanges of like-kind property (involving properties other than corporate stock, notes, etc.) or on gain realized on an involuntary conversion of property (e.g. through condemnation by the government, fire, etc.) if the proceeds received are reinvested in similar property.[32] In each case, the corollary of non-recognition of gain is that the property acquired takes the same tax basis as that of the property transferred (the so-called "ex-

---

29. Sec. 1211,1212. Generally, the capital gain and loss rules apply only to transactions which constitute a "sale or exchange," Sec. 1222, although provisions such as Sec. 1034A deem a sale or exchange to exist in situations where an actual sale or exchange may not be present. Congress increasingly has subjected sophisticated financial transactions and dealers in stocks to constructive realization regimes. *See, e.g.,* Sec. 475, 1256, 1259.
30. Sec. 1221.
31. Sec. 1250, 1254, 1252 and 1255.
32. Sec. 1031,1033.

changed basis" rule). As a result, the "tax-free" exchanges are actually tax-deferred exchanges, since the gain will be recognized on the ultimate sale or exchange of the property acquired.

2.2.4 CREDITS AGAINST TAX

The tax rates prescribed in Section 11 are applied to taxable income determined under the foregoing rules. Against the resulting tax liability, however, certain credits are allowed. Again, the credits are of two types.

The first group of tax credits includes those that are structural in nature. Included are the credits for taxes paid to other countries and for withheld taxes paid to the US on amounts paid to nonresident aliens or foreign corporations.[33]

In the second group are credits provided to encourage or subsidize particular activities. The most important of these for corporations is the general business tax credit. This credit in turn is the sum of a number of separate tax credits, each of which provides a tax credit equal to a specific percentage of qualifying costs.[34] The amount of the allowable credit is limited to the greater of the corporation's minimum tax liability (see 2.2.5) or 25% of the corporation's regular income tax liability in excess of $25,000.[35] Allowable credits in excess of the limits may be carried back one year and forward twenty years.[36]

The tax credits that make up the general business credit include twelve different credits, among which are:

(1) a work opportunity credit for corporations that employ workers who are members of specified "target" groups which have experienced chronic unemployment or who have been on state or federal welfare rolls;[37]

(2) credits for certain investments in qualified energy conservation or conversion property or in qualified alternative energy property, such as solar or wind energy devices;[38]

(3) a credit for the cost of producing alcohol-based fuel;[39]

(4) a credit for investment in low-income housing projects.[40]

---

33. Sec. 27, 33.
34. Sec. 38(a),(b).
35. Sec. 38(c).
36. Sec. 39.
37. Sec. 51. The normal deduction for wages paid to such workers must be reduced by the amount of the work opportunity credit claimed by a taxpayer. Sec. 280C. The mathematical result of this reduction is the same as if the amount of the tax credit were included in taxable income. A "temporary" tax credit also is provided to employers of long term welfare payment recipients. Sec. 51A.
38. Sec. 46, 48.
39. Sec. 40. The amount of this credit is directly included in taxable income. Sec. 87.
40. Sec. 42.

A tax credit also is provided for incrementally increasing costs for qualified research activity.[41]

2.2.5   ALTERNATIVE MINIMUM TAX: CORPORATIONS

2.2.5.1   *Background*

Since 1969, the US has imposed a minimum tax — albeit in various forms — on corporations. The general thrust of the minimum tax has been to bring back into the tax base tax-favored items of income and deduction which a given taxpayer has been deemed to have been using in excess. A taxpayer subject to the minimum tax thus has the value of tax preferences for which it has qualified reduced or eliminated.

The alternative minimum tax (AMT) was given its present structure in 1982. Subsequent legislation expanded its scope, and these developments, combined with the narrowing of the gap between the "regular tax" top rate (35 per cent) and the AMT rate (twenty per cent), have converted the AMT from a stop-gap measure against excessive use of tax preferences into a nearly complete income tax system that exists side-by-side with the regular tax system previously described. The AMT system employs a single flat rate lower than the regular tax rate, but it is applied to a tax base that more closely approximates economic income. Accordingly, many corporate taxpayers find themselves subject to the AMT, a fact which affects both domestic corporations and foreign corporations doing business in the US.

2.2.5.2   *The AMT base*

The AMT tax base is calculated by beginning with taxable income, determined as described in 2.2.2. The taxable income figure is then increased as the result of certain "adjustments". The most significant of these adjustments are:
  (1) The depreciation rate for tangible personal property is reduced from 200 per cent to 150 per cent.[42]
  (2) An alternative net operating loss deduction is provided which limits the amount of such deductions to 90 per cent of alternative minimum taxable income (AMTI) determined without regard to the deduction.[43]
  (3) An "adjusted current earnings" (ACE) adjustment requires that a corporation increase its AMTI by 75 per cent of the amount, if any, by which its ACE exceeds its AMTI (determined without regard to the ACE and

---

41. Sec. 41.
42. Sec. 56(a)(1)(A)(ii).
43. Sec. 56(a)(4), (d).

net operating loss adjustments).[44] The result of the ACE adjustment is to bring into the AMT base items excluded from the regular tax base.

After the above adjustments have been made, certain items of tax preference are then required to be added to AMTI. These items include tax preferences granted to the oil and gas industry and otherwise tax-free interest on certain state and local bonds issued for the benefit of private businesses.[45]

Once the adjustments and tax preferences have been added to regular taxable income, AMTI has been determined. A $40,000 exemption is then allowed to corporations, but the exemption is phased out if the corporation's AMTI exceeds $150,000. Once a corporation's AMTI exceeds $310,000, no exemption is available.[46] In addition, the AMT does not apply at all to "small corporations," those which had average gross receipts for the preceding three-year period of less than $5 million and whose gross receipts do not exceed $7.5 million in any year after the three-year period test is met.[47]

2.2.5.3   AMT rate

For corporations, the AMT rate is a flat twenty per cent.[48]

2.2.5.4   Credit against AMT

Only the foreign tax credit may be used against the AMT but the allowable credit is limited to 90 per cent of AMT. Any excess may be carried back and forward.[49]

2.2.5.5   Final tax liability

If the AMT so computed exceeds the taxpayer's regular tax for the year, the excess is added to the taxpayer's regular tax to determine the taxpayer's final tax liability.[50]

2.2.5.6   Minimum tax credit

A taxpayer may be subject to the AMT system in some years and to the regular tax system in others. AMT tax liability may have arisen as the result of differ-

---

44. Sec. 56(c), (g)
45. Sec. 57.
46. Sec. 55(d)(2), (3).
47. Sec. 55(e)(1), (2).
48. Sec. 55(b)(1)(B).
49. Sec. 55(b)(1)(B), 59(a). For treaty aspects of the partial denial of the foreign tax credit, *see* 11.3.
50. Sec. 55(a).

ences in treatment of timing items (e.g. depreciation) in the two systems. It would thus be possible for a taxpayer to be subject to AMT and to regular tax on the same item of income. To prevent this result, a tax credit is provided for AMT incurred with respect to timing (but not exclusion) items which may be carried over and taken in a year when the taxpayer is subject to regular tax liability.[51] In these timing situations, the twenty per cent AMT thus serves as a prepayment on the 35 per cent regular tax ultimately due.

2.2.6 TRANSACTIONS BETWEEN CORPORATIONS AND SHAREHOLDERS

Under US tax rules, a corporation is an entity separate and distinct from its shareholders. As a result, corporate earnings are taxed to the corporation; distributions from the corporation are taxed to the individual shareholders.

The *formation* of a corporation is generally accomplished tax-free. That is, the transfer of property to a corporation results in no current tax to the shareholders if the transferor-shareholders are in control (80 per cent) of the corporation immediately after the transfer. The corporation realizes no gain on the issuance of its stock. The shareholders have a tax basis in their stock equal to the aggregate bases of the property transferred to the corporation.[52]

Distributions of cash or property by a corporation to its shareholders constitute taxable dividends to the shareholders to the extent of the corporation's earnings and profits (current and accumulated).[53] In general terms, "earnings and profits" (a technical tax concept) correspond closely to the accounting concept of "earned surplus" of a corporation.[54] If the corporation distributes property with a fair market value in excess of basis, the corporation must recognize gain as if it had sold the property to the distributee. As a result, taxable income is realized both at the corporate level and at the shareholder level in such transactions.[55]

---

51. Sec. 53.
52. Sec. 351, 358, 362,1032. Property other than stock and certain types of preferred stock (so-called "boot") do not qualify for tax-free treatment and the value of such property or stock is taxable to the recipient shareholder. Sec. 351(b), (g), 356(a),(e).
53. Sec. 316. Dividends paid are not deductible by the corporation but interest paid on corporate debt is deductible. This distinction places enormous pressure on classifying sophisticated securities as debt or equity. The resolution of the issue is a factual matter ultimately resolved by the courts. In some instances, Congress has provided statutory rules, or authorization for Treasury regulations, to limit the deductibility of "interest" where the security involved and/or characteristics of the corporation cause the security to appear more like equity than debt. See Sec. 385, 163(e),(j), and (l). The debt-equity problem is intractable in a classical (non-integrated) corporate/shareholder tax regime such as that employed by the US where the corporation is treated as a taxable entity separate from its shareholders.
54. Sec. 312.
55. Sec. 311(b), 61.

For both individual and corporate shareholders, the amount of the dividend is the cash or fair market value of the property distributed. If the distribution is not out of earnings and profits, then the shareholder reduces basis in his stock by the amount of the dividend and, if the distribution is in excess of that basis, such excess is taxed as capital gain income. For corporate shareholders, a dividend received deduction is provided, as noted at 2.2.2.2.[56]

In general, a distribution of the corporation's own stock (a "stock dividend") is nontaxable to the shareholder. However, in a number of situations involving changes in a corporation's capital structure, the receipt of a stock dividend, actual or deemed, does constitute ordinary income to the shareholder.[57]

A *redemption* of stock (i.e. a purchase by the corporation of its own stock from a shareholder) results in capital gain to the redeemed shareholder provided that the distribution by the corporation is not essentially equivalent to a dividend. Rules are provided for determining whether a particular distribution falls on the ordinary dividend or on the capital gain side of the line. As in the case of a dividend distribution, the transfer of appreciated property by a corporation to redeem its own stock will give rise to recognition of gain by the distributing corporation.[58]

Distributions in *partial* or *complete liquidation* of a corporation also are treated as *exchanges* which qualify for capital gains treatment to individual shareholders. Again, the corporation recognizes gain on the distribution of appreciated property in liquidation.[59] The liquidation of an 80 per cent owned subsidiary is tax-free to the corporate parent and the subsidiary; correspondingly, the parent takes a transferred basis in the assets acquired in the liquidation.[60]

The Code permits a variety of corporate *reorganizations* to be effected on a tax-free basis. In general, these provisions are designed to permit business transactions involving certain corporate readjustments to be consummated without a tax being incurred by the participating corporations or their shareholders at the time of the transaction. The theory of these provisions is that the readjustments, while they may produce changes in the structure of a business enterprise, do not involve such fundamental changes in the nature or character of the relation of the owners of the enterprise to the assets of the enterprise as to warrant a tax on the accrued gain or allowance of a loss deduction. The nonrecognition provisions cover a wide range of transactions ranging from statu-

---

56. Sec. 301(b)-(c), 243.
57. Sec. 305. *See also* Sec. 306 as to the treatment of preferred stock distributed by a corporation.
58. Sec. 302, 311(b). *See also* Sec. 304 which provides ordinary income treatment on gain resulting from purchases by one corporation of stock in a second corporation that is controlled by the same shareholders who control the purchasing corporation.
59. Sec. 302(b)(4), 311, 331, 336.
60. Sec. 332, 337, 334(b)(1).

tory mergers to exchanges of stock for stock, stock for assets, recapitalizations of a single corporation, or a mere change in the form or name of the corporation.

In a qualifying reorganization, neither the shareholders of the corporations involved nor the corporations themselves recognize any gain or loss. As a corollary, special basis rules are required to reflect the nonrecognition of gain. In general, the shareholders substitute the basis in their old stock as the basis in the new stock. At the corporation level, assets acquired in a reorganization carry over the same basis to the acquiring corporation as they had in the hands of the transferring corporation. In certain types of reorganizations, the receipt of cash or other property is permitted in addition to the receipt of stock in the acquiring corporation. In such cases, the cash or value of other property is taxed at the time of the reorganization, the gain generally being classified as capital gain.[61]

Special rules are also provided to permit certain tax-free divisions of existing corporations. These rules are quite restrictive since corporate divisions present the possibility that cash and other liquid assets may be distributed to shareholders as capital gains rather than as ordinary dividend income.[62]

In qualifying acquisitive reorganizations, special rules are provided to carry over the corporate attributes of the transferring corporation to the acquiring corporation, such as its earnings and profits account and net operating loss carryovers.[63]

The reorganization provisions are discussed in greater detail in 7.3.1.2 where reorganizations involving US and foreign corporations are considered.

Consolidated returns may be filed by corporate groups where the parent corporation owns at least 80 per cent of the stock of its subsidiary corporations. Under the consolidated return rules, income and deductions of the various members of the group are consolidated and the net income of the group is subject to tax. Dividends within the corporate group are not taxable. Regulations provide detailed rules for the tax treatment of inter-company transactions.[64] A foreign corporation in general may not be a member of a consolidated return group and, therefore, the significance of the consolidated return rules is limited to domestic corporate groups.[65]

---

61. *See* Sec. 354, 356-358, 361-362; *Commissioner v. Clark*, 489 US 726 (1989).
62. Sec. 368(a)(1)(D), 355.
63. Sec. 381. Strict limitations are imposed on the deductibility of net operating loss carryovers by an acquiring corporation, whether in a taxable or tax-free acquisition, by Sec. 382-384 and 269.
64. The consolidated return rules are contained almost entirely in Treasury Regulations which have nearly the same authority as a Code provision. *See* Treas. Reg. Sec. 1. 1502-1 and following for the highly complex rules governing consolidated returns.
65. However, a foreign taxpayer may own the stock of a US parent which in turn has US subsidiaries and the US group may file a consolidated return.

2.2.7 PENALTY TAXES

2.2.7.1 Accumulated earnings tax

During most of US tax history, the top corporate rate has been lower than the top individual rate. As a result, the total tax burden on the corporation and its shareholders could be minimized by retaining profits in the corporation for as long as possible before subjecting them to the second tax at the shareholder level. In order to discourage such accumulations, Sections 531-537 were adopted and impose an "accumulated earnings tax" on certain corporate retentions. The tax is applied to every corporation "formed or availed of for the purpose of avoiding the income tax with respect to its shareholders . . . by permitting earnings and profits to accumulate [beyond the reasonable needs of the business] instead of being divided or distributed." The determination of the reasonable needs of the business involves a complex factual inquiry into all aspects of the corporation's business.[66] US corporations with foreign shareholders and foreign corporations with US shareholders are subject to the tax, although in the latter case only with respect to the corporation's US source income. Foreign corporations doing business in the US which have only foreign shareholders generally are not subject to the tax. (*See* 5.5.8.1.)

2.2.7.2 Personal holding company tax

The US, since 1934, has had a special set of provisions dealing with accumulations by personal holding companies, so-called "incorporated pocketbooks". The provisions are intended to force dividend distributions which are subject to the higher individual rates.[67]

Under the personal holding company tax provisions, a penalty tax is imposed on the "undistributed personal holding company income" of a corporation which qualifies as a personal holding company. Personal holding company income in general consists of dividends, interest, royalties, annuities, and certain rents. The personal holding company provisions are directed at closely held corporations which, in terms of the statute, means that five or fewer individuals must own (directly or by attribution) more than 50 per cent of the stock of the corporation. Corporations which run afoul of the personal holding company tax can avoid the tax by payment of a so-called "deficiency dividend". The deficiency dividend can be deducted at the corporate level and hence will elimi-

---

66. *See, e.g., Bardahl Mfg. Corp. v. Commissioner,* T.C. Memo 1965-200.
67. The personal holding company tax rules are contained in Sec. 541-547. A corporation can be used as an investment vehicle and avoid any problems under the personal holding company tax if the corporation is subject to single level taxation under Subchapter S. *See* 2.5.

nate the personal holding company penalty tax liability. The shareholders correspondingly include the deficiency dividend in income.[68]

The personal holding company tax can apply to any US corporation regardless of the source of its income and regardless of whether a significant part or all of its shareholders are foreign. The application of the penalty tax to foreign corporations investing in the US is considered at 5.5.8.2.

2.3　The individual income tax

2.3.1　TAX RATES

Individuals are subject to marginal tax rates ranging from 15 per cent to 39.6 per cent. Separate rate schedules are provided for married couples filing joint returns, married couples filing separate returns, heads of households, and single persons. The brackets for heads of household (generally involved where a single parent maintains a household with dependent children) are about halfway between those for joint returns and single persons. The rate brackets are adjusted annually for inflation.[69]

2.3.2　THE TAX BASE

The individual tax rates are applied to *taxable income*. The starting point in computing taxable income is *gross income* (gross receipts minus the cost of goods sold). From this figure are first subtracted allowable *business deductions* and certain *adjustments* to arrive at *adjusted gross income*. From adjusted gross income are then subtracted certain *personal deductions*. The taxpayer is then allowed a deduction for *personal exemptions* to arrive at the final figure for taxable income.

2.3.2.1　*Gross income*

Gross income includes income "from whatever source derived".[70] However, as discussed in 2.2.2.1 certain statutory exceptions are provided. The principal exclusions are interest on state and local bonds; contributions to and income earned by qualified employee retirement plans and the value of certain other fringe benefits of employees; the accrued gain in property transferred by gift or bequest; receipts of gifts, bequests and proceeds of life insurance; compensation for injuries or sickness; certain scholarships and fellowship grants; and all

---

68. Sec. 561-565.
69. Sec. 1(a)-(c), (f).
70. Sec. 61.

or part of the gain on the sale or exchange of residences.[71] By administrative action, benefits paid under certain programs to further social welfare objectives of the government are also excluded from gross income.

2.3.2.2   Capital gains and losses

As a result of the 1997 Act, there is a maze of preferential rules applicable to gains realized on the sale or exchange of a "capital asset" by an individual. In simplified form the preferential capital gain regime is as follows:[72]

(1) The general rule is that gain realized on the sale of a capital asset held for more than eighteen months is taxed at a maximum 20 percent rate. This rate benefits all taxpayers for whom rates above 20 percent would apply if the gain were taxed like "ordinary income" such as compensation or investment income. For individuals in the 15 percent rate bracket, the capital gain rate is reduced to 10 percent.

(2) Capital assets held for more than one year but not more than 18 months and so-called "collectibles" are subject to a 28 percent maximum rate (thus benefitting only taxpayers whose ordinary income is taxed at rates higher than 28 percent).

(3) Beginning in 2001, the 20 and 10 percent rates in (1) are reduced to 18 and 8 percent respectively if the asset sold has been held by the taxpayer for more than five years. But since the provision applies only to assets acquired after the year 2000, taxpayers are given the election to treat capital assets as having been sold on January 1, 2001 and recognize gains (but not losses) on those assets. If the election is made, the five-year holding period begins running on that date.[73]

(4) Gain on the sale of depreciable real estate is taxed at a 25 percent rate to the extent that gain is attributable to prior depreciation deductions which reduced basis and at a 20% rate on the balance of any gain.

(5) One-half of the gain realized on the sale of qualified "small business stock" is excluded from income. The balance of the gain is taxed at a maximum 28% rate (thus providing a maximum 14% rate on the total gain). The taxpayer can avoid current gain recognition if within 60 days she reinvests the sales proceeds from qualified "small business stock"

---

71. The provisions excluding receipts from gross income appear generally in Sec. 101 and following.
72. Sec. 1(h) sets forth rules for capital gains. The text summary masks the extraordinary complexity of the calculation required under Sec. 1(h). For a convenient description of these calculations, see Posin, *The Big Bear: Calculating Capital Gains After the 1997 Act*, 76 Tax Notes 1450 (1997).
73. For taxpayers in the 15% bracket, the five-year holding period begins on the date of acqusition, even if before 2001.

held for more than 6 months in qualified small business stock issued by another corporation.[74]

(6) If the asset sold is the taxpayer's principal residence, then gain up to $250,000 ($500,000 for married taxpayers) is excluded from income if specified conditions are met.[75]

(7) If the asset sold has been held for less than 12 months, the gain is taxed at the taxpayer's ordinary income tax rates.

The other capital gain rules described in 2.2.3 generally continue to apply to individuals, except that capital losses in excess of capital gains may not be carried back, but may be carried forward indefinitely.

Arguments for preferential treatment of capital gains on tax policy grounds generally are unconvincing and there is no discernible rationale at all for the preferential scheme described above. One clear result, however, is the addition of inordinate complexity in the Code.

2.3.2.3 Deductible expenditures — business and investment

For an individual, the deductions allowed from gross income in arriving at adjusted gross income generally are the same as those allowed to corporations described in 2.2.2.2 and 2.2.2.5.

In addition to the ordinary and necessary expenses of a trade or business, an individual is allowed as a deduction all ordinary and necessary expenses paid or incurred for the production or collection of income, and for the management, conservation, or maintenance of property held for the production of income.[76]

2.3.2.4   Expenditures not deductible

The group of expenditures that are disallowed as deductions, described in 2.2.2.3 above, are in general also disallowed as to individuals. In addition, individuals are denied deductions for personal, living, or family expenses except as provided in 2.3.2.6 below.[77]

---

74. Sec. 1202, 1045. Detailed requirements are imposed that must be met if a corporation's stock is to qualify as "small business stock." A taxpayer electing the rollover provision takes the same basis in the new stock as she had in the stock sold.

75. Sec. 121.

76. Sec. 212. Such costs, although costs of producing income, are technically deducted from adjusted gross income and then only to the extent they exceed two per cent of the taxpayer's adjusted gross income. Sec. 67.

77. Sec. 262.

2.3.2.5 *Special limitations on tax shelter losses and interest deductions*

2.3.2.5.1 Limitation of deductions to amount at risk

Under long-standing US rules, an individual is permitted to deduct currently costs incurred in engaging in a trade or business or investment activity even if borrowing represented the source of the invested funds. The same result held even if the borrowing was "nonrecourse", i.e. the lender agreed to look for repayment of the loan only from the property securing the loan and not from other assets of the borrower. Thus, for example, an individual who purchased a building entirely with borrowed funds which he had no obligation to repay personally could begin taking depreciation deductions before making any principal payments on the loan. This mismatch between investment and deductions was one of the foundations upon which "tax shelters" were created, especially when accelerated deductions were involved.

To deal with the above situation, "at risk" rules in general limit a taxpayer's current deductions from an activity to the amount by which the taxpayer's personal assets are at risk with respect to the activity. A taxpayer is at risk to the extent she has made an actual investment of cash or property or has borrowed on the basis of personal liability to invest in an activity. If the deductions from an activity for a current year exceed the taxpayer's at risk amount for that year, the excess cannot be deducted but must be deferred until future years when the taxpayer has increased her at risk amount (which can also be produced by the realization of net taxable income from the activity). As a result, deductions attributable to nonrecourse borrowing cannot, in general, be taken until principal payments are made on a nonrecourse loan. An important exception to the general rule is permitted in the case of real estate where nonrecourse borrowing from third party lending institutions is treated as at risk.

Although the at risk rules were developed in the context where current *accelerated* deductions were being generated by nonrecourse borrowing, the rules also apply to deny current deductions for the ordinary and necessary expenses of a trade or business to the extent the taxpayer is not at risk.[78]

2.3.2.5.2 Limitations on the deduction for interest expense

Prior to 1969, interest expense could (with certain rather limited exceptions)[79] be deducted without regard to the use which the taxpayer made of the borrowed funds. Subsequently, Congress imposed increasingly stringent limitations on

---

78. Sec. 465. Similar at-risk rules limit the current utilization of certain business tax credits. Sec. 49.

79. The principal exceptions were provisions that denied deductions for interest expense incurred to purchase or carry tax-exempt bonds (Sec. 265) or, in certain instances, to pay premiums on annuity or life insurance policies (Sec. 264).

the deductibility of interest expense. The limiting rules require allocation of interest expense to particular categories of income or activities and several different allocation methods are employed. The result is a set of rules which are based on no discernible rational principle for treating interest expenses in an income tax system.

The following discussion summarizes briefly the existing limitations.

1. *Trade or business interest* expense is deductible without regard to any of the limitations on interest expense.[80]

2. *Investment interest* expense can be deducted only to the extent of investment income for the taxable year; any excess is carried forward to future years when the taxpayer has investment income.[81]

3. *Passive activity interest* expense is limited by the rules discussed in 2.3.2.5.3.

4. *Qualified residence interest* is deductible in full. In general, interest on funds borrowed on the basis of a mortgage on the taxpayer's principal residence and on one secondary residence qualifies for full deductibility, although the total debt cannot exceed $1 million.[82]

5. *Personal interest* is interest other than that described in categories 1-4, above, and is nondeductible in its entirety.[83] Thus, interest incurred to purchase consumer durables, on income tax deficiencies, or to finance vacations is all nondeductible.

As a general rule, interest expense is placed in one of the above categories by *tracing* the borrowed funds. Thus, investment interest is determined by tracing borrowed funds into properties which generate investment income, e.g. dividends, interest, rents, and capital gains. Since money is fungible, the tracing approach to classification of interest expense requires a suspension of belief in economic reality as well as the imposition of complex administrative and record-keeping burdens on taxpayers and tax administrators.[84]

Other provisions impose separate limitations on different categories of interest expense. Thus, for example, Section 263A(f) requires that interest expense incurred during the production period of property (such as a building) be capitalized and added to the basis of the property. Under this provision, interest is allocated to the appropriate property under both a *tracing* and a *stacking* procedure. Debt that can be specifically traced to a particular activity must be allocated to it (e.g. a loan obtained to construct a building). If production

---

80. Sec. 163(a), (h)(2)(A).
81. Sec. 163(d).
82. Sec. 163(h)(2)(D),(3).
83. Sec. 163(h)(1)-(2). A limited deduction is allowed for interest expense on debt incurred to finance qualified higher education costs, an item that normally would be classified as personal interest. Sec. 221.
84. Temp. Treas. Reg. Sec. 1.163-8T,-9T and -1OT, provide rules for placing interest expense in the above categories and some simplifying procedures to ease administrative problems involved in the tracing approach.

expenditures exceed that amount of debt, then other debt of the taxpayer is allocated to the property (and interest thereon is required to be capitalized in that property). In other words, where a taxpayer is engaged in the production of long-lived properties, such as buildings, all debt of the taxpayer must first be stacked against the costs of producing that building to the extent of those costs.[85]

In other situations, important in the international context, interest expense is allocated on the theory that money is fungible and still different allocation rules are employed. *See* 4.4.3.1.

The above tabulation does not exhaust — although it may have exhausted the reader — the list of rules applicable to the treatment of interest expense. For example, complex rules are also employed to determine the amount of interest currently deductible with respect to debt obligations that are issued or purchased at a discount. *See* 2.7.

2.3.2.5.3 Limitations on the deduction of passive activity losses

Despite the at-risk rules, the limitations on investment interest, the alternative minimum tax, and the reduction in value of all tax preferences by the lowering of marginal tax rates, Congress in 1986 felt compelled to add still another set of provisions to impose further limitations on "tax shelters". These rules are contained in the provisions limiting the current deduction from passive activities to the amount of the taxpayer's passive activity income. In other words, deductions generated by passive activities cannot be used to "shelter" personal service, active trade or business, or portfolio investment income.[86] Any excess passive loss is carried over to be deducted in a subsequent year in which the taxpayer has passive income, including gains from the sale of the passive activity that itself generated the prior excess losses.

An "activity" is "passive" with respect to a taxpayer if it involves the rental of property or if it is a trade or business in which the taxpayer does not "materially participate". The quoted terms are defined in tortuous detail in the Code and Regulations.[87]

There are several noteworthy aspects to the passive activity loss regime. First, it requires allocation of deductions among several classifications of income. When coupled with the interest expense deduction rules discussed above, it can be seen that the US has overlaid its "global" system of income taxation with very substantial elements of a schedular system. This overlay has

---

85. *See* Treas. Reg. Sec. 1.263A-8 for the rules implementing the capitalization of interest requirements of Sec. 263.
86. Sec. 469. Similar limitations apply to tax credits generated by passive activities.
87. *See* Treas. Reg. Sec. 1.469-0 to 11.

produced an extreme level of complexity in the US income tax system. Second, as in the case of the at-risk rules, the passive activity loss rules deny deduction of economic costs currently incurred to produce income — a result incompatible with a global income tax regime. Finally, in a truly remarkable turn in US tax legislation, Congress required that the Treasury issue Regulations producing the opposite result from that of the general statutory rules where "necessary or appropriate" to carry out the purposes' of the passive activity loss rules.[88]

2.3.2.6 Deductible expenditures — personal

Certain deductions are permitted even though they do not represent costs of producing income.

The expenses which are deductible regardless of the nature of the expenditure — the "itemized personal deductions" — include interest on qualified personal residences (discussed above), certain state, local and foreign taxes, casualty losses, charitable contributions, medical expenses and contributions to qualified individual retirement plans. In several instances, limitations are imposed on the deductible amounts.[89]

Most taxpayers do not itemize the above personal deductions by virtue of a "standard deduction". The standard deduction for married taxpayers filing a joint return is $5,000 and is $3,000 for single persons, figures which are adjusted annually for inflation.[90] The standard deduction amount, when added to the personal exemptions discussed below, insures that persons with incomes below governmentally established poverty levels will not incur any income tax liability.

Special rules are provided for a category of "mixed" business-personal expenditures. These expenditures involve activities in which there is a significant personal element, but as to which there is also a business or investment element. Generally speaking, the Code provides arbitrary rules for determining the extent of deductibility (and hence the business-relatedness) of these types of expenses. Examples of mixed business-personal expenditures, which are partly deductible, include moving expenses, travel and entertainment expenses, work clothing, offices maintained in a personal residence, vacation homes which are rented out for part of the year, and so-called "hobby" situations where it is unclear whether the taxpayer is actually engaged in the activity to

---

88. Sec. 469(j). *See* Temp. Treas. Reg. Sec. 1.469-2T(f).
89. *See* Sec. 163, 164, 165(c), 170, 123, 219. If a taxpayer's adjusted gross income (AGI) exceeds $100,000, the deductions are reduced by 3 per cent of the amount of AGI above $100,000. Sec 68.
90. Sec. 63(c).

make a profit.[91] The amounts that are allowed as deductions under these rules generally either are subtracted from adjusted gross income to arrive at taxable income (and are thus subject to a floor equal to 2 per cent of adjusted gross income) or are limited to the gross income produced by the activity.

After the foregoing deductions have been subtracted from adjusted gross income, the taxpayer is then entitled to one $2,000 deduction (adjusted annually for inflation) for himself, his spouse and each dependent. These deductions are the so-called *personal exemptions*.[92]

With the subtraction of the personal deductions from adjusted gross income, the individual taxpayer has arrived at taxable income.

2.3.3   CREDITS AGAINST TAX

The tax rates described in Section 1 of the Code apply to taxable income determined under the foregoing rules. Against the resulting tax liability, however, certain credits against tax are allowed. As in the case of corporations, the credits are of two types.

The first group of tax credits are structural in nature and include the credits for taxes withheld by the individual's employer, estimated taxes previously paid, and income taxes paid to other countries.[93]

In the second group are credits provided to encourage or subsidize particular persons or activities. These include, for example, the general business credit discussed in 2.2.4 above, a tax credit for costs of child care incurred to enable the taxpayer to work outside the home, a refundable earned income credit, a tax credit for the elderly, a $500 tax credit per each child of the taxpayer under age 17, and tax credits for costs of higher education.[94]

2.3.4   ALTERNATIVE MINIMUM TAX: INDIVIDUALS

As in the case of corporations, individuals are subject to the AMT and pay the AMT if it exceeds their regular tax liability. In general, the adjustments and tax preferences described at 2.2.5 are also applicable, although the AMT rates for individuals are 26 per cent up to AMT of $175,000 and 28 per cent above that amount. The special lower rates described in 2.3.2.2 apply to capital gains,

---

91. *See* Sec. 217, 274, 280A, 183.
92. Sec. 151-152. The personal exemptions are phased-out for high income taxpayers, e.g., above $150,000 AGI for married taxpayers.
93. Sec. 31, 6315, 27.
94. Sec. 21, 32, 22, 24, 25A.

however. Many of the personal costs deductible for regular tax purposes are not deductible for AMT purposes, and a basic exemption ($45,000 for married taxpayers) is phased out above specified income levels (e.g., married taxpayers with over $150,000 of income).[95]

2.3.5 TRUSTS AND ESTATES

Under US tax principles, trusts and estates are in general not treated as separate entities. Thus, in the case of a simple trust that distributes all of its income currently, the trust pays no income tax and the beneficiary includes the distributed amount in his own income. In more complex trusts which accumulate all or part of the trust income, the trust does pay tax on the income in the year accumulated.[96]

In some cases, the grantor of a trust retains such extensive controls or powers over the trust that she is considered to remain the owner of the trust property for income tax purposes. Under the "grantor trust" rules, the creator of the trust is taxable on the trust income each year and, in effect, makes a gift of the trust income to the beneficiary who in fact receives it.[97]

If a trust derives capital gain income, the trust itself pays the tax thereon unless such gains are specifically allocated to an income beneficiary by the trust instrument. In the case of grantor trusts, capital gains derived by the trust generally are taxed to the grantor.

The treatment of foreign trusts and foreign beneficiaries is discussed at 5.7.

2.4 Partnerships

Under US tax principles, the partnership is not treated as a separate taxpaying entity. Partnership income and deductions "flow through" to the individual partners, whether natural persons or juridical entities, and are taxed to them in accordance with the principles outlined in the preceding sections. The partnership itself is treated as an accounting entity for purposes of computing the partnership's net income or loss which is then apportioned to its partners.

---

95. Sec. 55(b)(1)(A) and (3), (d)(1) and (3).
96. The rules described in the text are contained in Sec. 641–667 of the Code. The US tax treatment of trusts, which can be quite complex in its technical detail, is described in McDaniel, Ault, McMahon and Simmons, *Federal Income Taxation* (Foundation Press: Mineola, N.Y., 1994) at pp. 1235-1248.
97. *See* Sec. 671-677. The grantor trust rules are described in detail in McDaniel, Ault, McMahon and Simmons, note 96 above, at pp. 1215-1234.

Accordingly, the partnership must file a tax return which fundamentally operates as an information return with respect to the items of partnership income and deduction.[98]

In general, income and deductions realized at the partnership level retain their tax character when passed through to the partners.[99] Thus, for example, if the partnership realizes an item of tax exempt income, that income remains tax exempt in the hands of the partner. Since the partnership earnings are taxed to the partners whether distributed or not, a partnership distribution to a partner ordinarily does not generate any further tax to the partner when received.[100]

The US tax rules applicable to partnerships treat the partnership in some cases as simply an aggregate of the individual partners while for other purposes the partnership is treated as a separate entity, independent of its individual members. For example, certain tax elections are made by the partnership as an entity rather than by the individual partners.[101] On the other hand, some limitations on deductions are applied to the individual partners rather than to the partnership itself, treating the partnership as an aggregate of the partners involved.[102]

Because no entity level tax is imposed on earnings or on gains from sales of assets, the partnership is a highly favored form for doing business and carrying on investment activities, for US persons and foreigners alike. The check-the-box rules, discussed at 2.1.2, will make partnerships even more attractive as investment vehicles. In addition, Regulations provide great flexibility in allocating items of income, gain, deductions and credit among the partners.[103] These rules permit the partners to control the timing and allocation of income and deductions to a degree that is not possible with an entity taxed as a corporation. Finally, unlike a corporation, a partnership generally can be liquidated without current income tax consequences,[104] again in marked contrast to a corporate liquidation which normally produces two levels of tax.[105]

---

98. Rules governing partnerships are set forth in Sec. 701-761. Virtually all states have enacted legislation establishing "limited liability companies" (LLCs). An LLC has the corporate characteristic of limited liability but for tax purposes may be treated either as a partnership or a corporation. The text discussion of partnerships applies equally to an LLC which is taxed as a partnership. It applies also to any entity that has elected to be taxed as a partnership pursuant to the rules described in 2.1.2.

99. Sec. 702(b).

100. This is not true if the total of partnership cash distributions to the partner exceed the partner's share of partnership income and the partner's original investment in the partnership. In such cases gain may be recognized by the partner.

101. *See* Sec. 703(b).

102. See Treas. Reg. Sec. 1.702-1(a)(8)(iii).

103. Treas. Reg. Sec. 1.702-1(b)(2).

104. Sec. 731-735.

105. To offset in part the great tax advantage of the partnership form, a category of "publicly traded partnerships" was created which are taxable as corporations. Sec. 7704. Taxation as a corporation under these rules is not difficult to avoid, especially for passive investment partnerships. In addition, Sec. 771-777 set forth simplifying rules for so-called "electing large partnerships" (100 partners or more).

2.5   S Corporations

Another entity is the so-called "S Corporation"[106] in which, like a partnership, all items of income, deduction and credit are taken into account by the shareholders ratably to their stock ownership.

The S corporation regime was originally developed for small business corporations. Accordingly, several eligibility requirements are imposed which are not applicable to C corporations or partnerships. The S corporation (i) can have no more than 75 shareholders, all of whom must be individual US citizens or residents (or certain qualified trusts and tax exempt organizations) and (ii) can have only one class of stock. An S corporation which has a 100 percent owned subsidiary must treat all tax attributes of the subsidiary as its own.[107]

While an S corporation is often referred to as a corporation taxed like a partnership, such a statement is misleading. First, unlike a partnership, an S corporation realizes gain on all distributions of appreciated property, just as does a C corporation.[108] Second, all the rules applicable to C corporations (not the partnership rules) apply to S corporations in situations not dealt with by specific S corporation rules. Third, as a result, the S corporation does not permit the flexible allocations of tax items among shareholders as does the partnership.

An S corporation can be a vehicle through which US businesses and investors carry on transactions abroad. The form is of no utility to a foreign corporation or a nonresident alien individual since neither can be a shareholder in an S corporation.

2.6   Other flow through entities

2.6.1   REGULATED INVESTMENT COMPANY (RIC)

Certain types of investment companies, including mutual funds, may elect to be taxed on a flow through basis even though they otherwise are classified as corporations. All distributed income of the corporation is taxed only to the shareholders; the RIC is subject to taxation only on undistributed income. A qualifying RIC must maintain a diversified portfolio and 90 per cent of its gross

---

106. Corporations subject to the corporate tax regime described in 2.2 are referred to as "C" corporations. The rules governing S corporations are set forth in Sec. 1361-1378.
107. Sec. 1361. There is no limit on the quantative size of an S corporation, whether measured in terms of income or assets.
108. The effect of this rule for an S corporation, however, is generally to accelerate the tax on the gain. Two levels of tax are usually avoided because the shareholders' basis in their stock is stepped up by the corporate level gain recognition and then reduced by the amount of the distribution. In some situations, however, corporate and shareholder level tax can both be incurred.

income must be derived from dividends, interest and gains from the sale of stock or securities. The governing provisions spell out in great detail other requirements that must be satisfied by the RIC.[109]

2.6.2   REAL ESTATE INVESTMENT TRUST (REIT)

A REIT is treated as a flow through entity if the detailed requirements of Sections 856-860 are satisfied. The most important of the requirements are that 75 per cent of the REIT's gross income must be derived from passive real estate activities (the balance can only be from other passive investments such as stocks and bonds), the ownership interests must be widely held, and 95 per cent of the REIT'S taxable income must be distributed as dividends. If the statutory requirements are met, distributions from the REIT are taxed only to the owners of the interests in the REIT.

2.6.3   REAL ESTATE MORTGAGE INVESTMENT CONDUIT (REMIC)

A REMIC itself is not subject to tax; the holder of an interest in the REMIC is taxed directly on the REMIC income, whether distributed or not. The REMIC provisions (contained in Sec. 860A -860E) were enacted to facilitate the pooling of real estate mortgages in an entity which could issue more than one class of ownership interest.

2.7   Accounting aspects

Income and deductions are accounted for in the US tax system under a special set of a tax accounting rules. While there are many instances in which tax and financial accounting methods correspond, the tax accounting principles nonetheless represent a separate body of rules. There is no general requirement of conformity between tax and book accounting.

There are two general methods of accounting for income and deductions: the cash method and the accrual method. Under the *cash method* an income item is recognized in the year in which cash (or its equivalent) is received and an expense item is deductible in the year in which it is paid. (The expense must constitute a currently deductible expense rather than a capital expenditure.) Under the *accrual method* of accounting, the taxpayer includes items of income in the year in which a right to the payment arises and subtracts deductions in the year in which an expense is incurred. The accrual method of accounting is used by

---

109. The RIC provisions are contained in Sec. 851-855, 860.

most business operations and is required for C corporations and unincorporated businesses which operate with an inventory.[110] While the tax accrual method corresponds in general outline to financial accounting there are important differences. An overriding principle in the tax accounting area is that the accounting method chosen must "clearly reflect income".[111]

Whatever the general accounting method of a taxpayer, there are a number of rules covering specific situations. For example, whether on the cash or accrual method, the taxpayer may account for certain sales of assets under the so-called "installment sale" method whereby the purchase payment received each year on the sale of an asset is treated in part as return of investment and in part as income.[112]

The US has extensively developed rules relating to the "time value of money". The general effect of these provisions, where applicable, is to place both parties to a transaction on an accrual basis, even if one or both otherwise is entitled to use the cash method of accounting or both parties on a cash basis even if one or both otherwise would be an an accrual basis. The most important of the time value of money provisions are those dealing with "original issue discount".[113] In its simplest form, original issue discount arises, for example, where a corporation issues a 10-year bond with a face amount of 1,000 but, because it carries a below-market nominal interest rate, an investor will pay only 900 for the bond. The 100 differential is in fact interest and both issuer and investor are required to account for that interest on an accrual basis. Thus, the borrower is entitled to deduct the interest on an accrual method over the 10-year period of the bond and the investor must include the same amount in income each year, even though no interest payment reflecting the discount is made until year 10. The original issue discount rules apply to a wide variety of situations involving financial instruments and must be considered in virtually every transaction involving the issuance of debt.[114]

Similar time value of money rules apply in the case of leases of property, the performance of services, and special situations such as nuclear decommissioning costs.[115]

Income must be accounted for on an annual basis, usually the calendar year, though the corporate taxpayer is generally free to choose a fiscal year differing

---

110. Treas. Reg. Sec. 1.446-1(c)(2)(i). Increasingly, Congress has restricted the ability of business taxpayers to use the cash method of accounting. *See, e.g.*, Sec. 448.

111. Sec. 446(b).

112. Sec. 453, 453A and 453B. Generally, if a taxpayer holds installment debt in excess of $5 million, the taxpayer must pay an interest charge on the deferred tax.

113. Sec. 1272-1275.

114. Treasury Regulations issued under Sec. 1272 to 1275 provide detailed rules for application of the original issue discount provisions.

115. Sec. 467, 468A.

from the calendar year.[116] By and large, the annual accounting concept is followed quite rigorously and events which change the tax treatment of an item in a subsequent year are reflected in that year rather than through a recomputation of the tax liability for the earlier year. Here too, however, there are exceptions which treat integrated transactions on a unified basis even if they take place over several tax years.[117]

In general, income must be calculated and tax paid in US dollars.[118] This is true both for US taxpayers taxable on their worldwide income and foreign taxpayers taxable on income from US sources. The US rules regarding transactions in foreign currency are discussed in Chapter 10.

2.8   Statute of limitations and penalties

In general, a three year statute of limitation applies to tax matters.[119] A special six year period applies if the taxpayer omits from gross income an amount in excess of 25 per cent of the income shown on the return and the omitted amount is not disclosed in the return.[120] There is no time limit if a return is not filed or if the return is false or fraudulent. The taxpayer likewise has three years from the time the return was filed or two years from the time the tax was paid, whichever is later, to file a claim for refund.[121] Tax deficiencies carry an interest rate geared to the prevailing interest level as do successful refund claims, although the deficiency rate is higher than the refund rate.

There are a wide variety of civil and criminal penalties for tax underpayments and tax evasion. Due to the low rate of audits of individual income tax returns (less than 1 per cent per year), increased reliance has been placed on civil penalties imposed on taxpayers and tax advisors even though no tax evasion is involved.[122]

---

116. With some exceptions, partnerships, S corporations and personal service corporations must use the calendar year. Sec. 706(b), 1378, 441(i).
117. *See,* e.g. Sec. 1341.
118. Sec. 6316.
119. Sec. 6501(a).
120. Sec. 6501(e).
121. Sec. 6511(a).
122. Sec. 6651-6724. For example, Sec. 6662(b)(2) imposes a "no fault" penalty for any substantial understatement of tax liability. The penalty equals 20 per cent of the understatement. An understatement is substantial if it exceeds 10 percent of the amount of tax properly required to be shown on the return. The penalty can be avoided only if the taxpayer has disclosed the item giving rise to the understatement on his income tax return and has some legal authority for the position taken on the return.

Chapter 3
Jurisdictional principles

As noted in Chapter 2, Section 1 of the Internal Revenue Code imposes a tax on the "taxable income" of every individual. Taxable income in turn is derived from the Section 61 definition of gross income, i.e. "all income from whatever source derived." The term "source" embraces within its meaning both the type of income derived and the geographical location within which the income is produced. As a result, in the first instance, the literal scope of the US income tax on *individuals* is to tax all individuals in the world on their worldwide income! However, subsequent provisions make it clear that the assertion of worldwide taxing jurisdiction is only meant to include individuals who are US citizens or residents. For these taxpayers, US taxing jurisdiction is based on their personal relationship or status with respect to the US; the geographical source of their income is irrelevant. Partnerships, trusts and estates, whose taxation in very general terms approximates that of individuals, are likewise subject to US worldwide taxing jurisdiction if they are "domestic" entities, i.e. if they have substantial contacts with the US.

Nonresident aliens and foreign partnerships, trusts and estates are also subject to US tax. For such taxpayers, however, the US tax jurisdiction is based on the *geographic source* of the taxpayer's income. These taxpayers are in general only subject to tax on income from sources within the US. Their business income from US sources is taxed in much the same way as that of a US citizen or resident, while their investment income is subject to a special set of tax rules.

As respects *corporations,* the assertion of US worldwide tax jurisdiction is based solely on the place of incorporation. A corporation incorporated under the laws of some other country is treated for US tax purposes as a foreign corporation. Foreign corporations, like nonresident alien individuals, are subject to US tax on the basis of the US *source* of their income.

While the US asserts taxing jurisdiction over the foreign income of its citizens and residents, it alleviates the so-called "international double taxation" which may arise when another country also seeks to tax a portion of that income, through a foreign tax credit. The credit is available to US citizens and residents and domestic corporations who pay taxes on foreign income to other countries. In addition, an indirect credit is provided to US domestic corporations which receive dividend income from foreign corporations in which they own at least ten per cent of the voting stock.

The US in some instances also looks to the nationality or residence of a foreign corporation's shareholders in determining the appropriate pattern of taxation. In the case of *controlled foreign corporations* (that is a foreign corporation more than 50 per cent of whose voting stock or value is owned by US individuals or corporations), the normal US jurisdictional rules, which would allow deferral of US tax on the foreign income earned by a foreign corporation until its distribution to its US shareholders, are modified for certain types of undistributed income of the foreign corporation. In such cases, the US shareholders of the "controlled foreign corporation" are subject to tax on their allocable share of the described income, even though it is not currently distributed to them.[1] Special treatment is also provided for "foreign personal holding companies" and "passive foreign investment companies" (PFICs), again with the object of currently taxing to the US shareholders the undistributed taxable income of the foreign corporation or, in the case of PFICs, imposing an interest charge on deferred taxes when a distribution is made.

A number of provisions are intended to protect the assertion of US taxing jurisdiction, such as Section 482 (dealing with allocation of income and deductions among enterprises controlled or owned by the same interests in order clearly to reflect income) and Section 367 (imposing a tax in certain situations where a US person enters into what would otherwise be a tax-free organization, reorganization or liquidation involving a foreign corporation).

The US has entered into a number of bilateral tax treaties which modify the above general pattern of United States income taxation of international transactions.

The foregoing discussion describes in the broadest terms the general pattern of US rules dealing with foreign income and foreign taxpayers. That general description masks technical provisions that are extraordinarily complex in interpretation and operation. To some degree, this complexity is to be expected since international transactions themselves — especially as conducted by multinational corporations — are necessarily complex. But the greatly increased complexity added by recent legislation has strained the ability of taxpayers to comply with and tax administrators to enforce the US rules that apply to international transactions. In the following Chapters, we turn to an analysis of the most important of these provisions and the technical problems that have arisen in implementing them, viewed both from the standpoint of the tax administrator and from the standpoint of taxpayers who must live and operate within those rules.

---

1. In one sense the controlled foreign corporations provisions introduce a different test to determine whether a corporation is a "domestic" corporation, i.e. the place of incorporation test gives way to one focusing on the residence or nationality of the shareholders. However, this generalization is not completely accurate, since it is the US shareholder and not the corporate entity which is subject to US tax. Some of the policy considerations behind the controlled foreign corporation provisions are considered in 7.2.8.

Chapter 4
Source rules

4.1   General

The Code in Sections 861-865 and the Regulations issued thereunder set forth with considerable specificity the rules for determining the source of income for US tax purposes. The exclusive function of these rules is to establish whether income is derived from sources within the United States ("US source income") or from sources without the United States ("foreign source income"). Other sections of the Code dictate the operative results that flow from the source determination.

The two most important substantive areas that depend on the source rules are: (1) the tax treatment of nonresident aliens and foreign corporations, which in general are taxed only on US source income; and (2) the limitations applicable to the foreign tax credit allowed to a US taxpayer, which are fixed by the amount of the taxpayer's foreign source income, determined under US source rules. In general, the same source rules apply in both situations though in some cases the source of a particular item of income depends on whether it is received by a foreign taxpayer or a US taxpayer.

In addition, the applicability of a number of other Code provisions depends on whether income is determined to be from US or foreign sources.

4.2   Application of source rules to specific items of gross income

Sections 861 and 862 set forth rules for determining the source of specified types of gross income.[1] Section 865 has special rules for gross income from the

---

1. The reader should be aware that lurking behind the seemingly straightforward list of income items set forth in 4.2.1 through 4.2.7 is a host of difficult definitional problems. For example, the term "interest" includes not only direct interest paid but also imputed interest under Section 483 and original issue discount under Section 1273. "Dividend" is a term of art in US tax law, being defined in Sections 301 and 316. Since Treas. Reg. Sec. 1.861-3(a)(1) refers to Section 316, it is possible for some distributions to be treated as dividends for corporate law purposes, but still not constitute "dividends" for source rule purposes; conversely, a distribution which is treated as a dividend under Section 316 (even though in corporate law terms it is not a dividend) is a dividend for source rule purposes. There is also an uncertain and much litigated line in US tax jurispru-

sale of personal property. Section 863 provides source rules for items of income that are not otherwise specified.

4.2.1 INTEREST

In general, interest received on an obligation issued by a US resident or domestic corporation constitutes US source income.[2] There is, however, an important exception to the general rule. If 80 per cent or more of the US obligor's gross income is derived from the active conduct of a foreign trade or business, then the interest is treated as foreign source in its entirety when received by an unrelated party. The determination whether the exception is applicable is made by considering the ratio of active foreign business income to the total income of the US obligor for the three-year period preceding the year in which the interest is paid (the "testing period"). If the interest is received by a related party,[3] the interest has a foreign source only to the extent it is derived from active foreign business income. Thus, if a US obligor has 90 per cent of its income from an active foreign business in the testing period, all interest paid to an unrelated party is treated as foreign source to the recipient. Only 90 per cent of the interest paid to a related party is so classified. If less than 80 per cent of the income in the testing period is derived from an active foreign business, then all of the interest is US source regardless of the status of the recipient.

Another exception to the general rule that interest from a US obligor constitutes US source income is provided for interest paid by foreign branches of US banks.[4]

Interest paid by a foreign obligor in general has a foreign source to the recipient. However, interest paid by a US branch of a foreign corporate obligor is treated as US source.[5] For purposes of the foreign tax credit, interest paid by a

---

dence between compensation for personal services and receipts from royalty income or the sale of property. The classification of the receipt under US tax principles will determine which of the source rules described in paragraphs 4.2.3, 4.2.4, or 4.2.6 will be applicable.

2. Sec. 861(a)(1).
3. In general, a related party is one connected to the obligor directly or indirectly by a ten per cent or more ownership interest. *See* Sec. 861(c)(2)(B)
4. Prior to 1986, interest paid to nonresident aliens and foreign corporations on deposits with US banks which was not connected to a US business was treated as foreign source and thus not subject to tax. The 1986 Act changed the source rule to treat such interest income as US source and modified the substantive taxing rules to exempt such interest from tax in the hands of foreign recipients. *See* 5.4.5.1. *See also* the discussion of the exemption for US source "portfolio" interest in 5.4.5.3.
5. Sec. 884(f)(1)(A) treats such interest as "paid by a domestic corporation" thus giving it a US source. Source rules for interest income are thus the same whether the interest is paid by a US branch or a US subsidiary of a foreign corporation. *See* 5.5.6 for a discussion of the attribution of interest payments to a US branch.

United States-owned foreign corporation to its US shareholders is treated as US source interest income to the extent that it is allocated to US source income of the paying corporation.[6]

4.2.2 DIVIDENDS

Dividends from US corporations constitute US source income regardless of the income composition of the corporation.[7] Dividends from foreign corporations generally will be foreign source income. However, dividends paid by a foreign corporation conducting a trade or business in the US constitute US source income if 25 per cent or more of the corporation's gross income from all sources was, for the preceding three years, effectively connected with the conduct of a trade or business in the US. If the 25 per cent limit is exceeded, only a portion of the dividend is US source income, determined by applying the ratio described in 4.2.1.[8] For foreign tax credit purposes, Section 904(g) treats dividends from a United States-owned foreign corporation as US source income to the extent derived from US source income of the paying corporation.

4.2.3 PERSONAL SERVICES INCOME

In general, US source income includes all income derived from personal services performed in the US, regardless of the residence of the payor, where the contract was entered into, or where the payment was made. However, compensation derived from services performed within the US will constitute foreign source income if (1) it is received by a nonresident alien who is temporarily in the US for not more than 90 days in a year, (2) it does not exceed $3,000, and (3) the services are performed for a foreign payor not engaged in a trade or business in the US (or for a foreign business operation of a US person).[9]

---

6. Sec. 904(g). This rule prevents the US shareholder from "converting" US source income to foreign source interest income by routing it through a US-owned foreign corporation.
7. Sec. 861(a)(2). Prior to 1986, a dividend paid by a US corporation which had less than twenty per cent US source income was treated as foreign source in its entirety. The 1986 Act eliminated this rule. However, special taxing rules apply to dividends paid to foreign shareholders where the domestic corporation has substantial foreign business income. *See* 5.4.5.2.
8. Sec. 861(a)(2)(B). US source dividends paid by foreign corporations which are subject to the branch profits tax discussed in 5.5.5 are not subject to tax when paid to nonresident aliens and foreign corporations. Sec. 884(e)(3).
9. Sec. 861(a)(3). The foreign employer will not be regarded as engaged in a US trade or business by virtue of the activities of the employee which are examined for purposes of applying the source rule. Treas. Reg. Sec. 1.861-4(a)(3).

Compensation for personal services performed outside the US is foreign source income.[10]

4.2.4 RENTS AND ROYALTIES

All rents and royalties from property, tangible and intangible, located or used in the US are US source income.[11] Included are rents or royalties for the use in the US of intangible assets such as patents, copyrights, and secret processes.[12] If the transfer of the rights to the intangible is treated as a sale rather than a license for tax purposes, the royalty source rule (and not the sale source rule, see 4.2.6) applies to any payments which are contingent on factors such as use and productivity.[13]

Rents and royalties from property located or used outside the US are foreign source income.[14]

---

10. Sec. 862(a)(3). Treas. Reg. Sec. 1.861-4(b)(1) provides that where services are performed in part within and in part without the US an apportionment of the amount paid between US and foreign sources must be made "on the basis that most correctly reflects the proper source of income under the facts and circumstances of the particular case." Apportionment on a time basis is one, but not the only, acceptable method of apportionment under the Regulation. For examples of application of the allocation rules in personal services situations, *see* Rev Rul. 74-108, 1974-1 Cum. Bull. 248 (payments by US soccer team to foreign player); *Stemkowski v. Commissioner,* 690 F.2d 40 (2nd Cir. 1982)(hockey player's income allocated between Canada and the US on the basis of all days of service, including training camp and playoffs). Special rules apply to services rendered in connection with international transportation. *See* Sec. 861(a)(3) (last sentence), 863(c).
11. Sec. 861(a)(4). In Rev. Rul. 80-362, 1980-2 Cum. Bull. 208, the Internal Revenue Service took the position that the royalty source rule applied to source in the US royalty payments where a foreign third party received the payments from a foreign licensee which had in turn relicensed the intangible for use in the United States. In *SDI Netherlands BV v. Commissioner,* 107 TC 161 (1997), the Tax Court rejected the "cascading" royalty approach of Rev. Rul. 80-362 in a somewhat similar factual situation. The interposed foreign company, which received royalties both from US and foreign sources, was not a "conduit" and the court refused to "flow through" the source of the royalties received by the company to the royalties paid in order to make them partially US source.
12. Transfers of rights to intangibles often have elements of license, sale and personal services intertwined in the same transactions. The exact classification of the amounts received is important since the applicable source rules are different for each category. Similar issues arise concerning the treatment of payments received in connection with computer programs. Suppose, for example, that the taxpayer has the copyright on a computer program and grants a right to a foreign customer to make 50 copies of the program for use by its employees at one location (a "site license"). Is the transaction a license, generating foreign source royalty income, or should it be viewed as the equivalent of the sale of 50 disks, which would be treated under the rules on sourcing sales income discussed in 4.2.6? Proposed Regulations have been issued dealing with a number of these questions. *See* Prop. Treas. Reg. Sec. 1.861-18(h) Ex. 10 (1996) (site license treated as a sale of the copyrighted property and not a license).
13. Sec. 865(d)(1)(B).
14. Sec. 862(a)(4).

4.2.5 GAINS FROM DISPOSITION OF REAL PROPERTY

Gains from the disposition of "United States real property interests" constitute US source income. Gains from sales of real estate located outside the US are foreign source income.[15]

4.2.6 GAINS FROM SALE OF PERSONAL PROPERTY

As a general rule, gain from the sale of personal property is sourced at the residence of the seller.[16] There are, however, a number of exceptions to the general rule.

With respect to inventory (i.e. property held for sale to customers), gain generally is sourced at the place where the sale takes place.[17] The Regulations provide that the place of sale is generally the country in which the rights, title and interest of the seller pass. If the seller retains a bare legal title, then the sale occurs where the risk of loss passes. If tax avoidance was the primary purpose for structuring a transaction in a particular manner, the Treasury will look to all the surrounding circumstances to determine where the substance of the sale occurred.[18]

Gain on depreciable property is sourced under the inventory rule except that gain attributable to previously taken depreciation deductions is sourced in the United States if the depreciation was taken as a deduction against US source income[19]

In general, other gain attributable to a sale by an office or other fixed place of business established outside of the taxpayer's country of residence has its source where the office is located.[20]

Gain on the sale of stock in an affiliated foreign corporation realized by a US resident is sourced outside the US if the foreign corporation derives the bulk of its income in the country in which the sale takes place.[21]

---

15. Sec. 861(a)(5); Sec. 862(a)(5).
16. Sec. 865(a). For purposes of applying this source rule, special provisions determine the residence of an individual which depend in part on the location of his principal place of business. Sec. 865(g)(1)(A)(i). A corporation is a resident of the country under the laws of which it is created. Sec. 865(g)(1)(A)(ii).
17. Sec. 861(a)(6). This source rule only applies to inventory (1) purchased by the taxpayer or (2) produced and sold by the taxpayer entirely within or entirely outside of the US. In the case of inventory produced within the US and sold outside (or the converse) the income is allocated partly to US source and partly to foreign source under Sec. 863. *See* 4.3.2.
18. Treas. Reg. Sec. 1.861-7(c). *See US v. Balanovski,* 236 F.2d 298 (2d Cir. 1956), for an example of the application of these principles.
19. Sec. 865(c).
20. Sec. 865(e). In the case of a US resident, the gain must be subject to a foreign tax of at least ten per cent. In the case of a nonresident with a US office, the gain will not be US source under this rule if the property is sold outside the US and an office of the taxpayer in the foreign country materially participated in the sale. *See* 5.3.5.
21. Sec. 865(f).

4.2.7 UNDERWRITING INCOME

Income derived from insuring US risks is US source income. All other under-writing income is foreign source income.[22]

4.3 Application of source rules to other items of income

4.3.1 GENERAL

Section 863(a) gives the fiscal authorities broad power to allocate or apportion between US and foreign sources items of gross income other than those enumerated above.[23] Regulations under Section 863(a) have been issued dealing with the source of income from "notional principal contracts" where payments are calculated on a notional principal amount and based on some external index (see 10.3.2)[24]. Such income is generally sourced at the residence of the tax-payer unless the contract is associated with a business abroad.

Scholarship income, which is taxable in certain circumstances, also has a special source rule under Section 863(a) Regulations. In general, it is sourced based on the residence or status of the grantor. However, a special rule treats as foreign source any payments by a US grantor to a foreign person for activities to be performed outside the US, thus avoiding a potential US tax on much US-based educational support.[25]

Regulations concerning natural resources extracted in the United States orig-inally gave a US source to all of the income, despite the fact that the sale of the property took place abroad. The natural resources Regulations were held in-valid by the Tax Court and a Court of Appeals and the IRS subsequently issued Regulations which allocate the income between US and foreign sources based on the fair market value at the export terminal.[26]

4.3.2 INCOME PARTLY FROM US SOURCES AND PARTLY FROM FOREIGN SOURCES

Section 863(b) authorizes Regulations to deal with income derived "from sources partly within and partly without the United States." The most important rule in this area involves income from the sale of goods manufactured within

---

22. Sec. 861(a)(7).
23. *See* Rev. Rul. 66-291, 1966-2 Cum. Bull. 279, applying this authority to determine the source of income derived from winning a prize in a contest sponsored by a US company.
24. Treas. Reg. Sec. 1.863-7.
25. Treas. Reg. Sec. 1.863-1(d)(2)(iii).
26. *Phillips Petroleum Corp. v. Commissioner*, 97 TC 30 (1991), aff'd without opinion, 96-1 USTC 50,006 (10th Cir. 1995); Treas. Reg. Sec. 1.863-1(b).

the United States and sold without, or vice versa. Under Treas. Reg. Sec. 1.863-3(b), the taxpayer can elect between the "50/50" method and the "Independent Factory Price" ("IFP") method to source income from export sales of manufactured goods.[27] Under the 50/50 method, one-half of the taxpayer's income is considered attributable to "production activity" and one-half to "sales activity." If all of the production activities are in the US, all of the production income is US source. If there are production activities both within and outside the US, the income is allocated on the basis of the relative tax basis of the production assets.[28] With respect to the sales activities, the income will be allocated according to the title passage rule (4.2.6) unless the property is sold for consumption in the United States, in which case the income will be US source.[29] Thus, in general, a minumum of 50% of all export sales income will be foreign source.[30]

The taxpayer can also elect to allocate income between production and sales activities using the IFP method. This method can be used if the taxpayer has regular sales through independent distributors. The sales price to the independent distributor will determine the amount of the income attributable to production activities with the remainder being attributable to sales. Thus, for example, if the taxpayer produces goods with a cost of goods sold of 80 and sells them to an unrelated distributor for 100 and also sells the same or similar goods directly for 110 to a retail outlet, the US source production income would be 20 and the foreign source sales income would be 10[31]

Section 863 also contains rules to allocate income from transportation and communications to sources within and without the US.

4.4 Allocation of deductions to arrive at taxable income

4.4.1 BACKGROUND

The foregoing rules have involved the determination of the source of "gross income." The proper allocation of deductions to arrive at taxable income from a

---

27. Treas. Reg. Sec. 1.863-3(a)(2),(b). A third method, based on the taxpayer's books and records, is available with the consent of the IRS.
28. Treas. Reg. Sec. 1.863-3(c)(1)(ii).
29. Treas. Reg. Sec. 1.863-3(c)(2).
30. The 50/50 rule will normally allocate more income abroad than would have resulted from the application of normal "arm's length" principles. See 8.1. It is highly unlikely that the foreign income allocated under the 50/50 rule will be subject to tax in the foreign jurisdiction so that the allocation results in increased foreign tax credits for the US seller with no increase in foreign taxes paid. See 6.6. The 50/50 rule is thus a tax subsidy for US exports.
31. Treas. Reg. 1.863-3(b)(2)(iv) Ex. 1. Prior to their revision in 1996, the Regulations required the taxpayer to use the IFP method if an IFP could in fact be established through unrelated party sales. This position was upheld by the courts. *Phillips Petroleum Corp. v. Commissioner*, 97 TC 30 (1991), aff'd without opinion, 96-1 USTC 50,006 (10th Cir. 1995). The abandonment of the requirement to use arm's length principles when the arm's length result can be clearly established underlines the subsidy character of the rule.

US or foreign source is an independent question. Sections 861(b), 862(b), 863(a) and 863(b) each contain provisions granting broad authority to the Treasury to issue regulations for the allocation of deductions, losses and expenses between US and foreign sources.

Thus, unlike the statutorily-based provisions for determining the source of gross income items, the rules with respect to the allocation of deductions are contained primarily in Treasury Regulations. The length and complexity of the allocation of deduction Regulations have grown substantially since the first serious attempt to develop Regulations was made in 1977.

The Regulations provide general rules applicable to all types of deductible expenditures. In addition, specific rules are detailed for certain types of deductible items, notably interest, research and development costs, and overhead expenses.

4.4.2 GENERAL RULES

Under the general rules of the Regulations[32], deductions must first be allocated to a class of gross income. The Regulations list the classes of gross income among which deductions must be allocated. Those classes include the types of income described in 4.2 but, in some cases, group several of those income items into a single class (for example, gains derived from dealings in property) and add some additional classes of income. As a basic proposition, deductions are to be allocated to a class of gross income based on the "factual relationship" between the deductions and the class of gross income. It is not necessary that in a given year the taxpayer actually have realized income in the class to which the deductions relate; it is only necessary that the property or activity has generated, or will reasonably be expected to generate, gross income. Thus, for a given year, deductions allocable to a class of income may exceed the income actually realized in that class.[33]

In summary, at the first level, deductions are to be allocated to the class of income to which they are "definitely related" on a factual basis; deductions not definitely related to a class of income are ratably allocated to all gross income.[34]

Once deductions have been allocated to the appropriate class of gross income it may then be necessary to make an apportionment of the deductions. Apportionment of deductions is required between the statutory grouping of gross income and the residual grouping of gross income. A statutory grouping is comprised of the gross income from a specific source which must be deter-

---

32. Treas. Reg. Sec. 1.861-8.
33. Treas. Reg. Sec. 1.861-8(a)(2), (3); 1.861-8(b); 1.861-8(d)(2); 1.861-8(g), Ex. 24.
34. Treas. Reg. Sec. 1.861-8(b)(5).

mined in order to arrive at taxable income. For example, if a US corporation has both US and foreign source income, and it is necessary to determine its foreign tax credit limitations, the relevant statutory grouping is foreign source income and the residual grouping is US source income. For a nonresident taxpayer, the statutory grouping would be "effectively connected income" (see 5.3) and all other income is in the residual grouping. Thus, the items of income assigned to a particular statutory grouping depend upon which operative section of the Code is under consideration.[35]

Apportionment of deductions between a statutory grouping and the residual grouping is required in two situations:

(1) where a class of income to which deductions are allocated is in part in the statutory grouping and in part in the residual grouping; and

(2) where the class of income contains more than one statutory grouping.

If a class of gross income is entirely within one grouping, no apportionment is required.

As in the case of the rules governing the allocation of deductions to particular classes of income, the apportionment of deductions between statutory and residual groupings is to be made on the basis of the "factual relationship" of the deductions and the groupings. Factors are provided that are to be taken into account in effecting an apportionment, such as a comparison of the units sold that are attributable to each grouping, a comparison of the gross sales and receipts attributable to each grouping, or the costs of goods sold attributable to each grouping. Deductions not definitely related to any class of gross income must be apportioned on the basis of gross income in the statutory grouping to total gross income[36] but, given the specificity of the apportioning rules, this type of deduction presumably will occur infrequently.

An example will illustrate the operation of the allocation and apportionment rules. Assume that a foreign taxpayer manufactures goods abroad and sells them through a US sales branch. Under the principles discussed in 4.3.2, the gross income from production and sales will be divided between a US source portion and a foreign source portion. Expenses incurred with respect to the sales activities in the US are "definitely related" to the US income and costs of manufacturing are similarly related to the foreign source income; the expenses thus would be allocated to those classes of income accordingly. Since the sales costs are all related to the class of gross income which is wholly within the statutory grouping, i.e. effectively connected income, they would also all be apportioned to that grouping. Similarly the manufacturing costs all would be allocated to the residual grouping. However, general management expenses of the taxpayer which related to both sales and manufacturing would be allocated

---

35. Treas. Reg. Sec. 1.861-8(a)(2), (4).
36. Treas. Reg. Sec. 1.861-8(c)(1).

to the class of income which included both US and foreign source income; accordingly, it would then be necessary to apportion the deductions for these costs between the statutory grouping of effectively connected income and the residual grouping based on the factors discussed above.

4.4.3 SPECIAL RULES

The foregoing rules are modified in the case of certain specified types of deductions. The most important of these are the deductions for interest, research and development costs, and home office oversight expenses.

4.4.3.1 Interest

4.4.3.1.1 General

Interest expense generally is required to be allocated to all classes of gross income.[37] The provision is based on the theory that money is fungible.[38] In a few narrowly defined cases, however, the fungability theory is abandoned and interest expense is allocated to a specific item or class of income.[39] Once interest expense has been allocated to a class of income, it must be apportioned be-

---

37. See Temp. Treas. Reg. Sec. 1.861-9T to 13T. The allocation and apportionment rules which apply to interest (including original issue discount, see 2.7) also apply to "interest equivalents", defined as any expense or loss which is "substantially incurred in consideration of the time value of money." Temp.Treas. Reg. Sec. 1.861-9T(b)(1)(i). Thus the implicit interest element in some currency and interest rate swaps is treated as interest expense for purposes of the allocation and apportionment of deduction rules.

38. See Temp. Treas. Reg. Sec. 1.861-9T(a): "[I]n general, money is fungible and . . . interest expense is attributable to all activities and property regardless of any specific purpose for incurring an obligation on which interest is paid.... The fungibility approach recognizes that all activities and property require funds and that management has a great deal of flexibility as to the source and use of funds. When [money is borrowed for a specific purpose, such] borrowing will generally free other funds for other purposes and it is reasonable under this approach to attribute part of the cost of borrowing to such other purposes." Compare the discussion in 2.3.2.5.2.

39. Under Temp. Treas. Reg. Sec. 1.861-10T(b), interest on so-called "nonrecourse" debt, i.e. debt on which the borrower is not personally liable, is generally allocated to the income from the property securing the debt if certain conditions are met. The same approach is taken to interest expense incurred in connection with certain "integrated financial transactions." In such cases, the interest is allocated directly to the corresponding income amount. Thus if the taxpayer incurs a borrowing to invest in a financial asset, the return on which will be used to amortize the debt, the interest expense will not be required to be apportioned if a number of technical conditions are fulfilled. Temp. Treas. Reg. Sec. 1.861-10T(b). In addition, where a US parent corporation borrows money which it "on-lends" to its foreign subsidiary, it may be required to allocate some of the third party interest expense directly to the foreign source interest income it receives from the subsidiary. These rules, dealing with "excess related group indebtedness", are extremely complex and are intended in very general terms to approximate the results which would have obtained if the foreign subsidiary had borrowed directly (where all of its interest expense would have been allocated to foreign source income) rather than from the US parent. Treas. Reg. Sec. 1.861-10(e).

tween the statutory grouping and the residual grouping. The apportionment method to be applied is the asset method.[40] Under this method, to determine the amount of interest expense to be apportioned to US source income, for example, the taxpayer's total interest expense is multiplied by a fraction, the numerator of which is the tax book value (or "tax basis") of the assets used in the United States and the denominator of which is the tax book value of the taxpayer's total worldwide assets. The balance of the interest is apportioned to foreign source income.[41]

4.4.3.1.2 Foreign Taxpayers

In response to the special situation of foreign corporate taxpayers with US branches, particularly banks, Treas. Reg. Sec. 1.882-5 applies a different set of interest expense allocation rules to such entities. These rules adopt a concept of the fungibility of capital (rather than of money.) The taxpayer is required in effect to establish the appropriate amounts of "equity" and "debt" capitalization in the US branch and allocate the interest expense accordingly. In outline, the "debt" capitalization is determined by first valuing the assets of the US branch, using the approach of the branch profits tax discussed in 5.5.5. "US-connected liabilities" are then calculated, on an elective basis, either by using the actual worldwide ratio of liabilities to assets of the foreign corporation or a fixed ratio (50% in the case of nonbanks and 93% for banks.) The applicable ratio is applied to establish the level of US-connected liabilities. This amount of liability is then compared with the amount of liability actually shown on the US branch's books. If the booked liabilities exceed the US-connected liabilities under the allocation approach, the interest expense generated on those liabilities is correspondingly reduced, in effect allocating an additional portion of the foreign corporation's equity capital to the US operations. In the converse situation, where US-connected liabilities exceed booked liabilites, the head office is deemed to have partially funded the US office with capital borrowed elsewhere and the interest deduction is increased by attributing additional interest expense to the excess US-connected liabilities. An alternative method of interest calculation takes in account the situation where the US branch (typically a bank) has foreign currency dominated assets.[42]

---

40. Sec. 864(e)(2).
41. In addition, Sec. 864 specifically requires that assets generating tax exempt income are not to be taken into account in making the allocation. Further, in determining the tax basis of stock in a foreign corporation held by a US corporation, the basis must be increased by any undistributed earnings of the foreign corporation accumulated while the taxpayer has held the stock. Also, for an affiliated group of domestic corporations, the members of the group are treated as a single corporation, thus allocating the total interest expense of the group over the group's total assets. This group rule prevents US taxpayers from isolating interest expense in a member of the domestic group which does not have any foreign source income.
42. Treas. Reg. Sec. 1.882-5(e).

Similar rules apply to individual foreign taxpayers. Under Temp. Treas. Reg. Sec. 1.861-9T, interest expense will only be deductible if the liability generating the interest expense is shown on the taxpayer's books or is secured by US property. In addition, no deduction is allowed to the extent that liabilities exceed 80% of the value of the US assets, thus in effect requiring an 20% "equity" investment in the US business. Special rules apply to partnerships and in general make the allocation at the partnership level. A foreign corporation which is a partner must apply the allocation rules of Treas. Reg. Sec. 1.882-5, above.

4.4.3.2 Research and development expenses

Special rules are also provided for the treatment of research and development expenses. The Regulations are based on the premise that research and development "is an inherently speculative activity, that findings may contribute unexpected benefits, and that the gross income derived from successful research and experimentation must bear the cost of unsuccessful research and development."[43]

As a result, research and development expenditures are considered under the Regulations to be connected to appropriate product categories and therefore are allocable to items of gross income as a class that are related to the product category. Product categories are specified and include such classifications as mining, construction services, transportation services and the like. For manufactured products, the classification is in terms of groups such as engines and turbines, drugs, lighting and wiring, etc. The income that is considered related to a product category includes not only sales income but royalties and dividends as well in the appropriate circumstances.

Once the allocation of the deduction to classes of income related to product categories has been made, the deduction then may have to be apportioned between the relevant statutory grouping of gross income and the residual grouping of gross income. First, where research and development ("R&D") expenses are incurred "solely" to meet legal requirements, the expenses are allocated entirely to the jurisdiction where the requirements arise. This means that expenses incurred, for example, to comply with US Food and Drug Administration regulations will all be allocated to US source income and will not affect the US taxpayer's foreign tax credit computation. With respect to other R&D costs, the "sales method" generally applies which focuses both on sales and the "geographic source" where the R&D activities take place. Where over 50% of the R&D costs are incurred in one geographic source, 50 % of the costs are allocated to that source. This reflects the theoretical view that R&D costs are more likely to be of benefit in the country in which the expenses are incurred. It also responds to the practical consideration that foreign jurisdictions may be reluctant

---

43. Treas. Reg. Sec. 1.861-17(a)(1).

or unwilling to allow a deduction for R&D costs incurred outside the jurisdiction. In these circumstances, a US allocation to foreign source income would not be matched by a corresponding deduction in the foreign jurisdiction. [44] After the exclusive geographical allocation is made, the remaining costs are allocated under a sales formula which compares sales revenues within the product category involving the statutory grouping to total product sales.[45] Thus, for example, if a US taxpayer incurred 500 of R&D costs in the US and had total sales in the product category of 2,000 with 1600 of those sales in the US, 250 of the R&D costs would be allocated to US source income under the exclusive geographic location rule and the remaining 250 would be allocated 50 to foreign income and 200 to US income on the basis of sales. In applying the sales formula, appropriate adjustments are made to take into account sales by controlled subsidiaries where those corporations could be expected to benefit from the R&D.

An optional allocation method based on gross income is also available if the taxpayer so elects.[46] Under this method, 25% of the R&D costs are allocated to the place of performance of the research activities and the remainder is allocated on the basis of gross income in the relevant product category. However, the amounts allocated under the gross income method must result in an allocation to the statutory and residual groupings which are at least 50% of the amount which would have been allocated under the sales method.

4.4.3.3 Other expenses

The Regulations provide specific rules (although not in the detail employed for interest and research and development deductions) for home office or oversight costs attributable to dividends received from a foreign corporation; legal and accounting fees and expenses; income taxes; losses on the sale, exchange or other disposition of property;[47] and the net operating loss deduction.

---

44. The exclusive allocation based on the geographic location of the R&D activities has a long and checkered history. In the original 1977 Regulations, 30% of the R&D costs were allocated on a geographic basis. Moved by complaints from US taxpayers that this allocation did not sufficiently reflect the value of R&D expenditures in the US, Congress suspended the operations of the Regulations and allowed all R&D costs incurred in the US to be allocated to US source income. This suspension lasted until 1986, when temporary rules in subsequent years allowed variously 50% and 64% of the expenses to be allocated on a geographic basis. The 50% rule in the present Regulations is the current compromise. The taxpayer can allocate more than 50% of the costs to the jurisdiction where the activities take place if it can establish that the research will have only limited or delayed benefit in other jurisdictions.
45. Treas. Reg. Sec. 1.861-17(c)(l).
46. Treas. Reg. Sec. 1.861-17(b)(1)(ii), (d).
47. Treas. Reg. Sec. 1.861-8(e)(7) provides that losses on the disposition of a capital asset shall be allocated to "the class of gross income to which the asset ordinarily gives rise". In *Black & Decker Corp. v. Commissioner*, 986 F2d 60 (4th Cir. 1993), the court applied this Regulation to allocate the loss on the sale by a US corporation of stock of a foreign subsidiary to foreign income since the dividends on the stock would have been foreign source income. The court disregarded the

Section 864(e)(6) requires that expenses incurred by an affiliated group of domestic corporations be allocated on a consolidated basis unless the expenses are directly related to a specific income producing activity, thus preventing the US taxpayer from isolating expenses in subsidiaries which have no foreign source income.

As noted above, the allocation rules in the Regulations primarily affect the computation of the limitations on the foreign tax credit, discussed in 6.6. However, the rules are also important with respect to determining "effectively connected" taxable income of foreign taxpayers (5.3), foreign base company income under the Subpart F rules (7.2.4), and numerous other provisions discussed in succeeding chapters which rely on the determination of US and/or foreign source taxable income.[48]

---

fact that no dividends were actually paid on the stock and rejected the taxpayer's argument that the purpose of establishing the subsidiary was not to generate foreign source dividends but to promote the sale of the taxpayer's US-produced products in foreign markets.

Since gains on the sale of capital assets are typically sourced to the residence of the taxpayer, in situations like *Black & Decker* there is an asymmetry between the treatment of gains and losses. In Sec. 865(j)(1), Congress expressly authorized (or more accurately invited) the Treasury to issue Regulations dealing with the treatment of losses on sales of personal property and Regulations have been proposed which would coordinate the treatment of gains and losses on such assets. Prop. Treas. Reg. Sec. 1.865-2 (1996) provides that loss on the sale of stock will in general be sourced in the same way as gain, that is, to the residence of the taxpayer. To prevent "dividend stripping" of foreign income in the form of a dividend followed by a domestic loss on the sale of the stock, a recapture rule is provided which would treat the loss as foreign source to the extent of dividends received within two years before the sale.

48. See the listing in Treas. Reg. Sec. 1.861-8(f), and illustrations in Treas. Reg. Sec. 1.861-8(g), Ex. 22 and Ex. 23.

Chapter 5

Income taxation of nonresident aliens and foreign corporations

5.1 Introduction

A number of structural building blocks are involved in determining the US tax liability of a foreign person. There are three basic concepts involved: (1) the nature and source of the taxpayer's income; (2) the taxpayer's activities in the US, i.e. whether he is engaged in a US trade or business; and (3) the relation between his income and his US activities, i.e. whether his income is "effectively connected" with a US trade or business. It is within the framework of these three variables that the pattern of US taxation is established. Source of income and income classification issues were discussed in Chapter 4. The following materials first discuss the other two elements in the statutory pattern, the trade or business concept and the effectively connected concept, and then examine in more detail the pattern of taxation for nonresident aliens, foreign corporations, partnerships and trusts. In Chapter 11 the impact of tax treaties on the domestic taxing rules will be considered.

5.2 The "trade or business" concept

5.2.1 BACKGROUND

A foreign taxpayer who is engaged in a US trade or business has achieved a substantial level of economic penetration in the US. He is not merely a passive investor but has become a direct participant in the economic life of the country.

The significance of a US trade or business for the tax treatment of foreign persons has varied over the years. The US tax system has always distinguished between the investment income from US sources of a foreign taxpayer and the business income attributable to the foreign taxpayer's trade or business carried on in the US. The investment income has generally been subject to a flat rate of tax on gross income, withheld at the source, while the net business income has been taxed at regular individual or corporate rates. However, prior to 1966, if a foreign taxpayer was engaged in a US trade or business, under the so-called force of attraction principle, the US taxed investment income at regular rates, even though it had no connection with the foreign taxpayer's US trade or business. The investment income was "attracted" to the US trade or business and taxed accordingly.

In 1966, the United States abandoned the force of attraction principle. Under the 1966 legislation, only investment income that is effectively connected with the conduct of a trade or business in the US is subjected to the full individual or corporate rates applicable to business income. The mere existence of a US trade or business is not sufficient to subject the investment income to the normal tax rates. Investment income not effectively connected with a US trade or business is in general taxed at the 30 per cent statutory withholding rate or lower treaty rates. While the existence of a trade or business in the US no longer affects the taxation of unrelated investment income, the trade or business concept plays an important role in the US taxation of foreign individuals and corporations. It determines the basic pattern under which the foreign taxpayer's income will be taxed, as discussed more fully in 5.4 and 5.5.[1]

5.2.2 THE EXISTENCE OF A TRADE OR BUSINESS

Although the term "trade or business" is employed in several different sections of the Internal Revenue Code, the statute does not contain a general definition of the phrase. Instead, the determination whether an activity constitutes a "trade or business" is left to a case-by-case resolution by the fiscal authorities and the courts.[2]

In the context of the rules governing foreign individuals and corporations, the fundamental distinction to be drawn is between commercial activity carried on in the US with some regularity versus passive investment. The polar models are a manufacturing plant operated in the US and the simple receipt of dividends paid on stock in a US company. But between these clear extremes, there is an infinite variety of activities which must be placed either in the trade or business or in the investment category.

---

1. The "trade or business" concept is somewhat analogous to the "permanent establishment" concept adopted in US tax treaties. Similarly, "effectively connected" corresponds to the notion of income "attributed to" the permanent establishment. *See* 11.5.4. While a determination that a foreign individual or corporation maintains a permanent establishment in the US will generally mean that a US trade or business exists, the reverse is not the case. The trade or business concept is broader than the permanent establishment rules and, therefore, a foreign individual or corporation can often be engaged in a trade or business in the US, but still be found not to maintain a permanent establishment there. *See,* e.g. *de Amodio v. Commissioner,* 299 F.2d 623 (3d Cir. 1962).
2. The Supreme Court has held that the term "trade or business" can have different meanings depending on which Code sections are involved. *Snow v. Commissioner,* 416 US 500 (1974). *See also Commissioner v. Groetzinger,* 480 US 23 (1987), note 8 ("We caution that in this opinion our interpretation of the phrase 'trade or business' is confined to the specific sections of the Code at issue here. We do not purport to construe the phrase where it appears in other places.")

The statute currently provides guidelines for resolution of the trade or business issue in three situations. Section 864(b) excludes from trade or business status:

(1) The performance of personal services for a nonresident employer under the same conditions that determine that compensation for personal services constitutes foreign source income[3] (*see* 4.2.3).

(2) Trading in stocks, securities or commodities through a US broker, if the foreign individual or corporation does not maintain a US office or fixed place of business through which the transactions are effected.[4]

(3) Trading in stocks, securities, or commodities for the foreign investor's own account, whether effected in the US directly or through agents.[5] This result holds even if the foreign investor maintains a US office and even if that office is the investor's principal place of business.[6]

Other statutory provisions treat certain activities as a trade or business:

(1) Section 871(c) provides that certain foreign students, teachers and exchange visitors "shall be treated as" engaged in a trade or business.[7]

(2) Sections 871(d) and 882(d) permit foreign individuals and corporations that own US real estate to elect to treat the income therefrom as trade or business income. The election applies only to real estate investments that, absent the election, would not constitute a trade or business under generally applicable principles.[8]

---

3. Sec. 864(b)(1); Treas. Reg. Sec. 1.864-2(b).
4. Sec. 864(b)(2)(A)(i), 864(b)(2)(B)(i), 864(b)(2)(C); Treas. Reg. Sec. 1.864-2(c)(1), (d)(1)
5. Sec. 864(b)(2)(A)(ii). The exemption does not apply to dealers in stock or securities. 864(b)(2)(B)(ii). Treas. Reg. Sec. 1.864-2(c)(2)(i) and (ii), (d)(2). It is unclear to what extent this exception applies to so-called venture capital investments where the foreign investor (or a partnership in which he is a partner) may be substantially involved in research, management and other activities in connection with the investment.
6. Sec. 864(b)(2)(C). Prior to the 1997 Act, a foreign corporation which had its principal office in the US was treated as engaged in a US trade or business when trading for its own account. Treas. Reg. Sec. 1.864-2(c)(2)(iii) provides examples of corporate functions that constitute a principal office. The quite detailed and formalistic rules in the Regulation established guidelines for a foreign investment company that desired to avoid US trade or business status by locating its principal office outside the US. This guidance led to the creation of the so-called "offshore investment funds", through which foreign investors invested in US stocks, bonds and commodities. If properly structured, profits on sales would be free of US capital gains tax (because, as explained in 5.3.2 only capital gains effectively connected with the conduct of a US trade or business are subject to US tax). In addition, if the country of incorporation selected had a favorable treaty with the US, the US tax on dividends and interest could be reduced or eliminated. These results made the offshore funds attractive to foreign investors but the benefits could only be realized if certain administrative tasks were performed offshore to avoid the "principal office" limitation. The 1997 Act eliminated this requirement, thus allowing offshore funds to carry on all of their activities in the US without being characterized as engaging in a US trade or business.
7. Treas. Reg. Sec. 1.871-9.
8. Treas. Reg. Sec. 1.871-10 details the procedures to be followed in making the election. *See also* Treas. Reg. Sec. 1.882-2(a). No other type of income is granted such an option. Rev. Rul. 74-63, 1974-1 Cum. Bull. 374. A similar election is provided in many US income tax treaties. See 11.6.3.

(3) Section 897(a) provides that gain or loss from the disposition of a "United States real property interest" shall be taxed "as if" the taxpayer were engaged in a US trade or business. *See* 5.3.3.

Apart from these specific statutory rules, the determination whether an activity constitutes a trade or business is made on a case-by-case basis, taking into account such factors as the taxpayer's motive (profit versus personal), quantitative aspects (frequency, substantiality and duration of the activities) and qualitative aspects (business versus investment).[9]

5.2.3 THE LOCATION OF A TRADE OR BUSINESS IN THE US

There is no Code provision that offers a comprehensive definition of when a trade or business is located within (or without) the US. A few specific examples are given. Thus, the performance of personal services in the US constitutes a trade or business located in the US.[10] As noted in 5.2.2, a foreign investor in the US can be considered to have a trade or business in the US when it is trading in stocks or securities through a broker or agent if the investor effects investment transactions through an office or fixed place of business located in the US. In addition, Section 864(c) and the Regulations issued thereunder, which set forth the "effectively connected" definition, contain a number of examples illuminating the business location issue. Those examples are considered in 5.3.2. Again, the issue whether a trade or business is located in the US is one to be determined on the basis of all relevant facts and circumstances. On the one hand, a foreign producer that ships directly to US customers does not have a trade or business located in the US.[11] At the other extreme, if a foreign corporation has

---

9. *See*, e.g. Rev. Rul. 73-522, 1973-2 Cum. Bull. 226 (nonresident alien who visited US once during the year to negotiate leases on real estate he owned was not engaged in trade or business); *Di Portanova v. US*, 690 F.2d 169 (Ct. Cls. 1982) (working interest in minerals did not involve a US trade or business). *See generally* Isenbergh, "The "Trade or Business" of Foreign Taxpayers in the United States", 61 *Taxes* 972 (1983).

An interesting current issue is the extent to which activities undertaken through the Internet will constitute a trade or business. Traditionally, soliciting US sales without any physical presence in the US does not amount to performance of a trade or business in the US. *Cf. Piedras Negras Broadcasting Co. v. US*, 43 B.T.A. 297, aff'd 127 F. 2d 260 (5th Cir. 1942). But perhaps the concept of physical presence is outdated in the light of the technological developments which make it increasingly irrelevant. For some current thinking on the question, *see* US Treas. Dept., *White Paper on Tax Policy Implications of Global Electronic Commerce* (Nov. 1996). The same issues arises in connection with permanent establishments in the treaty context and are discussed in 11.5.2.

Section 875 provides that a nonresident alien individual or a foreign corporation that is a partner in a partnership (or the beneficiary of an estate or trust) which is engaged in a US trade or business is considered also to be engaged in a US trade or business. On the other hand, grantors of trusts are not considered to be engaged in a US trade or business *merely* because the trustee is engaged in a US trade or business. Treas. Reg. Sec. 1.875-2(b).

10. Sec. 864(b)(1).

11. *See* Rev. Rul. 73-158, 1973-1 Cum. Bull. 337. But if the sales are effected through the foreign corporation's resident US agent, the foreign corporation may have a US-located business. Rev. Rul. 70-424, 1970-2 Cum. Bull. 150.

its principal office in the US and conducts all its activities there, it will obviously have a business situs in the US. But most situations will not be so clear cut and have to be resolved on the basis of the extent of the corporation's business functions carried on in the US.[12]

5.3 The "effectively connected" concept

5.3.1 GENERAL

The third of the critical definitional aspects of the US system for taxation of nonresident aliens and foreign corporations is the "effectively connected" concept. If a nonresident alien or foreign corporation has derived income from US sources (under the rules described in Chapter 4) and if that individual or corporation is engaged in a trade or business in the US (under the rules described in 5.2), then the actual tax treatment of the income depends on whether it is effectively connected with the conduct of a trade or business in the US.[13] Section 864(c) and the Regulations issued thereunder prescribe the tests to be utilized in determining whether or not income is effectively connected with a US trade or business.

The "effectively connected" rules involve four categories of US source income: (1) gain or loss from the sale or exchange of capital assets; (2) fixed or determinable annual or periodical gains, profits or income (described in Sections 871(a)(1) and 881(a)(1)); (3) gain or loss from the disposition of US real property interests;[14] and (4) all other income, gain or loss. The US system of imposing tax on such income derived by nonresident aliens and foreign corporations will be discussed in greater detail in 5.4 and 5.5. However, it will be useful to summarize the general pattern of taxation at this point to demonstrate the results that follow a determination that a particular class of US source income either is or is not income effectively connected with a US trade or business.

---

12. For examples, *see* Treas. Reg. Sec. 1.864-3(b).

13. In general, if a nonresident alien or foreign corporation at no time during the taxable year is engaged in a trade or business in the US, no income will be treated as effectively connected income. Sec. 864(c)(1)(B). However, if income which is attributable to the sale or exchange of property or the performance of services is received in a year in which the foreign person is not engaged in a trade or business but would have been treated as effectively connected if it had been received in an earlier year, then the income will remain effectively connected. For example, if the foreign person sells US business assets for deferred payments and receives the payments in a later year after the US business has been terminated, the gain will reman effectively connected. Sec. 864(c)(6). Similarly, if property ceases to be used in a US trade or business and is sold within ten years, the gain on the sale will reman effectively connected. Sec. 864(c)(7). This latter rule is of course extremely difficult to enforce if the property is removed from the United States.

14. Under Sec. 897(a), gain from disposition of US real property interests is deemed to be effectively connected.

Nonresident aliens		
Category of income	*If income is effectively connected*	*If income is not effectively connected*
1. Capital gains	Net income taxed at US individual income tax rates	No US tax unless the individual is in the US for 183 days[15]
2. Fixed or determinable income	Net income taxed at US individual income tax rates	Gross income taxed at flat 30% rate[16]
3. US real property interest gains	Net income taxed at individual rates (AMT rates)	Treated as effectively connected income
4. Other income	Net income taxed at US individual income tax rates	Treated as effectively connected income

Foreign corporations		
Category of income	*If income is effectively connected*	*If income is not effectively connected*
1. Capital gains	Net income taxed at regular corporate rate	No US tax
2. Fixed or determinable income	Net income taxed at regular corporate rates	Gross income taxed at flat 30% rate
3. US real property interest gains	Net income taxed at regular corporate rate	Treated as effectively connected income
4. Other income	Net income taxed at regular corporate rates	Treated as effectively connected income

---

15. Normally, in these circumstances the individual would be classified as a resident and thus subject to tax on worldwide income. The rule thus is only applicable to special categories of aliens such as students and diplomats. See discussion at 5.4.2.
16. Some items of fixed or determinable income are explicitly exempted from tax. See 5.4.5. The 30 per cent rate is often reduced by treaty. See 11.6.

Thus, in general terms, the effectively connected concept divides US source income between a foreign investor's two pockets. Income that is effectively connected (or is so treated) is placed in his business pocket and taxed at full US rates on a net basis; income that is not effectively connected is placed in his "investment" pocket and taxed at a flat rate on a gross basis.

5.3.2 CAPITAL GAINS AND FIXED OR DETERMINABLE INCOME

Section 864(c)(2) prescribes two tests for determining whether US source capital gain income and fixed or determinable income is effectively connected with the conduct of a US trade or business. The term "capital gain income" refers to gains (or losses) derived from the sale of exchange of a capital asset.[17] The term "fixed or determinable income" refers in general to interest, dividends, rents, salaries, wages, premiums, annuities, compensations, remunerations, emoluments and certain other gains.[18]

The tests to be applied to these two categories of income are (1) the "asset use" test and (2) the "business activities" test.

5.3.2.1 The "asset use" test

The "asset use" test is employed primarily to determine whether US source passive investment income, such as interest or dividends, constitutes effectively connected income.[19] For example, the US branch of a foreign corporation may conduct a manufacturing business and also derive dividend income from stock in a US company or capital gain from the sale of the stock. An asset, such as the stock in the above example, will be considered to be used in the conduct of a US trade or business — and the income, gain or loss derived therefrom thus effectively connected — if any one of three conditions is satisfied.[20]

(1) The asset is held for the principal purpose of promoting the present conduct of a trade or business in the US. For example, assume a foreign corporation that maintains a branch factory in the US acquires all the stock in a financially unstable US corporation that supplies a raw material essential to the foreign corporation's US manufacturing operation. The acquisition was made to insure the continued supply of the raw material to

---

17. The term "capital asset" is defined in Section 1221. *See* 2.2.3 and 2.3.2.2. For materials on the tests employed to determine whether an asset is (or is not) a capital asset, *see* McDaniel, Ault, McMahon and Simmons, *Federal Income Taxation, pp. 806-873 (1994)*.
18. Sections 871(a) and 881(a), discussed in 5.4 and 5.5, define "fixed or determinable income" in detail.
19. Treas. Reg. Sec. 1.864-4(c)(2)(i).
20. Treas. Reg. Sec. 1.864-4(c)(2)(ii).

the branch factory operation. Dividends paid on the stock, or gain or loss on the sale of the stock, will be considered effectively connected income because the asset producing the income promotes the present conduct of the US business.

(2) The asset is acquired and held in the ordinary course of business conducted in the US. Assume that in the above example the US branch factory commonly sold its products by taking trade notes receivable in payment. Interest income on the notes would constitute effectively connected income.

(3) The asset is otherwise held in a "direct relationship" to the trade or business conducted in the US.[21] The requisite "direct relationship" exists if the asset is presently needed in the business.

Thus, in the above example, assume the US branch factory requires a large cash balance to conduct its business. However, the amount required varies through the year as the result of the cyclical nature of the business. The US branch therefore invests the cash in short-term notes during these periods. Interest earned on the notes will be effectively connected income since the notes are required to meet present business needs. By contrast, if the cash were invested in securities in preparation for a future diversification or expansion by the US branch, its interest income would not be effectively connected since the securities would not be held to meet the present needs of the business.[22]

In addition, the Regulations create a presumption that a "direct relationship" exists if: (1) the asset was acquired from funds generated by the US trade or business; (2) the income from the asset is retained in the business; and (3) personnel in the US who are actively involved in the business exercise significant management and control over the investment of the asset. This presumption is, however, rebuttable by the taxpayer. Therefore, in the foregoing example, even if the investment securities were acquired out of funds generated by the US branch business, interest payments were retained in the business, and the managing officers of the US branch were responsible for supervising the investment, the income from the securities would not be effectively connected because the fact that the securities were acquired to meet future rather than present needs of the business would rebut the presumption of a "direct relationship" created by the Regulations.[23]

5.3.2.2   The "business-activities" test

The "business-activities" test is applied primarily to determine if income derived by dealers in stocks or securities, investment companies, those engaged

---

21. Treas. Reg. Sec. 1.864-4(c)(2)(iv).
22. Treas. Reg. Sec. 1.864-4(c)(2)(v), Ex. (1) and (2).
23. Treas. Reg. Sec. 1.864-4(c)(2)(iv)(b).

in the business of licensing patents, and service businesses constitutes effectively connected income.[24] Management of an investment portfolio does not fall within the business activities test unless that activity is the principal activity of the US trade or business. As in the case of the "asset use" test, the objective of the "business activities" test is to determine whether passive income — dividends, rents, royalties, etc. — "arises directly from" the US trade or business. Detailed rules are provided in the Regulations for application of the test to banking, financing and similar businesses conducted in the US.[25]

5.3.3 GAINS FROM THE DISPOSITION OF US REAL PROPERTY INTERESTS

Prior to 1980, properly advised foreign investors in US real estate could generally dispose of the property free of any US tax on the capital gain. A variety of techniques were used to achieve this result. These tax plans generally took advantage of the fact that, under normally applicable US tax rules, the US imposed no tax on capital gains, including gains from the disposition of real estate, unless the taxpayer was engaged in a US trade or business or, in the case of individuals, was present in the US for 183 days during the taxable year.

The rapid increase in the level of foreign investment in US real estate and agricultural operations which took place in the late 1970s led to closer scrutiny of these transactions by the US Government. Part of the response to the situation was the enactment of the Foreign Investment in Real Property Tax Act ("FIRPTA") of 1980.

Under Sectioin 897, gain or loss realized by a nonresident alien individual or foreign corporation from the "disposition" of a "United States real property interest" is taxed as if the foreign investor were engaged in a US trade or business and as if the gain or loss were effectively connected to that trade or business.[26] As a result, the ordinary US rates apply to such gains. The AMT rates are imposed on gain realized by nonresident alien individuals.[27] For foreign corporations, the regular corporate rate generally will be applicable.

A "United States real property interest" may be either (1) a direct interest in real property located in the US or (2) an interest (other than solely as a creditor) in a domestic "United States real property holding corporation" (RPHC). An RPHC is a corporation in which the fair market value of US real property interests owned by the corporation equals or exceeds 50 per cent of the sum of the fair market value of the corporation's US real property interests plus its for-

---

24. Treas. Reg. Sec. 1.864-4(c)(3).
25. Treas. Reg. Sec. 1.864-4(c)(5). *See* Rev. Rul. 86-154, 1986-2 Cum. Bull. 103 (securities held by branch of foreign bank in the US; various situations distinguished).
26. Sec. 897(a)(1).
27. Sec. 897(a)(2).

eign real property interests plus all other assets used in its trade or business.[28] If, under the foregoing test, a corporation was a domestic RPHC at any time during the five years preceding the disposition of the taxpayer's shares in the RPHC, the gain (or loss) is recognized by the foreign taxpayer.[29] Special rules apply to investment in US real estate through a real estate investment trust (REIT.).[30]

Thus, where a foreign investor owns US real estate directly or through a US corporation which is an RPHC, gain on a sale or exchange of either the property or the stock will be fully subject to US tax. Moreover, the techniques discussed in 2.2.3 and 2.2.6 for exchanging property on a tax-free basis generally are not available unless the property received in the exchange is such that the gain on its sale would be subject to US tax. The Act gave the Treasury broad authority to issue Regulations which determine the extent to which the various nonrecognition provisions discussed in Chapter 2 will or will not apply to exchanges of US real estate interests or stock in a domestic RPHC.[31]

Different rules apply where the US real property interest is owned by a foreign corporation. The gain on disposition of stock in a foreign corporation which owns a US real property interest is not subject to tax under Section 897. Instead, tax is deferred until the corporation itself disposes of the interest whether by sale or exchange, dividend distribution, or distribution pursuant to a redemption or liquidation. The tax is then imposed on the corporation.[32] The gain subject to tax is the difference between the fair market value of the interest at the time of distribution and its adjusted basis. Neither statutory tax-free exchanges nor the use of tax treaty elections, discussed above, can be used to avoid US tax on the disposition of US real property interests by a foreign corporation.

The FIRPTA provisions are reinforced by withholding requirements, as discussed at 5.8.2.2. Treaty implications of the legislation are considered in Chapter 11.

---

28. Sec. 897(c). Special "look through" rules are applied so that a corporation is treated as owning its pro rata share of the relevant assets of corporations controlled (50 per cent) by it. Attribution rules are applied to determine whether the requisite 50 per cent control exists.
29. The disposition of the stock in a domestic RPHC is not taxable, however, if the corporation has disposed of its US real property in a taxable transaction prior to the disposition of the stock. Sec. 897(c)(1)(B). There is also an exception if the stock of the RPHC is publicly traded and the selling shareholder owns five per cent or less of the stock. Sec. 897(c)(3).
30. See 2.6.2. Dividend distributions by a REIT attributable to real estate operating income are taxed as normal dividends; dividends attributable to gains on the disposition of US real property interests by the REIT retain that character in the hands of foreign investors and are taxed as effectively connected income. Sec. 897(h)(1). REIT shares are treated as US real property interests unless the REIT is domestically controlled. Sec. 897(h)(2).
31. Sec. 897(e); Temp. Treas. Reg. Sec. 1.897-6T.
32. Sec. 897(d). As discussed at 2.2.6, prior to 1986 corporate level gain was generally not recognized on the distribution of appreciated property by a corporation to its shareholders. The 1980 treatment of distributions of US real property interests held by foreign corporations was a precursor of the 1986 Act changes.

5.3.4   OTHER INCOME

US source income other than capital gains and fixed or determinable income is treated as effectively connected income if the taxpayer conducts a trade or business in the US. Such income will therefore be taxed at full US rates even though it has no actual connection at all with the trade or business actually conducted in the US. To this extent the "force of attraction" principle still has a limited application. For example, suppose a foreign corporation sells two products. It establishes a US branch to sell one of the products in the US. The other product is sold directly to US customers by the home office abroad, with the home office shipping directly to the US customers. The sales income of the home office is treated as effectively connected income even though it in fact has no connection with the business actually conducted by the US branch.[33]

5.3.5   FOREIGN SOURCE INCOME EFFECTIVELY CONNECTED WITH A US BUSINESS

The preceding materials have discussed the rules applied by the US to determine whether its full tax rates should be applied to US source income derived by nonresident aliens or foreign corporations. The detailed nature of those rules is intended to provide guidance and a relatively high degree of certainty so that foreign investors can determine in advance the tax consequences of US investment. In addition, the particularity of the rules is designed to insure that the United States is not utilized as a tax haven.

In furtherance of this latter objective, certain categories of *foreign source* income are treated as effectively connected with the conduct of a US trade or business and hence subject to full US tax rates. In general, foreign source income is not treated as effectively connected income. (Section 864(c)(4)(A).) However, Section 864(c)(4)(B) details specific types of income that will be treated as effectively connected with a US trade or business even though the income is determined to arise from a foreign source under the rules discussed in Chapter 4. The types of foreign source income selected for this special treatment include those that are especially susceptible to manipulation by taxpayers to obtain tax advantages. In the absence of Section 864(c)(4)(B), transactions

---

33. Treas. Reg. Sec. 1.864-4(b). As discussed in 5.2.2 above, an alien individual who is a partner in a US partnership which is engaged in a US trade or business is also considered to be engaged in a US trade or business. Under Treas. Reg. Sec. 1.875-1, such a nonresident alien partner is subject to full US income tax on any effectively connected income if the partnership "at any time during the taxable year" was engaged in a US trade or business. As a result a nonresident alien who becomes a limited partner on the last day of a taxable year could subject previously earned "other income" to full US tax since such income is treated as effectively connected income if the taxpayer is engaged in a US trade or business. *See Vitale v. Commissioner,* 72 TC 386 (1979), for an application of this result under pre-1966 law.

could be arranged so that the income was treated as from a foreign source under the source rules, even though the transaction in fact had substantial economic ties to the US. In a sense the results with respect to effectively connected foreign source income can be seen as a modification of the otherwise applicable source rules discussed in Chapter 4. Put another way, the types of income covered have such a relationship to the US that they should be treated as US source income and taxed accordingly. However, instead of formally changing the source rules in these situations, the Code applies the effectively connected concept to what is still technically foreign source income. This choice of technique has some important implications. For example, in some of its income tax treaties, the US has obligated itself to tax only US source income of foreign taxpayers. In such cases, the treaty provisions can prevent the application of the effectively connected concept to what is still technically foreign source income.[34]

Foreign source income will be treated as effectively connected with a US trade or business if it is "attributable" to an "office or other fixed place of business" in the US. Both of the quoted terms are defined in the statute (Section 864(c)(5)) and given detailed content by the Regulations.

The foreign source income that can be treated as effectively connected income if the above conditions are satisfied includes (1) rents or royalties and gain or loss from intangible property which is located or used outside the US if derived from the active conduct of a trade or business in the US;[35] and (2) dividends or interest and gain or loss from stocks or securities which are derived in the conduct of a US trade or business either by banks or other financial institutions or by a corporation whose principal business is trading in stocks or securities for its own account.[36] Thus, for example, if the US branch of a foreign bank makes a loan to a Mexican borrower, the interest income may be taxed under section 864(c)(4) if the statutory tests are met despite the fact that the interest income technically has a foreign source.

Under Section 865(e)(2), income from the sale of personal property (including inventory) attributable to a US branch of a foreign taxpayer in general has a US source where the sale occurs outside the US but is effected through the US office. Such income is treated as effectively connected US source income (regardless of where the title to the property passes) and is subject to tax under

---

34. *See* Rev. Rul. 74-63, 1974-1 Cum. Bull. 374 (pre-1986 law).
35. Treas. Reg. Sec. 1.864-5(b)(1).
36. Treas. Reg. Sec. 1.864 5(b)(2). The Regulations exempt income derived from incidental investment activity — portfolio investments — and specifically state that a holding company is not a corporation whose principal business is trading in stocks or securities. In addition, income described in categories (1) and (2) in the text does not constitute effectively connected income if the recipient owns more than 50 per cent of all the voting stock of the corporate payor or if the income constitutes subpart F income (7.2.4.1).

Section 882. However, if a foreign office of the taxpayer participates materially in the sale and the property is sold for use outside the US the income will have a foreign source and will not be subject to US tax.[37]

5.4 Taxation of nonresident aliens

5.4.1 GENERAL

The general pattern of taxation discussed in paragraphs 5.2 and 5.3 applies to *nonresident* aliens. *Resident* aliens are taxed on their worldwide income in the same manner as US citizens. (*See* Chapter 3.) Thus an individual's status as resident or nonresident is a crucial element in establishing the appropriate taxing regime. The following material deals with the determination of resident or nonresident status and then examines in more detail the rules for the taxation of nonresident aliens. The special rules that may apply when a long term permanent resident abandons his residence are considered in 5.4.7.

5.4.2 DETERMINATION OF STATUS AS RESIDENT OR NONRESIDENT

Section 7701(b) has detailed rules to determine the resident or nonresident status of aliens.[38] In general, an alien will be treated as a US resident if he meets any of the following three tests:

    (1) the permanent residence test;

---

37. Section 865(e)(2)(B). One effect of this rule is to allow the US to tax such income in certain circumstances under tax treaties which restrict the US taxing right to US source income. It also affects the foreign tax credit allowed to foreign persons. Sec. 906 (6.4.4). Sec. 864(c)(4) continues to apply to sales of inventory by individuals who are US residents for purposes of Sec. 865 because they have a "tax home," i.e., principal place of business, in the US but are nonresidents under Sec. 7701(b)(5.4.2).

38. Prior to the enactment of Sec. 7701(b) in 1984, an alien's status as resident or nonresident was a factual question involving his intention with respect to the length and nature of the stay in the US. An intention to remain for an indefinite period was sufficient to establish residence while an intention to leave the US after a relatively short period established nonresidence. The question of residence was frequently litigated and the courts considered a variety of factors in determining the alien's intention. The following are some representative cases: *Siddiqi v. Commissioner,* 70 TC 553 (1978) (resident alien status where taxpayer entered the United States for an expected stay of 4-5 years to study architecture; compensation earned from temporary employment taxable at full US tax rates); *Jellinek v. Commissioner,* 36 TC 826 (1961) (nonresident alien status despite filing a declaration of intention to become a US citizen where the taxpayer returned to the foreign country within a short period of time because of lack of US employment opportunities); *Park v. Commissioner,* 79 TC 252 (1982) (taxpayer resident where he had substantial business and social connections to US despite fact that visa limited stay).

(2) the 183 day test; or

(3) the cumulative presence test.

In all other circumstances, he will be treated as a nonresident.

5.4.2.1 *The permanent residence test*

If an alien has the status of having been lawfully accorded the privilege of residing in the US under US immigration laws,[39] he is treated as a resident alien until such status has been revoked or otherwise terminated. Resident treatment under this test does not require that the alien actually be present in the US at any time during the year in question as long as he was present in the US at any time in a prior year.[40]

5.4.2.2 *The 183-day test*

Even if an alien does not have permanent resident status, he will be treated as a resident for tax purposes if he is physically present in the US for 183 days or more in the calendar year and does not qualify as an "exempt individual". Exempt individuals are, generally speaking, teachers, students and trainees and foreign government officials. Residence begins at the time the alien is first present in the US and continues for the remaining portion of that calendar year. Residence ends on the day that the alien leaves the US if the alien at that time has a closer connection to a foreign country than to the US and is not a resident at any time during the next calendar year.[41]

5.4.2.3 *The cumulative presence test*

If the alien is not present in the US for 183 days in the current year, he still may be treated as a resident alien on the basis of his cumulative presence in the US over the current year and the preceding two years if he was present in the US in the current year for at least 31 days. In determining cumulative presence, days present in the current year are added to one-third of the days present in the first

---

39. In general, this means that an alien holds a valid "green card" entitling him to unrestricted permanent residence in the United States. Sec. 7701(b)(6).
40. Sec. 7701(b)(2)(A). Under prior law, permanent residence status was considered an important factor in determining intent but was not by itself controlling. Permanent residence status continues until it has been formally determined to be rescinded or abandoned. Thus an alien who continues to hold a green card after leaving the United States and moving to a foreign country will still be treated as a US resident until steps are taken to formally abandon his US resident status. *See* Treas. Reg. Sec. 301.7701(b)-1(b)(3) for the steps necessary to obtain a formal determination of abandonment of resident status.
41. Sec. 7701(b)(2)(B). Treas. Reg. Sec. 301.7701(b)-3 sets forth detailed rules for determining days of physical presence. There are exceptions for situations where the taxpayer is prevented from leaving for medical purposes or is in transit.

preceding year and one-sixth of the days present in the second preceding year. If the total equals or exceeds 183 days, the alien is treated as a resident unless he can establish that he has his "tax home" (generally speaking, his principal place of business) in a foreign country and has a closer connection to that country than to the US.[42] Thus, for example, if an alien was present in the US for 66 days in 1998, 33 days in 1999 and more than 160 days in 2000, he would be resident in the US for 2000 unless he could meet the "closer connection/tax home" test. Under the cumulative presence test, an alien can spend up to 121 days each year in the US without being considered a resident. In general, the residence starting and ending rules for the cumulative presence test are the same as described in 5.4.2.2 for the 183-day test.

5.4.3 INCOME TAXED AT 30 PER CENT RATE

If a nonresident alien individual is not engaged in a US trade or business, a flat rate of 30 per cent is imposed on four categories of income from US sources:

(1) Fixed or determinable annual or periodic income (generally passive investment income such as dividends, interest and royalties from patents and copyrights).[43]

(2) Original issue discount on certain debt obligations.[45]

(3) The excess of capital gains over capital losses if the taxpayer has been present in the US for 183 days or more during the taxable year.[46]

(4) 85% of Social Security benefits.

---

42. Sec. 7701(b)(3)(B). *See* Treas. Reg. Sec. 301.7701(b)-2 for the factors to be considered in establishing the "closer connection." To take advantage of the "closer connection" exception, the taxpayer must file a statement with the IRS detailing the basis for the claim. Absent a properly filed statement, the exception is generally not available. Treas. Reg. Sec. 301.7701(b)-8.

43. The items of income are specified in Sec. 871(a)(1)(A). *See also* Treas. Reg. Sec. 1.871-7(b). The phrase "fixed or determinable annual or period income" has been given a very wide interpretation. *See, e.g. Commissioner v. Wodehouse,* 337 US 369 (1949) (lump sum payment for literary rights). For a history of the provision, *See Barba v. US,* 2 Cl. Ct. 674 (1983). Sec. 1441 requires that US payors of fixed or determinable income that is not effectively connected income withhold US tax on that income at a rate of 30 per cent. *See* 5.8.2.1.
    With respect to transactions involving patents, know-how, and other intangibles, royalties paid under a license agreement are subject to the 30 per cent withholding tax. In addition, if the transfer of the intangible is formally structured as a sale rather than a license, but payments are contingent on the productivity or use of the intangible, the transaction is treated as a license and the payments are subject to withholding as royalties. *See* Sec. 871(a)(1)(D).

45. See 2.7. Under Sec. 1273, original issue discount is deemed to accrue currently during the period that an original issue discount obligation is outstanding. Such accrued discount income is taxed to nonresidents at the time any payments (whether principal or interest) are made on the obligation. In addition any accrued but untaxed discount income is taxed when the obligation is sold. Sec. 871(a)(1)(C). No tax is imposed on original issue discount obligations which have a term of 183 days or less. Sec. 871(g)(1)(B).

46. Sec. 871(a)(2). This section has little current application in light of the present statutory definition of resident. See 5.4.2. In normal circumstances, an alien who was present in the US for 183 days or more would be treated as a resident and subject to tax at normal rates on his worldwide

The 30 per cent rate is applied to income of the type discussed above even when the nonresident alien is engaged in a US trade or business, as long as the income is not "effectively connected" under the tests outlined in 5.3.[47]

Where the income is subject to the 30 per cent rate, the tax is imposed on gross income. Thus, no deductions are allowed even though attributable to the income subject to tax. In the case of capital gains, the tax is imposed on the gain reduced by losses.

5.4.4 INCOME TAXED AT FULL US TAX RATES

All income of a nonresident alien that is (or is treated as) effectively connected with the conduct of a US trade or business is subject to the progressive US tax rates normally applicable to residents.[48] As in the case of US individuals, the rates are applied to taxable income (rather than to gross income as in the case of items described in 5.4.3). Thus, gross income (as defined in Section 872) is reduced by the deductions that are "connected with income" which itself is "effectively connected" income (as specified in Section 873).[49] In addition, Section 873 allows gross income to be reduced by one personal exemption, the deduction for charitable contributions and personal casualty losses even though these items are not so "connected".[50] Finally, various credits against tax are allowed.[51]

---

income and Sec. 871(a)(2) would have no application. The section could apply, for example, to students and foreign government officials who are exempted from the residence definition but who meet the Sec. 871(a)(2) test.

47. Treas. Reg. Sec. 1.871-8(b)(1).

48. Gains, realized by the individual, from the disposition of US real property interests are deemed to be effectively connected income and are subject to the AMT rates. Sec. 897(a)(2).

49. The rules for allocating and apportioning deductions are those set forth in Treas. Reg. Sec. 1.861-8 and following and 1.863-1 through 5, discussed in 4.4. No deduction is allowed for an expenditure that is allocable to an item exempt from tax. *See* Treas. Reg. Sec. 1.873-1(a)(1), (5). Sec. 874 requires a nonresident alien to file a return in order to obtain the benefit of the deductions allowed by Sec. 873. *Brittingham v. Commissioner,* 66 TC 373 (1976), held that even though some return is filed, no deductions are allowed if it is not a "true and accurate" return. *See also, Espinosa v. Commissioner,* 107 TC 146 (no deductions where timely return not filed; no waiver for "good cause" allowed).

50. A nonresident alien is not given the benefit of the standard deduction amount discussed in 2.3.2.6 because personal deductions are generally not allowed to such taxpayers. Sec. 63(c)(6)(B). In addition, if the nonresident is married, the preferential married person's rate schedule is not available. If a nonresident is married to a US citizen or resident, however, Sec. 6013(g) and (h) permit the spouses to elect to treat the nonresident spouse as a US resident and file a joint return. They are required to include their worldwide income but are then entitled to claim personal exemptions for themselves and qualified dependents, the standard deduction amount, tax credits, the married persons rate schedule, etc., just as in a joint return filed by married US citizens or residents.

51. Treas. Reg. Sec. 1.871-8(d).

5.4.5 EXEMPT INCOME

A number of provisions exempt from tax under Section 871(a) specified categories of US source income received by nonresident aliens.

5.4.5.1 Bank deposits

Interest on bank deposits with US banks paid to nonresident aliens is exempt from tax if such interest is not effectively connected with the alien's US trade or business. Prior to 1986, the exemption was effected by treating such interest as foreign source income; the 1986 Act modified the source rules to treat such interest as US source income and made the exemption from tax explicit. Section 871(i)(2)(A).

5.4.5.2 Dividends from foreign business income

If a domestic corporation derives 80 per cent or more of its income from an active foreign business in the three year testing period preceding the year in which it pays a dividend,[52] the portion of the dividend deemed to be paid out of the foreign business income is not subject to tax under Section 871(a). Thus, for example, if a domestic corporation has 90 per cent of its income in the testing period from an active foreign business and pays a dividend to a nonresident alien shareholder, only ten per cent of the dividend will be subject to tax under Section 871.[53]

5.4.5.3 Portfolio interest

Section 871(h) exempts from tax under Section 871(a) US source "portfolio interest" received by a nonresident alien. With respect to interest on "bearer" obligations, i.e. obligations which are not issued in registered form, the interest can qualify as portfolio interest only if the obligations are issued in a manner which "targets" the issue to foreign markets and the interest is payable only outside the US.[54] If the obligations are issued in registered form, the interest qualifies as portfolio interest if the US borrower paying the interest receives a

---

52. For the mechanics of the three-year testing period, see 4.2.1.
53. Prior to 1986, dividends in the circumstances described in the text were treated as foreign source income. As in the case of bank deposits, the 1986 Act modified the source rule to treat such income as US source but made the payment to nonresidents exempt from tax. Sec. 871(i)(2)(B).
54. Sec. 163(f)(2)(B). Treas. Reg. Sec. 1.163-5(c) sets forth the procedures which must be followed for the issuance to qualify as "foreign targeted." The purpose of the foreign targeting requirements is to insure in so far as possible that the obligations will not be issued to US persons.

statement from the beneficial owner of the interest that the recipient is not a US person.[55] The interest cannot be received from a corporation or partnership in which the recipient has a ten per cent or greater interest, thus insuring that the interest is on a portfolio-type investment.

The portfolio interest exemption also does not apply to bank loans made in the ordinary course of business. In addition, the definition of portfolio interest does not include "contingent" interest where the interest is determined by reference to income, cash flow, sales, etc. of the debtor or a related person. Section 871(h)(4)(C). The enactment of the exemption for portfolio interest by the United States was an important step in the "race to the bottom" with respect to source taxation of interest income generally.

5.4.5.4 *Capital gains*

Capital gains of a nonresident who does not meet the 183-day presence test of Section 871(a)(2) and which are not connected with a US trade or business are not taxable.[56]

5.4.6 TREATIES

Treaty provisions agreed to by the US and another country may modify the rules described above. (See Chapter 11.)

5.4.7 TAXATION OF NONRESIDENT ALIENS WHO ARE FORMER US CITIZENS OR LEGAL PERMANENT RESIDENTS.

Special rules in Section 877 apply for the taxation of nonresidents who have lost their US citizenship or permanent residence status where that change in status is determined to have been for tax avoidance purposes. While the special regime in Section 877 has long existed for former citizens, it proved largely ineffectual. Congress, reacting to some highly publicized cases of tax motivated expatriation, substantially strengthened the provision in 1996 and extended it to long term permanent residents who abandon their US residence. In general terms, where the provision applies, former citizens and residents continue to be taxed for ten years at normal rates on all US source income and for these purposes the concept of US source is substantially broadened.

---

55. Prop. Treas. Reg. Sec. 1.871-14 (1996).
56. The capital gain distributions of a mutual fund (regulated investment company) are also exempt from tax. Rev. Rul. 69-244, 1969 2 Cum. Bull. 215.

5.4.7.1   Former citizens

If the loss of citizenship had as "one of its principal purposes" the avoidance of US taxation, then the extended pattern of taxation of Section 877 applies for ten years after the loss of citizenship. The question of purpose is a factual one but if the loss of citizenship would involve a "substantial" reduction in tax, the burden of proof of showing the lack of a tax avoidance purpose is on the taxpayer. In addition, if the taxpayer had an average income of more than $100,000 for the last 5 years or has a net worth of at least $500,000 at the time of loss of citizenship, he is deemed to have a tax avoidance purpose.[57]

5.4.7.2   Former residents

Under Section 877, "long term" permanent resident aliens who cease to be lawful permanent residents (see 5.4.2.1) are treated in general in the same way as expatriating citizens. However, there are no exceptions applicable to the presumption of tax avoidance purpose created by the income and net worth tests. An alien is a "long term" permanent resident if he had this status for eight of the fifteen years prior to abandonment of residence status. Similar rules apply if the alien remains a permanent resident (i.e., keeps his green card) but moves to a country which has a tax treaty which would prevent the US from asserting personal tax jurisdiction under the treaty. See 11.4.1.1.

A separate rule applies without regard to purpose to any resident alien (whether or not a lawful permanent resident) who, having been a resident for at least 3 years, abandons his residence and reestablishes residence within three years. Section 7701(b)(10). In that situation, Section 877 applies in the interim years.

5.4.7.3   Pattern of taxation

Where Section 877 applies, the former citizen or resident is taxed on his US source income at the higher of the normally applicable rates for residents or the rates for nonresidents for a 10 year period following the change in status. For these purposes, "US source" income includes gain on the sale of stock or securities in US corporations and US governmental obligations as well as personal

---

57. These rules are in response to the singular lack of success the IRS had in establishing a tax avoidance purpose under the previous version of Sec. 877. *See, e.g., Furstenberg v. Commissioner,* 83 TC 755 (1984). Certain categories of taxpayers are exempt from the deemed tax avoidance purpose in circumstances where it would be natural to assume that the expatriation was not tax avoidance motivated, for example, adopting the citizenship of the taxpayer's country of birth or of the taxpayer's spouse. However, to qualify for the exemption, the taxpayer must apply for an IRS ruling that a tax avoidance purpose was in fact not present. Sec. 877(c).

property located in the US. Such gain would normally be foreign source under Section 865 and hence not taxable to a nonresident. Gain on the sale of stock in a foreign controlled corporation owned at the time of expatriation is also treated as US source. Attempts to avoid the rules by contributing US property to a foreign corporation are anticipated by providing that in such cases the gain will remain taxable. In the case of ex-residents, an election can be made to take a tax basis in the assets equal to their fair market value at the time of becoming a US resident, thus limiting the US tax claim to appreciation which took place while the taxpayer was a resident. An earlier proposal would have made the expatriation a realization event, following the pattern in a number of other countries but Congress chose to extend the scope of Section 877 instead.

5.5 Taxation of foreign corporations

5.5.1 GENERAL

The US method of taxation of foreign corporations follows in most respects the rules applicable to nonresident alien individuals. Thus, in general, US source investment income is taxed at a flat 30 per cent rate if it is not effectively connected with the conduct of a US trade or business or at the normal corporate rates (generally 35 per cent) if it is effectively connected. The classification rules discussed at 2.1.2 determine whether a foreign organization will be subject to tax as a corporation.

5.5.2 INCOME OF FOREIGN CORPORATIONS TAXED AT 30 PER CENT RATE

If a foreign corporation is not engaged in a US trade or business during the taxable year, a tax of 30 per cent is imposed on its gross income from US sources that consists of (1) fixed or determinable annual or periodic income; (2) original issue discount and (3) gains from the sale or exchange of intangibles such as patents and copyrights to the extent that the gains are contingent on the productivity, use or disposition of the property sold.[58]

Even though a corporation is engaged in a US trade or business, income of the type described in the preceding paragraph is taxed at the 30 per cent rate if it is not effectively connected with the conduct of the US trade or business.

---

58. Sec. 881(a)(4). The definition of fixed or determinable annual or periodic income in Sec. 881(a) follows that in Sec. 871(a) discussed in 5.4.3.

5.5.3 INCOME OF FOREIGN CORPORATIONS TAXED AT NORMAL CORPORATION TAX RATES

The taxable income of a foreign corporation that is (or is treated as)[59] effectively connected with the conduct of a US trade or business is taxed at the normal US corporate rates. In determining taxable income, the starting point is gross income which is effectively connected with the US trade or business. Deductions are allowable to the extent that they are "connected with income" that is itself effectively connected income.[60] A charitable contribution deduction is allowed whether or not it is so connected. In addition, credits against tax are allowed.

5.5.4 EXEMPT INCOME

Interest on bank deposits, portfolio interest, dividends from US corporations from foreign business income and capital gains are exempt from tax if not effectively connected with a US trade or business. (*See* 5.4.5.)

5.5.5 BRANCH PROFITS TAX

5.5.5.1 *Background*

Prior to 1986, dividends paid by a foreign corporation conducting a trade or business in the US constituted US source income if 50 per cent or more of the corporation's gross income, for the preceding three years, was effectively connected with the US trade or business.[61] The amount of the US source dividend depended on the ratio of the effectively connected income to the total amount of income in the testing period. As US source income, the dividend was subject to tax in the hands of a nonresident alien or foreign corporate shareholder and the foreign distributing corporation was required to withhold US tax at the 30 per cent rate on the distribution. This so-called "second level" dividend tax was difficult to administer since it required calculation of the corporation's world wide income and imposed a withholding liability on a foreign corporation making a distribution to foreign shareholders. In addition, through proper planning, liability for the tax could be avoided by keeping the foreign corporation's

---

59. Gains from the disposition of US real property interests by a foreign corporation are treated as effectively connected with the conduct of a US trade or business. The term "disposition" includes dividend distributions and distributions pursuant to a redemption or liquidation.
60. Sec. 882(c)(1). See 5.4.4.
61. Sec. 861(a)(2)(B) (former version).

income below the 50 per cent threshold. The 1986 Act effectively eliminated the second level dividend tax and replaced it with the branch profits tax of Section 884.[62]

5.5.5.2 Structure of the branch profits tax

Section 884 imposes a 30 per cent tax on a foreign corporation's "dividend equivalent amount" which is defined as the foreign corporation's effectively connected earnings and profits.[63] This tax is in addition to the regular corporate income tax but, since the tax is based on earnings and profits, the corporate income tax is in effect deductible from the branch profits tax base. Thus if a foreign corporation has 100 of effectively connected earnings before corporate tax, it would pay 35 of regular corporate tax and then $100 - 35 = 65 \times 30\%$ or 19.5 of branch profits tax for a total tax burden of 54.5. Dividend distributions by the foreign corporation, even if constituting US source income under Section 861(a)(2), are correspondingly not subject to tax when paid to its foreign shareholders.

The branch profits tax can be deferred and, in certain circumstances, avoided altogether if the earnings potentially subject to tax are reinvested in the US business. Technically, under Section 884(b)(1) the amount of effectively connected earnings is reduced by the increase in "US net equity" for the year. US net equity is essentially the net investment in the assets used in the US trade or business.[64] Thus, in the example above, if the foreign corporation had 500 of net US assets at the beginning of the year and 565 at the end of the year, no branch profits tax would be due. The 65 of net earnings are deemed to have been reinvested in the US business.[65] If, however, the branch profits tax for a

---

62. Technically, the second level dividend tax is retained and the effectively connected income threshold is reduced from 50 to 25 per cent. Sec. 861(a)(2)(B). However, Sec. 884(e)(3) provides that the second level dividend tax is not applicable to any dividend paid by a foreign corporation which is subject to the branch profits tax. As a result, the branch profits tax replaces the second level dividend tax in all situations except those in which a treaty may prevent the application of the branch profits tax but allows a second level dividend tax. *See* 11.4.1.2 and 11.5.

63. As discussed at 2.2.6, earnings and profits is a technical US tax concept which is similar to but not identical with book income less income taxes paid. The notion that a branch can have its own earnings and profits apart from those of the corporation as a whole was unknown in US tax law until introduction of the branch profits tax. For aspects of the determination of the dividend equivalent amount, *see* Treas. Reg. Sec. 1.884-1(b).

64. The calculation is made in terms of tax basis and not fair market value. Sec. 884(c)(2). *See* Treas. Reg. Sec. 1.884-1(c).

65. The calculation of US net equity is not based on a tracing of the earnings but on the total change in the overall US investment. Thus if the foreign corporation in fact remitted the 65 of earnings to the home office but later in the same year transferred an additional 65 of funds to the branch for investment in the business, no branch profits tax would be due. Earnings are in effect "stacked" first against any increase in US net investment regardless of the actual source of the funds used for the investment. *See* Treas. Reg. Sec. 1.884-1(b)(2).

If a foreign corporation is a partner in a partnership which has effectively connected earnings and profits, its share of those earnings is subject to the branch profits tax. Treas. Reg. Sec. 1.884-1(d)(3).

prior year has been avoided through reinvestment and in the current year there is a reduction in US net equity, then the amount of the reduction is included in the branch profits tax base for the current year. Thus, to continue the above example, if in the following year the foreign corporation had an additional 65 of earnings after regular corporate tax and US net equity at the end of the year of 500, both the 65 of current earnings and the 65 of previous earnings on which tax had been deferred would be subject to the branch profits tax in that year.

If the foreign corporation completely terminates its US trade or business, the resulting decrease in US net equity will not trigger an imposition of the branch profits tax on any earnings which had previously escaped the tax through reinvestment.[66]

5.5.5.3 Treaty aspects

In general, the branch profits tax is not imposed where its application would conflict with a US treaty obligation. Section 884(e). This is the case where a treaty contains a nondiscrimination clause which prohibits "less favorable" treatment for the permanent establishment of a treaty country taxpayer when compared with a similarly situated US person. If the branch profits tax applied to the permanent establishment, the foreign taxpayer would be subject to both the regular corporate tax and to the branch profits tax while a similarly situated US corporation would only pay the regular corporate tax.[67] Thus in these circumstances the branch profits tax is not imposed. However, the treaty limitation only prevents the imposition of the tax if the foreign corporation is a "qualified resident" of the treaty country, i.e. the corporation is not being used

---

66. Temp. Treas. Reg. Sec. 1.884-2T. The theory behind this approach is that if the investment had been made through a US corporation which had reinvested its earnings and then subsequently liquidated, no dividend withholding tax would have been imposed on the liquidating distribution. Since the branch profits tax is a replacement for the shareholder level withholding tax, parallel treatment requires that the tax not be imposed when the foreign corporation's US branch operations are in effect "liquidated" through a termination of the US business. The branch can also be "liquidated" by transferring its assets to a US subsidiary corporation in a tax-free transaction. In the latter case, the accumulated earnings on which branch profits tax has not been paid carry over to the transferee corporation, thus supporting future dividend payments. *See* Temp. Treas. Reg. Sec. 1.884-2T(d).

67. It could be argued that since the branch profits tax is really a surrogate for the second level shareholder tax, the foreign corporation is in no different position than a US corporation with foreign shareholders where the corporate level tax applies to the corporate level profits and the withholding tax to corporate distributions. However, the Internal Revenue Service has taken the position that imposition of the branch profits tax, which technically falls on the foreign corporation and not the shareholders, does in fact constitute impermissible discrimination. Treas. Reg. Sec. 1.884-1(g)(3) gives a list of those treaties which prevent the imposition of the branch profits tax. If the treaty permits the imposition of the branch profits tax but stipulates certain conditions for its imposition, the tax will only be applied if the conditions are met. In addition, if the treaty provides for a reduced rate of tax for dividends paid by US subsidiaries to foreign corporate parents, that rate rather than the 30 per cent rate will be used for the branch profits tax. Sec. 884(e)(3)(A); Treas. Reg. Sec. 1.884-1(g)(4).

by residents of third countries for "treaty shopping."[68] Other aspects of the "treaty shopping" problem and the branch profits tax are discussed at 11.4.1.2 and 11.10.

5.5.6 BRANCH INTEREST TAX

5.5.6.1 *General*

In addition to the second level dividend tax described at 5.5.5, prior to 1986 the US also imposed a second level tax on interest paid to foreign recipients by a foreign corporation with substantial amounts of US effectively connected income.[69] The 1986 Act eliminated the second level interest tax and replaced it with the branch interest tax of Section 884(f).[70] Under Section 884(f)(1)(A) interest which is "paid by" a US branch is treated as if it were paid by a domestic corporation. That is, it will be deemed to be US source interest income under Section 861(a)(1) and subject to tax under Section 871(a) and 881(a) when received by foreign persons (unless some exception, for example, the exemption for portfolio interest applies). The statute does not indicate how to determine when interest is "paid by" the branch but extensive Regulations have been issued which deal with the question. In general, interest will be "paid by" the branch if it arises in connection with a liability which is identified in the foreign corporation's books and financial statements as a liability of the US business or is secured by US assets.[71]

Section 884(f)(1)(B) provides a special rule where the amount of the interest "paid by" the branch under Section 884(f)(1)(A) is less than the amount of the interest expense deduction allocated to the branch under Treas. Reg. Sec. 1.882-5. (*See* 4.4.) In this situation, the foreign corporation must pay tax on the difference between the "paid" interest and the "allocated" interest as if the difference were paid to it by a US subsidiary. That is, the difference is treated as interest from US sources, subject to tax as non-effectively connected US

---

68. A foreign corporation is a "qualified resident" and thus is potentially entitled to treaty protection if more than 50 per cent of its stock is owned by treaty country residents (or US persons) and less than 50 per cent of its income is used to meet liabilities to third-country residents. Sec. 884(e)(4) and Treas. Reg. Sec. 1.884-5. Foreign corporations whose stock (or whose parent's stock) is publicly traded on an established securities market in the treaty country are automatically treated as qualified residents. Corporations which cannot meet these "safe haven" tests can still be treated as qualified residents if they are engaged in an active business in the treaty country and in the US. Treas. Reg. Sec. 1.884-5(e).

69. Sec. 861(a)(1)(C) (former version). This section made the interest US source and hence subject to tax under Sec. 871 and 881.

70. Technically the section refers to interest paid by a "US trade or business" of a foreign corporation rather than by a "branch" but the tax is usually referred to as the branch interest tax.

71. Treas. Reg. Sec. 1.884-4(b)(1).

source interest income which the foreign corporation is deemed to have received, and which does not qualify for the portfolio interest exemption. The basic idea behind this special provision is that the US should be able to claim taxing jurisdiction over the amount of interest which is being deducted from the effectively connected corporate tax base. If the foreign corporation had invested in the United States through a US corporation, any interest paid by the US corporation would have been deductible from the corporate tax base but would have been subject to tax in the hands of the related party recipient. Section 884(f)(1)(B) reaches a similar result by treating the foreign corporation as the deemed recipient of the "excess" allocated interest which has been deducted in determining the amount of the effectively connected branch income.

For example, suppose that a US branch books and pays interest expense of 100 to a foreign lender. The 100 of interest would be treated as US source interest income and would be taxable to the foreign lender under either Section 871 or 881 (assuming no exceptions were applicable). The US branch would be required to withhold tax at the 30 per cent rate under Section 1441. Suppose, in addition, that the amount of interest expense allocated to the branch under Treas. Reg. Sec. 1.882-5 (4.4.3.1) in calculating its effectively connected income is 150. The 50 of "excess" interest is deemed to have been received by the foreign corporation as non-effectively connected US source interest income and is taxable at the 30 per cent rate under Section 881(a). Thus, all interest expense which was deducted for purposes of determining the effectively connected income of the branch would have been subject to tax as US source interest income.[72]

5.5.6.2   Treaty aspects

Section 884(f)(3) deals with the treaty aspects of the branch interest tax and provides rules similar to those applicable to the branch profits tax. If a foreign corporation with a branch in the US is a "qualified resident" of a treaty country which has a treaty provision prohibiting the US from imposing tax or reducing the rate of tax on interest paid by a treaty country corporation, then either no tax or the reduced rate of tax will be imposed under Section 884(f)(1)(A). If the foreign corporation is not a qualified resident of the treaty partner but pays interest to a foreign person who is entitled to treaty benefits, the recipient of the interest will be taxed in accordance with the terms of the treaty between the US and the recipient's country (assuming in turn that the recipient is a qualified resident of that country).[73]

---

72. For a case illustrating the operation of the branch interest tax, *see Taiyo Hawaii Company v. Commissioner*, 108 TC 590 (1997).
73. Sec. 884(f)(3)(B).

5.5.7 ALTERNATIVE MINIMUM TAX

Foreign corporations which are engaged in a US trade or business are subject to the alternative minimum tax discussed at 2.2.5. The tax base (book income) is limited to the taxpayer's effectively connected income and loss. Thus, only if an item of income or loss is treated as effectively connected will it enter into the book income computation.[74] In addition, if the foreign taxpayer does not maintain an appropriate financial statement dealing with its US activities, it can elect to compute the net book income on the basis of the taxpayer's earnings and profits which are attributable to income or loss that is effectively connected with the US trade or business as computed for purposes of the branch profits tax. (*See* 5.5.5.) The effectively connected earnings and profits are reduced by federal and foreign tax costs involved. The alternative minimum tax also applies to gains attributable to the disposition of US real property interests which are treated as effectively connected.

5.5.8 PENALTY TAXES APPLICABLE TO FOREIGN CORPORATIONS AND DOMESTIC CORPORATIONS WITH FOREIGN SHAREHOLDERS

5.5.8.1 *Accumulated earnings tax*

5.5.8.1.1 Foreign corporations with US income

As discussed at 2.2.7.1, Section 531 imposes a penalty tax on corporations which accumulate income to avoid the shareholder level tax. The tax is applicable to foreign corporations which accumulate US source income if any of the shareholders of the corporation are subject to tax on the distributions of the corporation.[75] In the case of foreign corporations subject to the branch profits tax, any distributions to foreign shareholders would be exempt from US income tax under Section 884(e)(3). (See 5.5.5.1.) Thus the accumulated earnings tax would not be applicable to such corporations owned entirely by foreign persons. In addition, in many circumstances, US treaties prevent the imposition of US "second level" dividend tax on distributions to foreign shareholders (See 11.6.1). Finally, Section 245 allows a 100 per cent dividends received deduction to US corporate shareholders in foreign corporations for dividends received out of US source effectively connected income of the foreign corporation. Thus

---

74. Treas. Reg. Sec. 1.56-1(b)(6)(ii).
75. Treas. Reg. Sec. 1.532-1(c).

in most circumstances the accumulated earnings tax will not be applicable to foreign corporations.[76]

5.5.8.1.2 Foreign shareholders in domestic corporations

In general, dividends paid by a US corporation to a foreign shareholder would be subject to US tax and thus the corporation could in principle be subject to the accumulated earnings tax if it did not make distributions.[77] However, the fact that the shareholder level dividend tax in many cases would be at a reduced treaty rate would be relevant in determining if the retention of earnings was to avoid the shareholder level tax.

5.5.8.2 *Personal holding company tax*

Foreign corporations may be subject to the personal holding company provisions discussed at 2.2.7.2. However, the computation of the tax is based on the "taxable income" of the corporation, thus automatically limiting the tax base to US source income in the case of a foreign corporation.[78] Even in the case when US source income is present, a foreign corporation is exempted from the personal holding company provisions if all of its stock is owned by nonresident alien individuals. Sec. 542(c)(7). If the foreign corporation has any US shareholders this exception is not available, but a general de minimis rule may still be applicable.

There are no special rules applicable to domestic corporations with foreign shareholders which otherwise qualify as personal holding companies. Thus, regardless of the level of foreign ownership or the source of the US corporation's income, the personal holding company tax provisions can be applicable.

5.5.9 COMPARISON OF BRANCH AND SUBSIDIARY OPERATIONS

As the preceding material has indicated, there are a number of differences between the taxation of foreign investment in the US through a branch of a foreign corporation and investment carried out through a US subsidiary. As

---

76. For foreign corporations with US shareholders who would be taxable on the distribution, the tax could be applicable, though of course the tax avoidance purpose would still have to be established. Even here, the tax is not applicable if the foreign corporation is a personal holding company, a foreign personal holding company or a passive foreign investment company. Sec. 532(b).

77. An exception is applicable in those cases in which the foreign-owned domestic corporation has substantial foreign business income (see 5.4.5.2).

78. Under Sec. 882(b), the foreign corporation's gross income in general only includes income from US sources.

regards the underlying corporate tax, business income is taxed at the same rates but the computation of the tax base differs. For a foreign branch, the source rules of Sections 861-65 determine the amount of gross income and the allocable share of deductions is established by Treas. Reg. Secs. 1.861-8 and following and 1.882-5. For a US subsidiary, the tax base is its worldwide income. Its share of income and deductions from dealings with related parties is determined on a direct basis under the arm's length principles of Section 482 (discussed in Chapter 8).

A second "level" of tax is collected from the business income of the branch through the imposition of the branch profits tax. That tax is payable currently to the extent that the US profits are not reinvested in the US business. The second level of tax on a US subsidiary's income is only collected when the US corporation actually distributes the income to the foreign shareholder. Thus the payment of the tax may be deferred, though excessive accumulations of income may run afoul of the accumulated earnings tax.

Historically, the bulk of foreign investment in the US has been through US subsidiaries. Branch operations have been mainly limited to foreign banks and other financial institutions which must operate in that form for regulatory reasons. Real estate investment in branch form has also been common. The extensive use of US subsidiaries has resulted in part for commercial reasons and in part because of the uncertainties surrounding branch income determination. Generalizations about the appropriate investment structure, however, are difficult to make. For example, treaty benefits discussed in Chapter 11 may alter the domestic rules in favor of one form of investment over the other. For individual or closely held private investment, estate tax considerations must also be taken into account. (*See* Chapter 12.) And naturally the tax regime in the investor's own country and its interaction with the US system must also enter into the analysis. The basic point is that the failure to coordinate more closely branch and subsidiary taxation makes the overall taxing pattern transactionally elective.

5.6 Taxation of foreign partnerships and foreign partners

5.6.1 FOREIGN PARTNERSHIPS

Since the US does not treat a partnership as a separate taxable entity (*see* 2.4), the partnership, whether foreign or domestic, simply serves to pass through partnership income and loss to the partners. In determining whether this pass-through pattern of taxation applies to a foreign legal organization, the entity classification rules discussed at 2.1.2 are applicable. Thus under the elective "check the box" rules, a foreign entity which is treated as a corporation under foreign law may be a partnership for US purposes. While such "hybrid" treatment has always been possible in principle, the ease of creating such entities under the "check the box" approach will make such structures much more common and raises both planning opportunities and traps for the unwary. The appropriate treatment of such "hybrid" entities involves a number of complex issues, many of which have not yet been fully resolved. Withholding tax aspects of hybrid entities are discussed in 5.8.2 and treaty aspects are considered in 11.4.1.2.

5.6.2 FOREIGN PARTNERS IN A US OR FOREIGN PARTNERSHIP

The taxation of a foreign partner on the income of a US or foreign partnership depends on the nature of that income. Under the conduit principle of partnership taxation, the partnership income retains its character in the hands of the individual partner. Thus, for example, if the partnership has income which is effectively connected with its US trade or business, the foreign partner is taxable on his share of such income under the rules described in 5.4 and 5.5. The partnership's US trade or business is attributed to the foreign partner.[79] If the partnership has income which, if received by the foreign partner directly would not be subject to tax, for example, non-effectively connected income from foreign sources, the foreign partner is not subject to tax on his share of such income. The foreign partner is taxed at the time the income is received or accrued by the partnership, depending on the partnership's method of accounting. (*See* 2.7.)

5.7 Taxation of foreign trusts and foreign beneficiaries

5.7.1 FOREIGN TRUSTS

5.7.1.1 *Classification issues*

A trust or other similar arrangement created under foreign law may be classified as a trust for US tax purposes under the Regulations discussed at 2.1.2.[80] If the purpose of the arrangement is to protect or conserve property for the beneficiaries, it will be treated as an "ordinary" trust and taxed according to US trust

---

79. Sec. 875(1).
80. As in the cases of foreign corporations, however, its treatment under foreign law is not determinative of the US tax classification.

taxation principles. On the other hand, if the purpose of the arrangement is to associate to carry on a business and divide the profits, it will not be treated as a trust for tax purposes despite the fact that it is legally organized in trust form.[81]

Assuming that the arrangement is classified as a trust, Sec. 7701(a)(30) and (31), as amended in 1996, provide rules for determining its status as "domestic" or "foreign".[82] A trust will be domestic if (a) a court in the US is able to exercise primary supervision over the administration of the trust and (b) US fiduciaries have authority to control all "substantial decisions" concerning the trust. All other trusts are treated as foreign. Thus, for example, if a trust is formed under US law subject to the supervision of a US court and has two trustees, one foreign person and one US person, it would normally be treated as a foreign trust if, as is usually the case, the trust instrument provided that decisions were to be made by a majority of the trustees. The single US trustee would not have the requisite control.[83]

5.7.1.2 Taxation of foreign trusts

As discussed at 2.3.5, US trusts are in general treated as conduits and the beneficiary is taxable on the distributed trust income. This result is accomplished by including amounts received by the trust in trust income initially but then giving the trust a deduction for the income which is distributed to beneficiaries. In the case of most domestic trusts, if income is accumulated and then distributed later, it is taxable to the trust and the beneficiary receives the distribution free of tax (in effect, as a gift).

Different rules apply to foreign trusts. The foreign trust is treated as a nonresident alien for purposes of initially determining its income. Thus it is not taxed on foreign source income and is subject to tax on US source income according to the pattern of rules discussed at 5.4. To the extent that the income is distributed currently, the trust is allowed a corresponding deduction. If income is accumulated by the trust and distributed to a foreign beneficiary at a later date, the tax paid at the trust level may be credited against the beneficiary's tax liability arising out of the accumulation distribution but will not be refunded at

---

81. Treas. Reg. Sec. 301.7701-4. Businesses operating in the legal form of trust are generally taxed as corporations (*see, e.g. Hynes v. Commissioner,* 74 TC 1266 (1980)), though classification as a partnership is also possible. There is very little authority on the classification of foreign legal entities organized in civil law jurisdictions which do not have the common law trust as an indigenous legal institution.

82. Prior to the changes in Sec. 7701(a)(30), cases and rulings looked at a number of factors including place of activity, residence of trustees, place of administration and the like to determine the status of a trust.

83. Prop. Treas. Reg. Sec. 301.7701-7(d),(e) (1997) provide more details on the application of the "court" and "control" tests.

the trust level.[84] The treatment of foreign trusts with US beneficiaries is discussed at 7.6.

The taxation of foreign estates is generally the same as the taxation of foreign trusts but income which is accumulated and later distributed is taxed only at the estate level.[85]

5.7.2 TAXATION OF FOREIGN BENEFICIARIES

Income which is distributed by a trust (whether foreign or domestic) is treated in the hands of the foreign beneficiary as having the same character as it had in the hands of the trust.[86] Thus the taxation of the beneficiary depends on whether the income was foreign source investment income, US source effectively connected income, etc. If the income is accumulated by the trust initially and then distributed, it retains its tax character when ultimately received by the beneficiary; any taxes paid by the trust are included in the beneficiaries' income and credited against their final tax liability. However, if the tax paid at the trust level exceeds the tax due at the beneficiary level, no refund is available to the beneficiary.[87]

5.7.3 FOREIGN GRANTOR TRUSTS

As discussed at 2.3.5, normally if the grantor of a trust retains certain control over or rights to the trust property, he will remain taxable on the trust income. This principle, when applied to nonresident grantors, led to significant tax avoidance possibilities through which a nonresident could establish a grantor trust with US beneficiaries (often with property "given" to the grantor by the beneficiaries) and the trust could then make distributions to the beneficiaries

---

84. Sec. 661(a), 665-668.
85. *See* Rev. Rul. 68-621, 1968-2 Cum. Bull. 286.
86. Sec. 652(a); Sec. 667(e). *See* Rev. Rul. 81-244, 1981-2 Cum. Bull. 151 (interest income on US bank deposit received by trust and distributed to nonresident beneficiary kept that character in the beneficiary's hands); *Martin-Montis Trust v. Commissioner,* 75 TC 381 (1980) (same). Where the income is investment income which is normally taxed on a gross basis to the foreign recipient, there is a question as to whether the amount includible when received as a trust distribution is reduced by the expenses incurred at the trust level. One case has allowed such treatment (under a prior version of the statute) but the result seems inconsistent with the general principles of pass-through taxation. *See Wittschen v. Commissioner,* 5 TC 10 (1945).
87. Sec. 666(e). This rule makes the timing of distributions important. For example, if a US trust with foreign source income distributes the income currently to its foreign beneficiary, there will be no tax at the trust level (because of the distribution deduction) and no tax at the beneficiary level (because the income is foreign source). However, if the income is accumulated and later distributed, it will be taxed to the US trust. Neither the trust nor the beneficiary can obtain a refund for the trust level tax when the income is distributed. The same principles apply to accumulated capital gains. *See, e.g. Maximov v. United States* 373 US 49 (1963).

which would not be subject to US tax.[88] The grantor theoretically would be subject to US tax on the trust income but could control the trust investment policy to avoid that tax. Often foreign tax would be avoided as well if the foreign jurisdiction treated the trust as a separate taxable entity. To counter such arrangements, Section 672(f), enacted in 1996, eliminates from grantor trust classification any trust (foreign or domestic) if the trust's income is not taken currently into account by a US person. Thus a trust established by a nonresident would not qualify as a grantor trust and would be subject to the normal pattern of taxation including the special rules applicable to foreign trusts with US beneficiaries discussed at 7.6.[89]

5.8 Procedural aspects

5.8.1 RETURN AND DISCLOSURE REQUIREMENTS

Every nonresident alien or foreign corporation which is engaged in a US trade or business must file a US tax return.[90] This return must be filed even though the taxpayer has no taxable income in his US trade or business. A US return must also be filed if the foreign taxpayer's US tax liability has not been completely covered by withholding at source. The filing of a return is a prerequisite for the allowance of any deductions otherwise available under the Code and, in addition, there are penalties for failure to file.[91] The return is generally due on or before the fifteenth day of the sixth month following the close of the taxable year (15 June for calendar year taxpayers). Special rules apply for employment income. In some cases estimated tax payments may be required.

There are a number of provisions requiring disclosure of information to various governmental agencies by foreign persons doing business in the US. Section 6038A requires information concerning any transactions between the foreign corporation and any "related entities."[92] The section is intended to help

---

88. *See* Rev. Rul. 69-70, 1969-1 Cum. Bull. 182 (income of foreign grantor trust set up by a nonresident alien was taxable to the grantor and not to the trust or the US resident beneficiary). For special rules treating foreign trusts set up by US persons as grantor trusts, *see* 7.6.2.
89. The special rules do not apply if the trust is a grantor trust because of the grantor's unrestricted power to revoke the trust or if the income of the trust can only be distributed to the grantor during his lifetime. Sec. 672(f)(2). Other aspects of the grantor trust rules as they apply to foreign grantors are described in Prop. Treas. Reg. Sec. 1.672(f)-1(a) (1997).
90. Treas. Reg. Sec. 1.6012-1(b), 2(g).
91. Sec. 874(a); Sec. 882(c)(2); Sec. 6651-52.
92. The detailed requirements of Sec. 6038A are set out in Treas. Reg. Sec. 1.6038A-1. A 25 percent foreign-owned corporation is required to furnish to the Service the information described in Sec. 6038A(b). This information includes (1) the name of each person that is a "related party" which has had any transaction with the reporting corporation; (2) the nature of the relationship with that party and (3) the nature of "any transactions" between the two corporations. Many

in policing intercompany pricing practices between related parties under Section 482. (*See* 8.3.) Under Section 6039C, the Treasury Department is authorized to issue Regulations requiring the disclosure of ownership by foreign persons of US real property interests[93] but no Regulations have as yet been issued. In addition, other nontax provisions also involve disclosure obligations. The Agricultural Foreign Investment Disclosure Act of 1978 (7 USC Secs. 3501-08) deals with foreign investment in agricultural land and the International Investment Survey Act of 1976 (22 USC Secs. 3101-08) imposes reporting requirements for foreign investors in US businesses.

5.8.2 WITHHOLDING AT SOURCE

5.8.2.1 Fixed or determinable income

Sections 1441 and 1442 impose a 30 per cent withholding tax on income such as interest, dividends, etc., and other fixed or determinable annual or periodical income paid to a nonresident alien, foreign corporation, foreign partnership or foreign fiduciary from US sources.[94] In the normal situation, this withholding at source fully satisfies the nonresident taxpayer's US tax liability and no tax return need be filed.

No withholding is required for income which is effectively connected with a US trade or business.[95] This rule mirrors the fact that effectively connected income is not subject to the 30 per cent tax, but is taxed at normal individual or corporate rates. Wages received by a nonresident alien employee for services performed in the US are subject to the usual wage withholding tax imposed on US citizens and residents rather than the 30 per cent rate.[96]

To be subject to withholding under Section 1441, amounts paid must be from sources within the US and thus no withholding is required on non-US source income, e.g. wages paid by a foreign employer to a nonresident alien employee who is only temporarily present in the US and meets the tests of Section

---

foreign-owned multinational groups with US operations have complained about the burdensome nature of the reporting requirements, especially in the light of the substantial penalties for noncompliance. *See* Treas. Reg. Sec. 1.6038A-4(a)(3).

93. Prior to its amendment in 1984, Section 6039C required extensive disclosure of foreign ownership in US real estate. Its scope was substantially limited after the introduction of withholding at source on dispositions of US real property interests. See 5.8.2.2.

94. Amounts paid to domestic partnerships with foreign partners are not subject to withholding by the payor but the partnership is required to withhold on the foreign partner's distributive share of the US source income (whether or not actually distributed). Similarly, withholding is required on US source income of foreign beneficiaries of a foreign or domestic trust. *See* Treas. Reg. Sec. 1.1441-2(a)(2).

95. Sec. 1441(c)(1). Withholding is required on effectively connected income of a partnership which is allocable to a foreign partner. *See* 5.8.2.3

96. Treas. Reg. Sec. 1.1441-4(b)(1).

861(a)(3) (*see* 4.2.3.). On the other hand, if the income is from US sources, withholding is required even if the foreign employer is not otherwise engaged in a US trade or business.

The 30 per cent withholding rate is often reduced or eliminated in United States tax treaties. (See Chapter 11.)

In general, for any exemption from or reduction in withholding tax to apply, various certifications of the recipient's qualification for the reduction or exemption must be supplied to the US withholding agent. Regulations adopted in 1997 substantially modified the US withholding tax procedures with respect to dividends.[97] The rule which allowed the US withholding agent to rely on the address of the payee of dividends to establish whether withholding is required was eliminated and dividends are subject to the normal withholding procedures.

In addition, a new withholding mechanism was established for "qualified intermediaries" which bases withholding on information supplied by, for example, a foreign financial institution holding investments for foreign taxpayers. The qualified intermediary must enter into a withholding agent agreement with the IRS setting forth the information which the intermediary is required to obtain from the foreign taxpayers, taking into account local "know your customer" rules which insure that adequate information has been obtained. In effect, the foreign intermediary takes over the functions of the US withholding agent.[98]

The 1997 Act dealt with the problem withholding in the case of "hybrid" entities (see 5.6.1). Under Section 894(c), a foreign person is not entitled to reduced treaty rates of withholding for income derived through an entity treated as a partnership for US purposes if three conditions are satisfied: (1) the income is not treated as an item of income to the foreign person by the treaty partners; (2) the treaty partner country does not tax the distribution of the income to the foreign person; and (3) there is no treaty provision dealing with income from a partnership. In addition, the 1997 Regulations follow foreign law classification in the case of hybrid entities to determine the appropriate treaty withholding rate. Thus if a foreign entity is classified as a corporation under the laws of the treaty partner country, that characterization will control the treatment for US withholding purposes, even if the US would classify the entity as a partnership under its domestic rules.[99]

---

97. *See*, Treas. Reg. Sec. 1.1441-2(b).
98. Treas. Reg. Sec. 1441-1(e)(3)-(5).
99. Temp. Treas. Reg. Sec. 1.894T-1(d). For example, suppose two residents of a treaty country formed a corporation in a tax haven which invested in US securities and the US treated the haven company under the "check the box" rules as a partnership while the treaty partner treated it as a foreign corporation. Under those circumstances, reduced treaty withholding would not apply since, under the characterization of the treaty partner, the income would not be received by a treaty country resident.

5.8.2.2 *Disposition of US real property interests*

Section 1445 sets forth detailed rules for withholding on the disposition of US real property interests. In general, the transferee of the real property interest is required to withhold ten per cent of the *amount realized* by the foreign transferor on the disposition of the property. Withholding can be avoided if the transferee receives from the transferor an affidavit that the transferor is not a foreign person or, in the case of the transfer of shares of stock of a domestic corporation, an affidavit from the corporation that it is not a US real property holding corporation.[100] No withholding is required if the stock of the corporation is regularly traded on an established securities market. Since the amount required to be withheld is based on the gross amount of the sales proceeds, it may exceed the tax liability on the foreign transferor's taxable gain. Section 1445(c) provides a mechanism by which the amount to be withheld can be reduced by obtaining an advance determination from the Internal Revenue Service of the maximum amount of the foreign transferor's tax liability. Section 1445(e) provides special rules dealing with withholding on distributions of US real property interests by domestic corporations, partnerships or trusts.[101]

5.8.2.3 *Withholding on foreign partners*

Section 1446 requires a partnership (domestic or foreign) to withhold tax at the highest marginal individual or corporate rate on a foreign partner's allocable share of the partnership's effectively connected income. The withheld tax is credited against the partner's US tax liability on the effectively connected income. In addition, withholding is required by domestic partnerships on a foreign partner's share of non-effectively connected US source fixed or determinable annual or periodic income whether or not the income is distributed.

---

100. Withholding is required if the transferee has actual knowledge that the affidavit is false. Sec. 1445(b)(7). In addition, if any agent of the transferor or transferee has knowledge that the affidavit is false, the agent is required to notify the transferee. If the notification is not furnished, the agent is required to withhold and is liable to the extent of its compensation received in connection with the transaction. Sec. 1445(d).
101. Procedures to be followed under Sec. 1445 are set forth in Treas. Reg. Sec. 1.1445-5.

Chapter 6

Taxation of foreign source income of US persons: the foreign tax credit

6.1   General

US citizens and residents and corporations organized in the US are subject to tax on their worldwide income. However, a number of rules apply to the income from foreign sources of such taxpayers. There are two fundamental sets of rules governing US taxpayers investing or doing business abroad. The first is the foreign tax credit mechanism, discussed in this chapter, which allows US taxpayers a credit against their US income tax liability for foreign income taxes paid on income from foreign sources. The second set is the transfer pricing provisions which are intended to allocate properly income and deductions between related parties. These rules are discussed in Chapter 8. In addition, there are a number of special provisions which are applicable to the foreign income or foreign activities of US taxpayers. These special rules are discussed in Chapters 7 and 9.

6.2   Treatment of foreign taxes in general

US citizens, resident aliens and domestic corporations who pay income taxes to foreign countries may elect annually either:

(1) to deduct those taxes from income as prescribed by Section 164(a)[1]; or

(2) to claim foreign income taxes paid or accrued as a credit against US income taxes[2] as allowed under Sections 901-908 and 960. If the taxpayer elects to utilize the foreign tax credit as to *any* income taxes, no foreign *income* taxes may be deducted under Section 164. However, the deductibility of all other types of taxes described therein is not affected by the election.

---

1. A deduction also is allowed for foreign real property taxes and any other foreign taxes incurred in profit-seeking activities.
2. Section 901 precludes utilization of the foreign tax credit to offset certain special US penalty taxes as, for example, the accumulated earnings tax and the personal holding company tax. The foreign tax credit may be used, however, to offset 90 per cent of the alternative minimum tax.

Generally speaking, it is to the taxpayer's advantage to elect the foreign tax credit rather than the deduction. The credit produces a dollar-for-dollar offset against US tax liability; the benefit of a deduction is limited to the amount of the foreign income taxes multiplied by the taxpayer's marginal US tax bracket (i.e. generally a maximum reduction for a corporation of 35 cents in US tax for each dollar of foreign tax paid).

6.3 Objectives of the foreign tax credit

Detailed rules are provided in the Code and Regulations to implement the foreign tax credit mechanism.[3] In considering those rules, it is important to keep in mind the functions which the foreign tax credit plays in the US international tax system.

Given the fact that the US taxes the foreign source income of its tax residents in full, some recognition must be given to the existence of foreign taxes which are also imposed on that income by foreign countries or else (1) a US taxpayer with foreign source income will bear a total tax burden greater than that of a taxpayer with only income from the US, and (2) because of the excess burden, foreign investment will be less attractive for a US taxpayer than domestic investment. The first point is essentially a question of equity in the treatment of US taxpayers regardless of the source of their income. It starts from the premise that foreign taxes are the equivalent of US taxes for equity comparison purposes. The second is a question of the attitude to be adopted regarding the impact that the tax system should have on investment decisions.

As to the first point, from the point of view of the US, equity in these terms is achieved if the foreign taxes paid by the US taxpayer with income from abroad are treated as equivalent to the payment of US taxes up to the level of taxation imposed by the US on a similar amount of income received by a taxpayer with income from sources within the US. The foreign tax liability replaces all or a portion of the US tax liability on the foreign source income and equality of treatment is assured.

Suppose, however, that the foreign taxes exceed the US taxes which would be applicable on the same amount of income. Here, the taxpayer with income from abroad bears a higher tax burden than a US taxpayer with the same amount of income from US sources if the credit is limited to the amount of US tax liability on the foreign income. This result does not occur because of the

---

3. The discussion of the foreign tax credit is necessarily brief and is intended to provide a general outline of the structure and operation of the credit. For a more extended discussion, *see* Kuntz & Peroni, U.S. International Taxation, ch. B4.

failure of the US to recognize the foreign tax liability. It simply reflects the fact that the foreign tax rate is higher than that selected by the US for the taxation of the income, whether domestic or foreign, of its tax residents. In such a case, the US is treating its taxpayers equally when viewed from the perspective of the general level of US taxation. Put another way, there is no international double taxation as long as the US recognizes the foreign tax liability up to the level of US taxation of the foreign income.

However, when considered from the perspective of the second point, the impact of total tax burden on foreign investment decisions, failure to credit (or refund) foreign taxes when they exceed the level of US taxation results in an additional tax burden on foreign investment by a US taxpayer when compared with purely domestic investment. Here a policy of tax neutrality (capital export neutrality) with respect to investment decisions would require a full crediting of foreign taxes without regard to their level in comparison with US domestic taxation. As will be seen, because of special limitations and special preferences, this result is not achieved by the US foreign tax credit mechanism.

The foreign tax credit method of dealing with the existence of a foreign tax liability can of course be contrasted with the exemption system used by many European countries. Under the exemption system, the foreign tax liability is recognized by exempting the foreign source income from domestic taxation. As a result, international double taxation is by definition avoided, but at the price of losing (1) equality of treatment of domestic taxpayers regardless of the source of their income when viewed from the perspective of the domestic system, and (2) tax neutrality with respect to foreign versus domestic investment decisions. Countries which have utilized the exemption method have insured that the foreign operations of their domestic taxpayers will not bear any other tax burden than that imposed by the country of foreign operation. This benefit (capital import neutrality) is seen by those countries as outweighing the equity and capital export neutrality factors. The distinction between the two systems can be overstated, however. If a US taxpayer is denied foreign tax credits because the foreign taxes paid exceed the US limitations, the US taxpayer is in the same economic position as if the US were an exemption country.

The above discussion illustrates the fact that no mechanism has been developed to deal with the problem of overlapping tax jurisdiction which will by itself accommodate all of the considerations here discussed. Therefore, many countries including the US provide other mechanisms (either directly or through the tax system) to achieve the objectives which cannot be realized through their basic structural mechanism for dealing with the problem of multiple jurisdictions taxing the same income.[4]

---

4. For discussions of the issues, *see* American Law Institute, *International Aspects of United States Income Taxation* (1987).

6.4 The direct foreign tax credit

6.4.1 ELIGIBILITY FOR TAX CREDIT

6.4.1.1 Persons eligible

Section 901(b) describes the categories of taxpayers eligible for the credit. US citizens and domestic corporations may credit income taxes paid to any foreign country. Alien residents are also entitled to the credit for taxes paid to any foreign country.[5] As discussed in more detail in 6.4.4, Section 906 allows a credit to nonresident alien individuals and foreign corporations for taxes paid to any foreign country or US possession with respect to income that is effectively connected with a US trade or business (*see* 5.3.5). Any of the above categories of eligible taxpayers that are members of a partnership, beneficiaries of a trust, or shareholders of an S corporation may also claim as a credit their proportionate share of the qualifying foreign taxes paid by the partnership, trust or corporation.[6]

6.4.1.2 Taxes eligible

The credit for foreign taxes is limited to *income* taxes.[7] In general, the character of the foreign tax is determined by its similarity to the US income tax. Detailed Regulations have been issued which deal with the question of when a foreign tax qualifies as an income tax. The determination whether a foreign tax qualifies as an income tax is a crucial part of the foreign tax credit mechanism. In general, Treas. Reg. Sec. 1.901-2 provides that a foreign levy is an income

---

5. Section 901(c) authorizes the President by Presidential proclamation to disallow the foreign tax credit to resident aliens who are citizens of a foreign country that does not allow US citizens resident therein a similar credit for taxes paid to the US or other countries. Before the President can take such an action, he must make findings that (1) the foreign country involved does not allow US citizens a credit similar to the US foreign tax credit, (2) the US has made a request to the foreign country to provide a tax credit to US citizens who are residing in it, and (3) it is in the public interest of the US to allow a foreign tax credit to citizens of the foreign country who are US residents only if the foreign country grants a similar credit to US citizens who are residents of the foreign country.
6. No foreign tax credit is allowed to individual investors in a US entity that is taxed as a C corporation under U.S. rules, see 2.1.2, even though the entity may be a valid partnership or trust under foreign law. Rev Rul. 72-197, 1972-1 Cum. Bull. 215 (same result under rules in effect prior to check-the-box regulations).
7. Technically the credit extends to war profits and excess profit taxes as well but in practice it is the income tax aspect of the credit which is important. The theoretical justification for limiting the credit to income taxes is that such taxes in general are not economically passed on by the US taxpayer and thus, with respect to those taxes, true economic double taxation has occurred. Rather than examining each situation to determine if in fact the tax has been passed on, the statute assumes that all (and only) income taxes are borne by the US taxpayer and are thus eligible for the credit. For a discussion of these issues, *See* American Law Institute, note 4, at 308.

tax only if the levy is a "tax" and the "predominant character" of the tax is that of an income tax in the US sense of the term. A levy is not a tax if the person paying it receives a specific economic benefit from the foreign country as a result of paying the levy.[8] A tax satisfies the predominant character test if it is likely to reach "net gain".[9] The Regulations in turn provide that the net gain requirement is satisfied if the tax is imposed (1) only on realized gains (although in some situations, such as taxation of imputed rent from home ownership, the requirement is satisfied even though there has not been a realization of gain in the US sense of the term); (2) on no more than gross receipts (i.e. an artificial posted price will not satisfy this element of the test); and (3) on net income (by allowing appropriate recovery of significant costs and expenses incurred to produce the gross receipts).

Under Section 901(i), a levy is not creditable if it is used to provide a subsidy to the taxpayer, a related person, or any party to the actual or a related transaction and the subsidy is determined by reference either to the amount of the tax or the tax base.[10]

The results reached in the Regulations may be changed by tax treaty.[11]

---

8. *See, e.g., Phillips Petroleum Co. v. Commissioner,* 104 TC 256 (1995) (Norwegian tax imposed only on oil producers not for a specific economic benefit). A taxpayer who is subject to a levy which is in part a tax and who also receives a specific economic benefit for part of the levy is a "dual capacity taxpayer." The amount of the creditable portion of the levy for such taxpayer is determined by rules set forth in Treas. Reg. Sec. 1.901-2A. In addition, Treas. Reg. Sec. 1.901-2(a)(3) provides that a foreign tax is not creditable if liability for the tax is related to the availability of a credit for the tax against the income tax liability of another country. This provision is aimed at so-called "soak up" taxes which are imposed by some countries when payments are made to nonresidents operating from a foreign tax credit system country but not when made to other nonresidents. *See, e.g.,* Rev. Rul. 87-39, 1987-1 Cum. Bull. 180 (Uruguay).

9. *See Texasgulf, Inc. v. Commissioner,* 107 TC 51 (1996) (discussion of "net gain" requirement in holding Ontario Mining Tax to be a creditable tax).

10. There have been a number of cases involving subsidies granted by the Brazilian government with respect to borrowings by Brazilians from foreign lenders. These cases provide further explication of the subsidy rule. *See, e.g., Nissho Iwai American Corp. v. Commissioner,* 89 TC 765 (1987) (Brazilian subsidy based on amount of withholding tax imposed on lender reduced taxes paid for foreign tax credit purposes); *Norwest Corporation v. Commissioner,* 69 F.3d 1404 (8th Cir. 1995) (US lender received interest from Brazilian borrowers which, in turn, received subsidies with respect to that interest; US lender entitled to foreign tax credit for withholding tax on the interest less the amount of the subsidy, the court rejecting the IRS view that none of the tax was creditable because of the subsidy); *Riggs National Corp. v. Commissioners,* 107 TC 301 (1996) (same result where government subsidies were provided during debt restructuring crisis of early 1980's). *Compare Foley v. Commissioner,* 87 TC 605 (1986) (direct incentive payments received under Berlin Promotion Law did not reduce taxes paid for foreign tax credit purposes); Rev. Rul. 86-134, 1986-2 Cum. Bull. 104 (Netherlands investment incentives did not reduce taxes paid for foreign tax credit purposes when provided as direct grants but did reduce taxes paid when converted to an identical tax credit provision).

11. For example, Rev. Rul. 78-424, 1978-2 Cum. Bull. 197, held that the UK petroleum revenue tax (PRT) was not a creditable income tax because the tax base included certain unrealized gains and was imposed on a field-by-field basis so that a taxpayer could have an overall loss on operations and still incur tax. The result in Rev. Rul. 78-424 was changed by the Third Protocol to the US-UK tax treaty which provides a limited tax credit for the UK PRT.

A "foreign country" includes any political subdivision thereof that levies and collects an income tax.[12]

6.4.2 IN LIEU OF TAXES

Section 903 also permits certain foreign taxes paid in lieu of an income tax to qualify for the credit under Section 901. A tax will be considered as imposed "in lieu of" an income tax if it is in substitution for, and not in addition to, an income tax otherwise generally imposed.[13]

6.4.3 TIME AND MANNER OF CLAIMING CREDIT

Generally, the year in which a taxpayer is entitled to claim the credit is determined by its method of accounting, i.e. cash or accrual. Section 905(a), however, permits a taxpayer to claim the credit in the year the foreign taxes accrued regardless of the method of accounting employed. But, if the foreign tax ultimately determined differs from that claimed as a credit, appropriate adjustments must be made.[14]

To be entitled to the foreign tax credit, the taxpayer must submit proof of (1) the amount of its total foreign source income; (2) the amount of its income from each country and the taxes paid or accrued thereto for which a credit is being taken; and (3) any other information necessary to enable the Internal Revenue Service to verify and compute the credit.[15]

6.4.4 NONRESIDENT ALIENS AND FOREIGN CORPORATIONS

The US subjects certain foreign source income to US tax. (*See* 5.3.5 above.) As noted earlier, one purpose of this provision is to prevent the US from becoming

---

12. *See* Treas. Reg. Sec. 1.901-2(g)(2).
13. Treas. Reg. Sec. 1.903-1 in effect exempts from the requirement that the tax be imposed on net income, gross withholding taxes on interest, dividends, royalties, etc. The Regulations give a number of examples of taxes meeting the "in lieu of" requirement.
14. Section 905(c) eliminates the need for adjustments if the foreign taxes are paid within two years of the close of the year to which the taxes relate where the actual taxes paid differ from the accrued amount because of currency fluctuations. If the payment is made after that time, an adjustment of the foreign tax credit is required. The original accrual must be reduced by that amount and then subsequently recomputed when the amount actually is paid. Temp. Treas. Reg. Sec. 1.905-3T and 4T provide procedures which must be followed in situations in which adjustments are required to be made.
15. Treas. Reg. Sec. 1.905-2, and Rev. Rul. 67-308,1967-2 Cum. Bull. 254, provide guidelines on the kind of evidence that a taxpayer should submit to substantiate a claimed foreign tax credit. Prop. Treas. Reg. Sec. 1.905-2(a)(2) and (b)(3)(1997) would relax some aspects of the substantiation requirements. For a case in which the taxpayer failed to meet the substation requirements with respect to foreign withholding taxes, *see Norwest Corporation v. Commissioner*, TC Memo 1995-453.

a tax haven as the result of the relaxation of its tax jurisdiction. However, the foreign source income that is taxed by the US under its effectively connected concept may also be taxed by the country of source and/or the country of domicile. Consistent with the purpose of the foreign tax credit, therefore, Section 906 grants a foreign tax credit under Section 901 to nonresident aliens and foreign corporations for taxes paid or accrued (or deemed paid or accrued under Section 902) to a foreign country or US possession with respect to that income. The limitations applicable to Sections 901 and 902 likewise apply to the credit allowable under Section 906.

6.5   The indirect foreign tax credit

The discussion in 6.4 concerned taxes paid directly by a US (or other qualifying) taxpayer to a foreign country. Section 902 treats foreign income taxes paid by described subsidiaries of US parent corporations as deemed paid by the parent. As a result, the US corporation becomes entitled to a credit under Section 901 for the taxes thus deemed paid by it. This is commonly referred to as the "indirect credit."[16]

More specifically, if a US corporation owns ten per cent or more of the voting stock[17] of a foreign corporation from which it receives a dividend,[18] it will be deemed to have paid the foreign income taxes paid by the subsidiary attributable to that dividend. As a result, the US parent is entitled to a foreign tax credit under Section 901 for the taxes paid by the foreign subsidiary. The US parent must also include the amount of the credit in its income (the gross-up requirement of Section 78). In effect, the US parent is treated as if the foreign subsidiary had paid it a dividend that included the tax due to the foreign country and the US parent had then paid the tax to the foreign country. Repatriated subsidiary profits thus have the same foreign tax credit effect as profits from direct foreign branch operations.

The indirect credit is also extended to taxes paid on dividends distributed by second, third, fourth, fifth and sixth tier foreign corporations if the parent of each meets the ten per cent voting stock requirement. However, in the case of

---

16. As in the case of the direct credit, the discussion provides an outline of the structure and operation of the indirect foreign tax credit. For a detailed analysis of the mechanism, *see* Kuntz and Peroni, note 3, ch. B4.09.
17. *See* Rev. Rul. 74-459, 1974-2 Cum. Bull. 207 (indirect credit not available for dividends paid on a 75 per cent nonvoting stock interest when the shareholder did not own ten per cent of the voting stock of the distributing corporation).
18. The ten per cent test is applied at the time the dividend is received by the US shareholder. Treas. Reg. Sec. 1.902-1(a)(1).

subsidiaries below the first tier, the US parent must have an indirect ownership in such subsidiaries of at least five per cent. In addition, for corporations below the third tier the corporation must be a controlled foreign corporation (7.2.3). For example, assume a US parent owns thirty per cent of the voting stock of a foreign corporation which in turn owns ten per cent of the voting stock of still another foreign corporation. Although the ten per cent test is met in each case, the US parent will not be entitled to an indirect credit for foreign taxes paid by the second tier subsidiary because the US parent has only an indirect three per cent interest in it (30 per cent of 10 per cent).

If the five per cent test is met with respect to subsidiaries below the first tier, then the foreign taxes paid by the first tier subsidiary include the taxes it is deemed to have paid with respect to dividends paid up by the lower tier corporations. Accordingly, the US parent will then get the benefit of those lower tier taxes as to dividend distributions it receives from the first tier subsidiary.[19]

In general terms, the amount of the indirect credit allowable to a US parent corporation is the ratio of the foreign income taxes paid by the foreign subsidiary which the dividend[20] paid bears to the subsidiary's undistributed earnings. For example, assume U.S. Corporation X owns all the stock of Foreign Corporation Y. In 1998, Y has 52 of undistributed earnings after payment of foreign taxes, has paid foreign taxes of 48, and distributes a dividend to X of 26. Corporation X is entitled to a foreign tax credit with respect to the dividend of 24 (48 × 26/52). Correspondingly, Corporation X must include in its income 5O (the 26 dividend received plus the 24 deemed taxes paid). At the end of the year, Corporation Y reduces its undistributed earnings by the 26 distribution and its foreign income taxes by the 24 deemed foreign tax credit allowed to Corporation X.

More technically, Section 902 provides that the allowable indirect credit is based on "post-1986 foreign income taxes"[21] and "post-1986 undistributed

---

19. Prior to the 1997 Act, only dividends from second and third tier subsidiaries could carry the indirect credit with them. Guidelines and examples of the operation of the indirect credit where second and third tier corporations are involved are set forth in Treas. Reg. Sec. 1.902-1(b), (c)(1). Similar rules will be developed for distributions from fourth, fifth and sixth tier subsidiaries.

20. The term "dividend" means a dividend as defined under US tax rules in Section 316. See 2.2.6; Treas. Reg. Sec. 1.902-1(a)(11). As to gains recognized on sales or exchanges of stock in a foreign corporation that are taxed somewhat like dividends, see Sec. 1248 discussed at 7.4.

21. The term "post-1986 foreign income taxes" means the sum of (1) the foreign income taxes incurred with respect to the year in which the dividend is distributed and (2) foreign income taxes incurred with respect to prior post-1986 taxable years for which a Sec. 902 credit has not previously been taken. Sec. 902(c)(2); Treas. Reg. Sec. 1.902-1(a)(8).

Sec. 986(a) requires that the amount of foreign taxes paid by a cash method foreign subsidiary be determined by translating the foreign currency into dollars using the exchange rate at the time of payment of the taxes. Accrual method taxpayers may use an average exchange rate for the year of accrual of the foreign taxes if the taxes are paid within two years after the taxable year to which the tax relates. See 10.2.2.2.

earnings."[22] Both taxes and earnings are thus "pooled" rather than being determined on a year-by-year basis as was the case before 1987.[23]

The operation of the indirect credit where lower tier subsidiaries are involved is illustrated by the following example: Assume US Corporation A owns all the stock of Foreign Corporation B which in turn owns all the stock of Foreign Corporation C. In 1998, Corporation C had before tax post-1986 undistributed earnings of 300, paid foreign tax of 90 and distributed a 100 dividend to Corporation B. During the same year Corporation B had 300 of before tax post-1986 undistributed earnings, made up of 200 from its own business operations and the 100 dividend from Corporation C. Corporation B paid 50 of foreign tax on its business income and distributed a dividend of 125 to Corporation A. Corporation B is deemed to have paid 42.857 of the foreign taxes paid by Corporation C (90 × 100/210). Corporation B thus actually paid and is deemed to have paid 92.857 of foreign taxes, composed of the 50 taxes actually paid and the 42.857 of taxes paid by Corporation C which are deemed paid by Corporation B. Corporation A then gets a credit against US tax of 46.428 determined by multiplying the 92.857 taxes paid and deemed paid by Corporation B by a fraction the numerator of which is 125 (the dividend actually paid by Corporation B) and the denominator of which is 250 (Corporation B's post-1986 undistributed earnings). Correspondingly, Corporation A must include the 46.428 in income under Section 78 in addition to the 125 dividend.

---

22. The term "post-1986 undistributed earnings" means the earnings and profits of the foreign subsidiary accumulated in taxable years beginning after 1986. The computation is made at the end of the taxable year in which the dividend is distributed. Sec. 902(c)(1); Treas. Reg. Sec. 1.902-1(a)(9). Accumulated earnings and profits are determined by using US tax rules. *US v. Goodyear Tire & Rubber Co.*, 493 US 132 (1989).

Under the IRS view, post-1986 undistributed earnings means the total amount of earnings of the foreign corporation determined at the corporate level; any special allocation of less than all earnings to a particular shareholder (which could thus reduce the denominator of the fraction and increase the allowable Sec. 902 credit) are disregarded. Treas. Reg. Sec. 1.902-1(a)(9)(iv). To the contrary is *Vulcan Materials v. Commissioner*, 96 TC 410 (1991).

Sec. 986(b) requires that the determination of post-1986 undistributed earnings be made in the subsidiary's functional currency (see 10.2.2.2) and, if necessary, translated into dollars using the exchange rate in effect on the date of the distribution (thus, no exchange rate gain or loss arises because of currency fluctuations between the year in which the earnings and profits arise and the year in which they are distributed as a dividend).

23. Distributions by foreign subsidiaries after 1986 are first deemed to have been paid out of post-1986 undistributed earnings and then out of pre-1987 earnings. *See* Treas. Reg. Sec. 1.902-1(b). Rules applicable to the latter category are set forth in Treas. Reg. Sec. 1.902-3.

The "pooling" of earnings and profits under Sec. 902(c)(1) is used only for determining the amount of the deemed foreign tax credit. It is not used for other purposes. For example, if a foreign subsidiary had a 50 deficit in earnings and profits in 1998 and 50 positive earnings and profits in 1999, a 50 distribution in 1999 would be a dividend to its US parent (because a "dividend" for US purposes results if there are distribution year earnings and profits even if there are no accumulated earnings and profits) but no foreign tax credit would be available because post-1986 undistributed earnings would be zero for Sec. 902 purposes. Treas. Reg. Sec. 1.902-1(a)(8)(i) and (b)(4) provide that the post-1986 taxes pool is not reduced by any foreign taxes attributable to the distribution.

The operation of the indirect foreign tax credit does require careful planning. As the foregoing example illustrates, where the tax rate of the lower tier corporation is higher than the tax rate of the higher tier corporation on their respective business operations, a dividend by the lower tier subsidiary to the higher tier subsidiary can increase the allowable foreign tax credit upon a dividend by the first tier subsidiary to the US parent corporation. On the other hand, if the tax rate of the lower tier subsidiary is lower than the tax rate of the higher tier subsidiary, a dividend by the lower tier subsidiary in effect reduces the foreign tax credit available on a dividend by the first tier subsidiary to the US parent corporation.

The foreign taxes deemed paid under Section 902 are treated under Section 901 in the same manner as foreign taxes paid directly and are subject to the same limitations.

6.6   Overall limitation on the foreign tax credit

6.6.1   HISTORICAL BACKGROUND

The foreign tax credit almost from its inception has been subject to a general limitation on the amount of the credit available for foreign taxes. While the forms of the limitation have varied, the basic purpose of the limitation has always been to prevent the crediting of foreign taxes against the US tax on income from US sources. As a result, foreign source income will be subject to the higher of the effective US or foreign tax rates. Prior to the Tax Reform Act of 1986, rather than tracing the actual foreign taxes paid to specific items or classes of income, and limiting the credit to the amount of the US tax on that income, the US adopted an approach which in general limited the credit for foreign taxes paid to a portion of the total US tax liability determined by the relation between foreign source income and total income. That system was significantly changed by the 1986 Act. It is helpful to review briefly prior changes in the US tax system to understand the reasons behind the 1986 actions.

Prior to the Tax Reform Act of 1976, a taxpayer could elect to compute the limitation on its foreign tax credit either on a country-by-country basis (the per-country limitation) or by aggregating all taxes paid to all foreign countries (the overall limitation).[24] Generally the per-country method was chosen by tax-

---

24. The following example illustrates the difference between two limitations. Assume US Corporation A had $1000 of income from Country X, $1000 of income from Country Y and $1000 of US source income. Country X imposed tax at a 60 per cent rate, Country Y at a 40 per cent rate, and the US at 50 per cent. The former per-country limitation would have allowed a credit for the full $400 of Country Y tax and $500 of the Country X tax (50% × $3000 = $1500; $1500 × $1000/$3000 = $500). Thus $100 of the Country X tax would be an excess foreign tax credit. Under the overall limitation, the allowable credit for both Country X and Country Y taxes

payers with losses in some countries and profits in others, because the losses did not prevent the crediting of taxes paid in the profit countries. On the other hand, the overall method was preferable for taxpayers operating at a profit in different countries, some with rates of tax higher than the US and some with rates lower. The overall method allowed the taxpayer to average the high and low rate countries and thus utilize currently the excess credits from the higher rate countries.

The Tax Reform Act of 1976 eliminated the per-country method and required all taxpayers to use the overall method. This action reflected a Congressional view that the combination of deductible losses from some countries and allowable foreign tax credits from others was creating an excessive tax benefit. Apparently, the averaging of rates achieved under the overall method was not seen as creating a similar problem. Requiring all taxpayers to use the overall method insured that foreign losses from a country first reduced other foreign source income before the tax credit mechanism came into play.

Even under the 1976 Act approach, certain types of income were removed from the overall credit computation and separate overall credit limit computations were required with respect to these categories. Interest income was a notable example of the separate treatment because of the ease with which its source could be manipulated. The problem of source manipulation was significantly increased by the 1986 Act reduction in the top US corporate income tax rate to 34 per cent. This action, it was assumed, would place many US corporations in a situation where their foreign taxes paid would exceed the US tax on the foreign income, with the result that they would be in an excess foreign tax credit position. Congress feared that this situation in turn would create too great an incentive for US corporations to manipulate receipts and deductions among various categories and sources of income in order to maximize foreign tax credit utilization. To prevent this reaction, the 1986 Act significantly expanded the categories ("baskets") of income for which separate foreign tax credit limitations must be computed. In general, the traditional overall limitation was retained only for income derived from manufacturing, production, sales and services carried out or performed directly by a US corporation or its foreign subsidiaries.

In addition, Congress was concerned about the averaging effect of the limitation within baskets. Thus, another theme that runs through the foreign tax credit limitation rules is the separation of items of high-tax income from items of low-tax income even though otherwise the two would fall within the same basket.

---

would be $1000 (50% × $3000 = $1500; $1500 × $2000/$3000 = $1000). Hence, there would be no excess credit under the overall method as compared to $100 under the per country method and Corporation A in effect used its excess foreign tax credit from Country X against the US tax on the income from Country Y.

6.6.2 THE GENERAL LIMITATION INCOME BASKET

As a technical matter, the computation of the overall limitation in Section 904(a) must begin by identifying the amounts allocable to eight separately defined baskets of income, with the balance falling into a residual category, the "general limitation income basket." It is, however, useful to begin analysis of the overall limitation with the general limitation income basket since in that category falls most manufacturing, sales and services income derived by US corporations from foreign operations.

The limitation in Section 904(a) provides that the total amount of the credit allowable under Section 901 may not exceed the proportion of the US tax on a taxpayer's worldwide taxable income that its foreign source taxable income bears to its total taxable income from US and foreign sources.[25] Where a US corporation derives all its foreign source income from active business activities, the operation of the general foreign tax credit limitation is relatively straightforward. For example, assume that a US corporation engaged in manufacturing operations has $2 million foreign source taxable income from country A on which it paid $500,000 in taxes, a $1 million loss in country B, and $1 million US source taxable income. The US tax on worldwide income is $700,000 (35% × $2,000,000). The maximum foreign tax credit that may be claimed in the current year by the corporation is $350,000 ($700,000 × $1,000,000/$2,000,000). Thus, even though the effective rate of tax in Country A is only 25 per cent, the full amount of tax paid may not be credited because of the effect of the loss in Country B. On the other hand, if the corporation had $500,000 income from Country A on which it paid $250,000 taxes (50 per cent rate), $500,000 from Country B on which it paid $100,000 taxes (20 per cent rate) and $1 million US source income, the full $350,000 would be creditable ($1,000,000/$2,000,000 × $700,000 = $350,000) since the use of the overall method allows the averaging of the foreign rates.

---

25. Taxable income for purposes of Sec. 904 is determined under US tax concepts and accounting rules. The amount of foreign taxes naturally is determined under the laws of the foreign country. If there are substantial differences, for example, in the items included in the tax base, this will affect the amount of currently available tax credit, even if the nominal tax rates are the same.

Generally, both the numerator and the denominator of the Sec. 904 fraction are determined by applying the rules discussed in Chapters 4 and 5. A special source rule, applicable solely for purposes of determining the allowable foreign tax credit, is contained in Sec. 904(g) which is intended to prevent artificially increasing the foreign tax credit limit by routing US source income through a foreign subsidiary to came back to the US as foreign source income. Special rules are required to integrate the treatment of capital gains and losses with the foreign tax credit. Those rules are contained in Sec. 904(b)(2), but have no significance for corporations as the same rate applies to capital gains and ordinary income. Individual taxpayers can be affected by the special rules since for this class of taxpayers a preferential rate is provided for capital gains.

6.6.3 THE SEPARATE "BASKETS"

In addition to the general limitation income basket, Section 904(d) specifies eight other categories or "baskets" of income for each of which a foreign tax credit limitation computation must be made. The mathematical application of the Section 904(a) limitation and the averaging effect discussed in 6.6.2 are the same but confined to the income and foreign taxes in each basket.[26] Thus, an excess foreign tax credit in one basket of income cannot spill over and offset US tax on income in another basket (in US tax jargon, no "cross crediting" is allowed). As noted above, the use of separate baskets of income for foreign tax credit limitation purposes pre-dated the 1986 Act, but that Act significantly increased both the number of baskets and the complexity of the limitation mechanism. In the following materials, the baskets are first considered as applied to income received directly by a US taxpayer; the application of the rules to income received and distributed by a foreign subsidiary are then considered.

6.6.3.1 The passive income basket

As discussed in 6.6.1, the basic US foreign tax credit mechanism contemplates that if foreign countries impose tax on a US corporation's business income higher than the 35 per cent US rate, an excess foreign tax credit will be created. That excess credit may be carried back and carried forward to be utilized in years when additional foreign source income taxed at less than a 35 per cent rate is realized. (*See* 6.7.) If it were possible, however, to generate additional foreign source income currently which was taxed at a low rate or not taxed at all, the averaging effect of the overall limitation fraction would permit the current crediting of the excess foreign taxes paid on the business income. Passive investment income, which is often subject to little or no foreign tax and whose source is readily manipulable, was used to achieve this result prior to the 1986 Act.

For example, assume foreign countries impose a tax of 50 per cent on $1 million of taxable business income of a US corporation. The corporation also has $1 million of US source income. In the absence of anything else, Section 904(a) would limit the allowable foreign tax credit to $350,000 ($700,000 × $1,000,000/$2,000,000). Total taxes of $850,000 would be paid and the corporation would have a $150,000 excess foreign tax credit. Suppose that the US corporation transfers assets generating $250,000 in passive income to a foreign country where the tax on the passive income is fifteen per cent. US source income is reduced to $750,000, total foreign source income is increased to

---

26. The methodology for allocating a taxpayer's foreign taxes among its baskets of income is spelled out in Treas. Reg. Sec. 1.904-6.

$1,250,000, and total foreign taxes paid thereon are $537,500 ($500,000 plus $37,500 on the passive income). The allowable foreign tax credit would then be $437,500 ($700,000 × $1,250,000/$2,000,000) (an increase of $87,500) and total US and foreign taxes would be $800,000 (a decrease of $50,000). While this result is simply a function of the averaging effect of the overall limitation, because the source of passive income is so easily manipulated by taxpayers, Section 904(d)(1)(A) requires that the overall limitation for foreign taxes on passive income be computed separately. Thus, in the above example, the passive income would be placed in the passive income basket, with the result that the US would impose a tax of $87,500 on the passive income against which a credit of $37,500 would be allowed. The US does not, therefore, have its tax on the passive income reduced by the excess credit generated by the business income.

The passive income basket, in general, includes dividends, interest, annuities, certain rents and royalties, and net gains from sales or exchanges of property that generate passive income.[27] Income equivalent to interest, such as loan commitment fees, is also included in the passive income basket. Net gains from commodity transactions are included in the passive basket unless realized by taxpayers actively and regularly engaged in such transactions. The passive basket includes net gains from foreign currency transactions,[28] unless the transactions are directly related to the business needs of the entity.

An important exception provides that rents and royalties derived from unrelated parties in the active conduct of a trade or business are excluded from the definition of foreign personal holding company income.[29] As a result, these items fall into the general limitation income basket.

The statute specifically excludes from the passive income basket:
(1) any income that is described in one of the other eight income baskets;[30]
(2) any export financing interest;[31]
(3) any high-taxed income;

---

27. Technically, "passive income" is defined in Sec. 904(d)(2)(A) by reference to the definition of "foreign personal holding company income", discussed at 7.2.4. The term includes income taxed under the foreign personal holding company provisions, discussed at 7.5.1, and under the passive foreign investment company rules, discussed at 7.5.2..
28. See 10.3.
29. *See* Treas. Reg. Sec. 1.954-1(e) and 2(d) and Treas. Reg. Sec. 1.904-4(b)(2) for rules with respect to related parties and whether rents and royalties are derived from the active conduct of a trade or business.
30. Sec. 904(d)(5) gives the Treasury broad regulatory authority to prevent manipulation of the character of income to try to achieve averaging effects that contravene the purposes of Sec. 904(d).
31. In general, this category includes interest derived from financing the sale for use or consumption outside the US of property manufactured or produced within the US so long as no more than 50 per cent of the fair market value of the property is attributable to products imported into the US. Sec. 904(d)(2)(G). Interest which qualifies for the exception falls into the general limitation income basket. The purpose of this exception is to avoid adversely affecting the level of US exports.

(4) any foreign oil and gas extraction income (see 6.8).

The "high-taxed income" exception is of some interest. Contrary to the general assumption underlying the passive income category, i.e. that passive income is subject to low foreign taxes, some passive income is subject to quite high foreign tax, e.g. withholding taxes on portfolio dividends. As a result, Congress felt it was not adequate merely to differentiate passive from other types of income but also passive income subject to low foreign effective tax rates from passive income subject to high foreign effective tax rates.[32] This so-called "high-tax kick-out", when it is operative, shifts income that otherwise would fall in the passive income basket to the general limitation income basket.

The high-tax kick-out rule operates mechanically and automatically if its conditions are satisfied. Under the rule, the foreign tax paid on the *net* passive income (gross income minus allocable deductions, both as determined under US rules) is compared to US tax on that income.[33] If the foreign tax exceeds the US tax, the passive income is "kicked-out" of the passive basket into the general limitation income basket. For example, assume that a US corporation receives $100 in passive income from a foreign corporation that is subject to a 30 per cent withholding tax. Under the US allocation of deduction rules (see 4.4), assume that 50 of the US recipient's expenses must be allocated to the 100 payment. The 50 of net passive income is subject to the high-tax kick-out because the 30 of foreign tax on the 50 of net income exceeds the US tax of 17.5 on that income (35% × 50). The high-tax kick-out thus operates when the effective foreign tax rate on passive income (determined under US rules) exceeds the US effective rate on that income, even though the nominal foreign rate is lower than the US rate.

6.6.3.2 The high withholding tax interest basket

Interest income (other than export financing interest) which is subject to a withholding tax that is five per cent or greater and is imposed on a gross basis is placed in a separate basket.

6.6.3.3 The financial services income basket

Income (other than passive income, export financing interest or high withholding tax interest) which is derived from the active conduct of a banking, financing or similar business or from ordinary investment activity by an insurance company is placed in a separate basket. Because of the difficulty of distinguishing passive from active income for financial institutions, the financial services

---

32. This differentiation insures that the US tax on low-taxed passive income will not be absorbed by the foreign tax on high-taxed passive income.
33. Treas. Reg. Sec. 1.904-4(c)(2) provides rules for the grouping of certain types of income for purposes of the high-tax kick-out rule. These regulations seek to ease the formidable task of applying the rule to each item of passive income.

income basket includes both types of income if the institution is "predominantly engaged" in the active conduct of a banking, insurance, financing or similar business.[34] If a financial entity does not satisfy the "predominantly engaged" test, its passive income remains in the passive income basket.

6.6.3.4   The shipping income basket

Income from aircraft and shipping operations is subject to a separate foreign tax credit limitation.[35]

6.6.3.5   The dividends from noncontrolled Section 902 corporations basket

If a US shareholder owns less than ten per cent of the stock of a foreign corporation, dividends from that corporation are placed in the passive income basket. If, however, the US shareholder owns ten per cent or more of the stock of a foreign corporation but, together with other ten per cent US shareholders, owns 50 per cent or less of that stock, dividends from such a "noncontrolled Section 902 corporation" fall into a separate limitation basket. Thus, foreign taxes imposed on the dividends, including both withholding taxes and deemed paid taxes under Section 902, may offset only US tax on that dividend income (including the gross-up under Section 78). Prior to 1997, a separate limitation applied to *each* noncontrolled Section 902 corporation from which a US shareholder received dividends. Thus, foreign taxes on dividends received from one noncontrolled Section 902 corporation could not be credited against US taxes on dividends received from a different noncontrolled Section 902 corporation even if their business activities were identical. Under the 1997 Act, dividends from all noncontrolled Section 902 corporations paid after 2002 and attributable to earnings and profits accumulated before 2003 may be aggregated into a single basket, although the separate corporation approach continues to apply to dividends from passive foreign investment companies (see 7.5.2). For post-2002 earnings, a look-through rule similar to that described in 6.6.3.7 applies to noncontrolled section 902 corporations so that a portion of a dividend from such a corporation is placed in the basket to which the ratable share of earnings and profits that generated the dividend would fall, e.g., active business income, passive income, etc.[36]

---

34. Treas. Reg. Sec. 1.904-4(e), adopts a very broad definition of qualifying income for financial institutions and provides that the "predominantly engaged" test is met if 80 per cent of an institution's gross income is qualifying income.
35. The income in this basket is that described in Sec. 904(d)(2)(D) and 954(f).
36. Prior to 2003, if a noncontrolled Sec. 902 corporation pays a dividend out of earnings and profits attributable to interest income on which a withholding tax in excess of five per cent was imposed, the excess is not treated as a foreign tax for purposes of determining the taxes deemed paid by the US recipient under Sec. 902. Thus, if a noncontrolled Sec. 902 corporation receives 100 of interest income which is subject to a ten per cent withholding tax, only five of the tax is

6.6.3.6   Other baskets

The US provides preferential tax treatment to income derived by subsidiaries of US companies engaged in foreign trade activities through a Domestic International Sales Corporation (DISC) or a Foreign Sales Corporation (FSC). See 9.2.3. and 9.2.2. for descriptions of the rules applicable to these entities. The US has thought it inappropriate to allow a credit for foreign taxes imposed on income which is in whole or in part excluded from or subject to deferred tax in the US. Accordingly, separate baskets are provided and separate Section 904(d) limitation computations are required for (1) dividends from a DISC paid from income treated as foreign source; (2) taxable income attributable to the foreign trade income of an FSC; and (3) distributions from an FSC out of earnings and profits attributable to foreign trade income or defined interest and carrying charges.

6.6.3.7   Look-through rules for controlled foreign corporations

A different regime applies to a US taxpayer that owns ten per cent of the stock of a foreign corporation in which it and other US ten per cent shareholders own more than 50 per cent of the stock of the foreign corporation (a "controlled foreign corporation" or CFC). If the US taxpayer receives dividends, interest, rents, or royalties from the foreign corporation, the taxpayer determines the proper basket for the income by "looking through" to the character of the underlying income of the foreign corporation out of which the payment was made.

Dividends received from a CFC are treated as income in a separate basket in the ratio of the CFC's earnings and profits in that basket to its entire earnings and profits. For example, assume US Corporation X received a 100 dividend from Corporation Y, a wholly-owned subsidiary incorporated in and operating exclusively in Country A. Corporation X has earnings and profits of 1,000 of which 800 is from its manufacturing operations in Country A and 200 is from dividends from a noncontrolled Section 902 corporation, also incorporated in Country A. Eighty (80) of the dividend to Corporation X is placed in its general

---

treated as a foreign tax paid by a 10-50 per cent US shareholder for purposes of computing its allowable Sec. 902 credit. The special limitation avoids the need to look through the noncontrolled Sec. 902 corporation in order to place each item of income in a separate basket. Nonetheless, it does require identification of that portion of the corporation's earnings and profits attributable to high-withholding tax interest. The special rule was thought necessary to prevent the crediting of high withholding taxes on interest income against the US tax on other types of income that otherwise could take place through the operation of the Sec. 902 deemed paid credit.

For post-2002 dividends paid out of post-2002 earnings and profits, a look-through rule is applied to all dividends from noncontrolled Section 902 corporations, thus rendering the special rule unnecessary.

limitation income basket and 20 is placed in its noncontrolled Section 902 corporation basket.[37]

A different method of allocating income from a CFC to the appropriate basket applies to interest, rents and royalties. In general, formulary methods are employed similar to those discussed at 4.4 with respect to the allocation of such items when incurred as expenses. Interest payments, however, must first be allocated to the passive income basket to the extent of the CFC's passive income before the formula is applied.[38]

6.6.3.8   De minimis rule

In general, if the separate category income of a CFC is less than the lesser of the $1 million or five per cent of its gross income, then all of its income will be treated as general limitation income. (*See* 7.2.5.)

6.6.4   THE TREATMENT OF LOSSES

6.6.4.1   Foreign losses

Prior to the 1986 Act, a US corporation which incurred an overall net foreign loss in a taxable year was subject to a special sourcing rule if in a subsequent year it realized foreign source income. Section 904(f)(1) provided that the prior loss, which offset US source income, was "recaptured" by treating as US source income that portion of the taxpayer's subsequent foreign source income equal to the lesser of (1) the amount of the prior foreign loss or (2) 50 per cent (or a larger percentage if the taxpayer so chooses) of the taxpayer's foreign source income.[39]

---

37. The application of the look-through rules to dividends imputed to the US taxpayer by virtue of subpart F provisions is considered at 7.2.5.
38. The complex allocation rules are set forth in Treas. Reg. Sec. 1.904-5(c)(2) and (3).
39. The problem to which Sec. 904(f)(1) was directed arose in situations in which a US corporation experienced current losses in its foreign operations and used those losses to reduce US tax on its US source income. In later years when income was derived from the operation, a foreign tax would be due unless the foreign country allowed a net operating loss carryover of the prior losses (as would the US in a similar situation). If the foreign country did not provide for a carryover of losses, foreign income and a foreign tax would be generated in later years and, under normal principles, a foreign tax credit would be available for those taxes. However, this result ignored the fact that the prior foreign losses had been used to reduce US taxable income so that a full crediting of the subsequent foreign taxes would give the US taxpayer a double benefit, i.e. a reduction of US taxes in earlier years and a foreign tax credit in later years.
   The operation of Sec. 904(f)(1) may be illustrated by the following example: Assume a corporation in year 1 utilized $500,000 of net losses from foreign sources to reduce US taxable income. In year 2 it realized foreign source taxable income of $1 million. Under the special source rule in Sec. 904(f)(1), $500,000 of the corporation's foreign income would be treated as US source income. As a result, the numerator of the Sec. 904(a) fraction would be reduced and so would the amount of creditable foreign taxes. In the above example, assume that the US corpo-

With the adoption in 1986 of the multiple baskets of income for foreign tax credit limitation purposes, it was necessary to provide more detailed rules as to how foreign losses were to be treated for Section 904(a) purposes. These rules are contained in Section 904(f)(5). The general rule is that foreign losses in one basket must first be used to reduce proportionately foreign income in any other basket. Only after this allocation may the excess of the foreign loss be used to reduce US source income. Subsequently, when foreign income is realized in the basket which generated the loss, that income must be recharacterized so that it offsets the losses previously taken in other baskets. This recharacterization rule in Section 904(f)(5) applies in addition to, not in lieu of, the recapture rule in Section 904(f)(1), described above.

The operation of the foreign loss rules in Section 904(f) can best be understood by considering the following examples:

Example (1): US Corporation X has a 100 foreign source loss in year 1 which is entirely within the general limitation income basket; it has no income in any other basket. Corporation X can deduct the 100 against its US source income in year 1.

When Corporation X realizes 100 foreign source general limitation income in year 2, only the recapture rule of Section 904(f)(1) is operative since no recharacterization of the income is required. That rule treats 50 per cent (or more if the taxpayer so elects) of the income as US source.

Example (2): Assume the same facts as in Example (1), except that in year 1 Corporation X also had 75 in its passive income basket. The 100 loss would first reduce the 75 of passive income and the 25 balance would offset US income. In year 2, 25 of the 100 of general limitation income would first be resourced as US income under the recapture rule and the balance of 75 would be allocated to the passive income basket under the recharacterization rule.

Example (3): In year 1, Corporation X has 200 of US income, twenty of foreign income in the passive income basket, ten of income in the noncontrolled Section 902 corporation basket, and a fifteen loss in the general limitation income basket. The fifteen loss must be allocated ten to the passive income basket and five to the noncontrolled Section 902 corporation basket. None of the loss is al-

---

ration had $1 million of US source taxable income in each of the two years. The deduction in year 1 produced a tax saving of $175,000 (35 per cent of $500,000). In year 2, the tentative US tax would have been $700,000 against which, absent the special rule, a maximum foreign tax credit of $350,000 ($700,000 × $1,000,000/$2,000,000) would have been available. Under the special rule in Sec. 904(f)(1) the maximum foreign tax credit in year 2 is reduced to $175,000 ($700,000 × $500,000/$2,000,000). Thus, the tax benefit granted by the US in year 1 is "recaptured" in year 2.

Under Sec. 904(f)(3), previously deducted losses will be recaptured if property used outside the US is disposed of, regardless of whether the gain on the disposition would be taxed. Thus, if a taxpayer disposes of such property in a tax-free transaction, an amount of previously deducted losses equal to the full amount of the gain must be recaptured in the year of the disposition.

located to the US income. Thus, for foreign tax credit limitation purposes, Corporation X has ten of passive income, five of Section 902 noncontrolled foreign corporation income and 200 of US income. As a result, Corporation X may not be able to claim a full credit in year 1 for the foreign taxes it paid on the income in the two positive income baskets.

In year 2, Corporation X has the same income except that it has positive income of 50 in the general limitation income basket. Since income in other baskets had been offset in year 1 by a general limitation income basket loss, ten of the year 2 income is recharacterized as passive income and five as noncontrolled Section 902 corporation income; the balance of 35 remains in the general limitation income basket. In year 2, therefore, Corporation X has 30 of passive income, fifteen of noncontrolled Section 902 corporation income and 35 of general limitation income. Excess credits generated in the first two baskets in year 1 can then be carried over and used in year 2. The actual foreign tax incurred in year 2 on the general limitation income is *not* recharacterized; it may be credited only against general limitation income in year 2 or succeeding years.[40]

The recharacterization rules in Section 904(f) mitigate the effects of rigid adherence to the foreign loss rules. For example, losses from a taxpayer's low-tax passive income basket might be required to be used to offset income in its general limitation income basket which is subject to a high rate of tax, thus creating an excess foreign tax credit situation. Conversely, if losses from a high tax basket reduce income in a low tax basket, the US Treasury loses its residual tax on the low-tax income. Recharacterization in this situation permits the Treasury to recover all or part of that tax.

6.6.4.2 US losses

If a US taxpayer has a US source net loss, that loss is allocated among, and thus reduces, the income in the various foreign income baskets proportionately to the income in each basket. Before a US loss is so allocated, a loss in any foreign income basket must first be allocated among the baskets.[41]

There is no recharacterization rule applicable to US source income earned in a subsequent year. Thus, for foreign tax credit limitation purposes, the effect of allocation of US losses is permanent. The failure to recharacterize US losses, at least to the extent they represent real economic losses, is arguably inappropriate and presumably was adopted because of revenue considerations.

---

40. Similar but more complex calculations are required if losses are sustained in more than one basket in a taxable year. Deductions must be apportioned among baskets to determine whether there has been a loss in that basket. Presumably, Treas. Reg. Sec. 1.861-8 (4.4) is to be applied in making the apportionment.
41. Sec. 904(f)(5)(D).

6.7   Carryback and carryover of excess credits

Allowable foreign tax credits in any of the separate baskets in excess of those creditable in the current year may be carried back two years and forward five years.[42] The credits can only be used in the basket from which they originated and then only to the extent there is "excess" limitation in that basket in the year to which they are carried.

6.8   Special limitations on the foreign tax credit

In addition to the limitations on the foreign tax credit discussed in 6.6, the amount of the credit may also be reduced by certain other limitations which are applicable to the natural resources industry[43] or which are intended to further non-tax objectives of the US.[44]

6.9   Relief for small investors

In 1997, Congress took an initial step to relieve small individual investors from the burden of complying with the full panoply of the Section 904 limitations. Under Section 904(j), individuals who incur not more than $300 ($600 in the case of joint returns) of foreign taxes imposed on their passive income from foreign sources are not subject to the rules of Section 904. Instead, such individuals may elect to take the credit up to the specified amounts without being concerned with which basket their foreign investment income should be placed. As a corollary, for individuals who elect to have Section 901(j) apply, no foreign tax credits may be carried from or to the taxable year.

6.10   Anti-abuse rule

Prior to the 1997 Act, taxpayers engaged in a variety of transactions designed to transfer the benefit of the tax credit for foreign withholding taxes from a taxpayer which could not use the credit to one which could. A tax-exempt pension fund, for example, in effect could sell the credit to a taxable entity which was in an excess limit position and thus could benefit from the credit. In simplified

---

42. Sec. 904(c).
43. *See* Sec. 901(e), (f); Sec. 907.
44. *See* Sec. 901(j) (denying a foreign tax credit for any taxes paid to a country whose government supports terrorism, does not have diplomatic relations with the US, or is not recognized by the US; such taxes are, however, deductible); Sec. 908, 999 (foreign tax credit must be reduced to the extent that the credit is attributable to income derived by the taxpayer from participating in or cooperating with an international boycott; amount of disallowed direct (but not indirect) credit is deductible).

form, just before the dividend record date of the stock in a non US corporation, a US tax-exempt entity would sell its stock in the company to a US bank for an amount which reflected the expected dividend. The bank would receive the dividend and the tax credit for withholding foreign taxes imposed on the dividend by the foreign corporation's government. The tax-exempt organization would receive enough to compensate itself for losing the dividend and would repurchase the stock immediately after the dividend record date for the value of the foreign corporation's stock now reduced because of the declared dividend. The bank would then take a loss on the sale. The combination of the loss plus the foreign tax credit insured a profit for the bank in a transaction for which there was no economic purpose other than creating foreign tax credits on dividends which would not have carried a tax credit to the tax exempt organization. Congress responded to this obvious tax avoidance transaction (and others similarly designed) by enacting Section 901(k). Under that provision, a US taxpayer cannot claim a foreign tax credit for dividend withholding taxes unless it has held the stock for more than 15 days during a 30-day period that begins 15 days before the dividend record date of the stock. (The time periods are extended to 90 and 45 days respectively for preferred stock). A simlar rule applies to the Section 902 indirect credit. An exception is made for securities dealers who are actively engaged in trade or business in the foreign country if certain qualifying conditions are met. Foreign taxes disallowed as a credit by Section 901(k) may be claimed as a deduction.

Because the parties to transactions such as that described above typically were unwilling to take any real economic risk of loss, it is expected that the holding period requirement will bring an end to such transactions.

6.11 A perspective on the foreign tax credit mechanism

After examining the "baskets" system of separate and overall limitations and the special limitations involved in determining the allowable credit for foreign taxes paid or incurred, one can reasonably ask whether there is anything left of the fairly straightforward principles that were asserted in 6.1 to undergird the foreign tax credit system. If a country adopts the foreign tax credit as its fundamental mechanism for adjusting international tax burdens, why are all the limitations required? An identification of the broad problems to which the varied limitations are addressed may shed some light on this question.

Any limitation on a foreign tax credit itself represents a deviation from the principle of capital export neutrality which is one object of the credit mechanism. But some limitation is required for several reasons. First, a limitation is necessary to protect the revenues of the US government. A pure credit mechanism would provide for full crediting of foreign taxes whatever the rate of foreign tax and refunds by the US government where foreign taxes exceeded US taxes (including US taxes on US income). This, of course, would put the US Treasury at the disposal of all foreign tax systems, a situation which neither the United States nor any other government has been willing to accept.

Hence, some limitation is required and the question is what form the limitation should take. A single overall limitation has the advantage of administrative simplicity and eliminates the necessity that foreign taxes be traced to specific items of foreign income, a requirement which would impose insuperable record-keeping burdens on taxpayers and would be impossible to administer by fiscal authorities.

On the other hand, an overall limitation in turn inherently involves an averaging of high and low tax rates on foreign income. When the US reduced its top corporate rate to 34 per cent in the 1986 Act, a general overall limitation could no longer be employed. The low US corporate rate would mean that most US multinational corporations would find themselves in an excess foreign tax credit situation. The concern then was that excessive pressure would be placed on the credit mechanism as US corporations sought to manipulate the source of income and deductions so that the averaging effects of the overall limitation would reduce or eliminate excess credit positions. The adoption of the system based on various "baskets" of income was intended to prevent manipulation for averaging purposes which Congress considered excessive. Averaging for "normal" business income was, however, still permitted. Given the fact that most trading partners of the U.S. rather quickly reduced their corporate tax rates to the 30-40% range, it can be questioned whether this justification for the multiple basket system is still valid, at least in the excruciating detail of its present form.

The justifications for the existing baskets and special limitations can be grouped in the following broad categories:

(1) Types of income that can be easily manipulated by taxpayers from country to country, with a resulting increase in the allowable foreign tax credit. The special baskets for passive income and for financial services income respond to this problem and in effect deny the use of the basic averaging mechanism to such income.

(2) Types of income with respect to which the US has granted preferential tax treatment. The basket governing FSC distributions and the special limitations with respect to natural resources income respond to this problem. The rules prevent the preferential tax treatment of such income by the US from being used to increase the available foreign tax credit through the impact of the preferences on the limitation mechanism.

(3) Types of income that are not subjected to the same tax rules abroad as are applied by the US. Failure to take these differences into account again can increase the allowable foreign tax credit at no increased US tax cost or exempt the foreign source income from tax altogether. The

107

          rule requiring recapture of overall foreign losses and the high withhold-
ing tax and shipping income baskets respond to this problem.

(4) Income earned in activities that run counter to foreign policy objectives
of the US. The rule denying the foreign tax credit for boycott related income responds to this problem by imposing a tax penalty on such income.

Thus, the various special limitations respond to what have been perceived as
defects in the operation of the credit when applied to the particular classes of
income involved. The use of the basket approach in turn responds to the averaging effect created by any overall limitation. While the number of baskets that
are presently employed by the US may be excessive — and many are of that
view — nonetheless some use of the basket approach appears necessary. The
resulting complexities of the foreign tax credit rules reflect the complexities of
the underlying US tax system and the international transactions to which the
credit mechanism must be applied.

Chapter 7
Treatment of foreign business operations and investments by US persons

7.1 Background

The materials in this chapter deal with special rules that apply to foreign business operations and investments by US persons. These rules are both in addition to and interact with the fundamental foreign tax credit rules discussed in Chapter 6.

Initially the materials deal with the treatment of US shareholders in "controlled foreign corporations." The emphasis is on business operations abroad although, as will be seen, some rules dealing with passive investment income are also considered.

Under the US tax principles previously discussed, the income of a foreign corporation with US shareholders is not taxed to the shareholder until repatriated, either in the form of a dividend or as a liquidation distribution. The appropriateness of the deferral of US tax which these principles can create has been seriously questioned ever since 1962. Legislation was proposed at that time which would have eliminated deferral for all US-controlled foreign corporations and taxed the foreign profits directly to the US shareholders on a current basis. After a lengthy and complex legislative process, the general elimination of deferral was rejected. However, deferral was curtailed through the so-called "subpart F" provisions for foreign corporations engaged in certain "tax haven" operations. In general, these provisions were directed at the use of foreign corporations which were used to accumulate certain types of income in a foreign "base" company located in a jurisdiction with little or no tax. The types of income included income from dealings with related parties which were channeled through the base company and passive investment income. The 1962 legislation attempted to distinguish between "legitimate" deferral of US taxation in foreign operations and deferral resulting from a manipulation of US tax rules. Accordingly, the lines drawn in reaching a compromise between those who favored complete elimination of deferral and those urging its retention were extremely detailed and complex and have been the subject of frequent legislative attention. The subpart F rules are considered in 7.2.

Given the fact that some US business activities can be carried on in a world of tax deferral where subpart F does not apply, a further set of rules is needed to place limits on the ability to taxpayers to move assets in and out of that world. These provisions are considered in 7.3 and 7.4.

The provisions granting tax deferral and then protecting against its abuse are among the most complex in the Code. The impact of the rules was reduced substantially but temporarily in 1986 by the reduction of the US corporate tax rate to a level well below that of most countries in which US companies carry on business operations. Tax deferral is of interest only if the foreign country rates are lower than those of the US. Following the US action in 1986, corporate tax rates in industrialized countries converged in the 30-40 percent range. In the case of tax havens and special preferential tax regimes, however, the anti-deferral provisions remain important.

Provisions governing passive foreign investments by US persons are then taken up in 7.5 and following. The theme running through the rules considered is the extent of current US taxation of passive foreign investment income.

The chapter concludes with a discussion of the US tax rules applicable to foreign trusts where US persons are involved.

7.2 Business operations through foreign corporations controlled by US persons: subpart F

7.2.1 BASIC STRUCTURE OF SUBPART F

A "US shareholder" that "owns" ten per cent or more of the "total combined voting power" of all classes of voting stock of a controlled foreign corporation (a "CFC") must include in income each year its *pro rata* share of the CFC's "951(a)(1) income" (authors' term).

A CFC is a foreign corporation in which more than 50 per cent of either the total combined voting power of all classes of voting stock or the total value of all stock is owned by ten per cent or greater US shareholders on any day during the taxable year of the CFC. The "951(a)(1) income" is taxed to the US shareholder in the year earned by the corporation; when it is subsequently distributed as a dividend, no further tax is imposed. A foreign tax credit is granted to the US corporate shareholder for the taxes it is deemed to have paid on the "951(a)(1) income" (and, of course, the US shareholder includes the amount of the deemed foreign tax credit in income also). The basis of the US shareholder's stock in the CFC is increased by the amount of any "951(a)(1) income" that is taxed by subpart F and decreased by subsequent distributions of previously taxed "951(a)(1) income."

Within this deceptively simple statutory framework lie a host of definitions, exceptions, limitations and qualifications.

7.2.2 TAX TREATMENT OF US SHAREHOLDER

A "US shareholder" is any US person (citizen, resident, partnership, corporation, estate or trust)[1] who owns directly or is treated as owning ("constructive ownership") at least ten per cent of the total combined voting power[2] of all classes of stock entitled to vote in a CFC. The US shareholder is taxed on its *pro rata* share[3] of the CFC's undistributed "951(a)(1) income".[4]

Constructive ownership of the stock of a CFC can result if a US person is a stockholder, partner, or beneficiary of a corporation, partnership, trust or estate that owns stock in a CFC.[5] Generally speaking, constructive ownership of CFC stock is determined by applying the attribution rules of Section 318 although some modifications are made.[6] While the attribution rules may push a US person above the 10 per cent stock ownership level, it is only taxed on its *pro rata* share of "951(a)(1) income" based on the stock it owns directly (or which is attributed to it from a foreign entity).

7.2.3 DEFINITION OF A CFC

A CFC is a foreign corporation in which more than 50 per cent of either the total combined voting power of all classes of stock entitled to vote or of the total value of all stock[7] is owned by "US shareholders," i.e. US persons owning di-

---

1. Sec. 951(b), 957(c), 7701(a)(30). Sec. 957(c) modifies the definition in the case of corporations organized in US possessions. For a shareholder that is taxed on the income of a CFC under Sec. 1247, 7.5.2, below, under the foreign personal holding company rules, 7.5.1, below, or under the passive foreign investment company rules, 7.5.2, below, Sec. 951(c), (d), and (f) and Sec. 1297(e) provide coordination of those provisions with the Sec. 951 rules.
2. As to what constitutes "voting power", *see* Treas. Reg. Sec. 1.951-1(g)(2).
3. Sec. 951(a)(2). For the definition of *pro rata* shares, *see* Treas. Reg. Sec. 1.951-1(e).
4. The constitutionality of Sec. 951 was upheld in *Garlock, Inc. v. Commissioner,* 489 F.2d 197 (2d Cir. 1973); *Estate of Whitlock v. Commissioner,* 494 F.2d 1297 (10th Cir. 1974); *Dougherty v. Commissioner,* 60 TC 917 (1973).
5. Sec. 958.
6. Sec. 958(c); Treas. Reg. Sec. 1.958-2. In general, under Sec. 318, a person is considered to be the owner of stock owned by close relatives (spouse, children, etc.), by his 50 per cent controlled corporation, or by a partnership or trust of which he is a partner or beneficiary. For purposes of subpart F, the percentage of stock ownership deemed to be controlling is reduced from 50 to 10 per cent.
7. Prior to 1986, only the voting stock requirement was employed. This test led to some controversy where the *value* of the stock held appeared to be more than 50 per cent although actual stock ownership was 50 per cent or less. *See,* for example, Rev. Rul. 70-426, 1970-2 Cum. Bull. 157;

rectly or by attribution 10 per cent of the voting stock of the CFC.[8] Thus CFC status may be avoided if there are eleven unrelated US shareholders who own ratably 100 per cent of the voting stock of a foreign corporation or if one or more US shareholders own exactly 50 per cent of the voting stock and 50 per cent of the total value of all stock of a foreign corporation, the balance being owned by foreign shareholders. A foreign corporation is a CFC if the more-than-50 per cent test is met on any one day during the taxable year.

7.2.4   INCOME TAXABLE TO US SHAREHOLDERS

A US shareholder of a CFC must include in income two principal types of income.[9]
   (1) its pro rata share of the CFC's subpart F income; and
   (2) the amount determined with respect to the shareholder under Section 956, i.e., the earnings invested by the CFC in US property for the year.

7.2.4.1   Subpart F income

The first major category of income currently taxable to a US shareholder is its *pro rata* share of the CFC's "subpart F income." Subpart F income, as defined in Section 952,[10] consists of two principal categories of income:

Garlock, Inc. v. Commissioner, supra note 4; *Estate of Weiskopf v. Commissioner,* 64 TC 78 (1975); *Koehring Co. v. United States,* 583 F.2d 313 (7th Cir. 1978) (holding that more than 50 per cent test was met although nominal stock ownership by US persons was 50 per cent or less). But compare *CCA, Inc. v. Commissioner,* 64 TC 137 (1975) holding the control test not satisfied where the US shareholders owned exactly 50 per cent of the stock and the foreign shareholders possessed real powers. The addition of the "value" test m 1986 resolved the legal issue, though factual disputes over the correct value remain.
   Only voting stock is considered in determining if a US person is a "US shareholder". The value test applies only to stock held by "US shareholders".

8. Sec. 957(a). The 50 per cent figure is reduced to 25 per cent in the case of certain insurance subsidiaries. Sec. 957(b).

9. There are two other categories of limited application: (1) *Less developed country income.* Prior to 1975, income which would ordinarily have been subject to current taxation was exempted from the subpart F provisions if it was invested in certain qualified investments in less developed country corporations. When the income was withdrawn from investment. it then became subject to tax. This exception to the application of subpart F was repealed in 1976. (2) *Shipping income.* Shipping income is treated as subpart F income but for taxable years beginning before 1987 was not currently taxed if reinvested in shipping operations. The income became taxable upon withdrawal of the income from investment under Sec. 951. Sec. 955. The exclusion of reinvested shipping income from subpart F income was repealed for taxable years beginning after 1986.

10. A CFC's subpart F income cannot exceed its current earnings and profits as defined in Sec. 964(a). Sec. 952(c)(1)(A). For taxable years beginning after 1986, deficits in earnings and profits from prior years generally cannot be used to reduce the current year's earnings and profits unless the deficits arose in the same activity. If the limitation of Sec. 952(c)(1)(A) applies in one year and there is an excess of earnings and profits over subpart F income in a later year, that excess is recharacterized as subpart F income in the later year. *See* 952(c)(2).

(1) insurance income;[11]

(2) foreign base company income.[12]

(See also 7.2.7 for additional special categories of subpart F income.) Even if income is within one of the two categories, it does not constitute subpart F income if it is effectively connected with the conduct of a US trade or business of the CFC (unless by treaty the income is exempt from tax or taxed at a reduced rate.)[13]

Subpart F income which is distributed currently to the US shareholders technically retains its character as subpart F income, and is taxed as such, despite its actual distribution.[14]

The term "foreign base company income" (FBCI) is defined in great detail in Section 954 and the Regulations issued thereunder. The basic arrangement sought to be brought within these rules is one in which a US parent creates a foreign subsidiary in a country that imposes little or no tax. The parent sells products to the subsidiary which then makes the sale to the ultimate customer. The various "sale" prices can be manipulated so that most of the profit winds up in the subsidiary in the non-tax country, thus avoiding both US and foreign tax. The same kind of arrangement can be structured involving the provision of services for a related party. The FBCI rules focus on sales or services provided outside the country of incorporation of the CFC since it is in those cases that the CFC is being used as a "base" company. Another situation at which the FBCI rules are aimed is the use of a foreign corporation as a holding company to accumulate passive investment income.

FBCI includes five categories of income:

(1) *Foreign personal holding company income.* This income consists of (i) dividends, interest, rents and royalties;[15] (ii) net gains from the sale or

---

Generally a CFC's earnings and profits are computed in the same manner as those of a US corporation. *See* Treas. Reg. Sec. 1.964-1. Subpart F income does not include earnings and profits that are attributable to foreign income that is blocked from repatriation by, for example, currency regulations of the foreign country. Treas. Reg. Sec. 1.964-2. In general US tax rules apply to determine the gross income and taxable income of a CFC. Treas. Reg. Sec. 1.952-2. Foreign currency fluctuations can affect the amount of a corporation"s earnings and profits for subpart F purposes, *see* 10.2 and Temp. Treas. Reg. Sec. 1.964-1T(g).

11. Sec. 952(a)(1). This category of subpart F income is defined in detail in Sec. 953; it is not discussed further in this book.

12. Sec. 952(a)(2).

13. Sec. 952(b).

14. Treas. Reg. Sec. 1.959-1(b). However, under Sec. 959, amounts distributed which were previously taxed under Sec. 951(a) are not included in the income of the US shareholder when received.

15. *See* Treas. Reg. Sec. 1.954-2.

Generally excluded from FBCI are dividends, interest, rents and royalties received by a CFC from *related* persons operating a trade or business in the CFC's country. (However, if an interest, rent or royalty payment decreased the payor"s own subpart F income, the exclusion is not applicable.) Sec. 954(c)(3); Treas. Reg. Sec. 1.954-2(b). In addition, rents and royalties received

exchange of property which gives rise to the income described in (i) or which does not give rise to any income;[16] (iii) gains from commodities transactions (other than by persons actively involved in the production, processing or sale of the commodities themselves as part of their ordinary business activities);[17] (iv) gains from certain foreign currency transactions (*see* 10.3);[18] and (v) income which is the equivalent of interest (e.g. loan commitment fees).[19]

(2) *Foreign base company sales income,* which consists of income from property purchased from or sold to a related person if the property is manufactured outside and *sold for use outside the CFC's country of incorporation.*[20]

(3) *Foreign base company services income,* which is income derived from performing services outside the CFC's country of incorporation for or on behalf of a related person.[21]

---

from *unrelated* persons are excluded if derived in the active conduct of the CFC''s trade or business. Sec. 954(c)(2)(A); Treas. Reg. Sec. 1.954-2(c) and (d).

Sec. 954(d)(3) defines the term "related person" for these purposes generally in terms of more than 50 per cent voting power or value. The definition of "related person" in Sec. 954(d)(3) prior to 1987 included partnerships that controlled foreign corporations but not partnerships that were controlled by foreign corporations. Taking advantage of this statutory defect, a U.S. multinational, the Brown Group, had its second tier Cayman Islands subsidiary (CI) form a partnership in which it owned an 88 per cent interest. The other 12 per cent was owned by two salespeople who had worked for Brown Group''s former sales representative in Brazil. The partnership became Brown Group''s sales agent and received all the commission income from Brown Group. CI reported its distributive share of the partnership income, but Brown Group did not report that income as subpart F income, asserting that the partnership was not a related party. Rejecting the IRS argument that the partnership entity should be ignored and CI treated as earning its share of partnership income, the taxpayer''s position was upheld by the court. *Brown Group v. Commissioner,* 77 F.3d 217 (8th Cir. 1996). A statutory change to Sec. 954(d)(3) would prevent that result for years after 1987. The situation, however, is one of those covered by the partnership anti-abuse rules in Treas. Reg. Sec. 1.701-2(e).

16. Gains from sales of property in this category that constitute inventory in the hands of the taxpayer or which are realized by a dealer in such property are not included.

17. Treas. Reg. Sec. 1.954-2(f).

18. Treas. Reg. Sec. 1.954-2(g).

19. Sec. 954(c)(1); Treas. Reg. Sec. 1.954-2(h). The 1986 Act eliminated an exception from foreign personal holding company income for interest, dividends, rents and royalties received by banks and insurance companies. Accordingly, such income is taxed currently despite the fact that it is not passive income and does not involve transactions between related parties. H.R. 2513, passed by the House of Representatives on November 18, 1997, would restore the exception for one year, taxable years beginning in 1998. *See* H. Rep. 105-318, 101st Cong., 1st Sess. (1997).

20. Sec. 954(d)(1). If the CFC purchases property from a related party but sufficiently transforms the property to constitute "manufacturing" by it, then the sale of that property does not result in foreign base company sales income. Treas. Reg. Sec. 1.954-3(a)(4). In some instances a branch of the CFC may be treated as if it were a subsidiary, and hence a related person, so that the subpart F rules apply to sales transactions between the CFC and its branch (normally such transactions are ignored for U.S. tax purposes). Sec. 954(d)(2); Treas. Reg. Sec. 1.954-3(b).

21. Sec. 954(e); Treas. Reg. Sec. 1.954-4.

(4) *Foreign base company shipping income,* which is income derived from the use of aircraft or vessels in foreign commerce outside the CFC's country of incorporation or from a space or ocean activity.[22]

(5) *Foreign base company oil related income.*[23]

In each category of income, the amount of FBCI is reduced by the deductions properly allocable thereto.[24]

The statute provides certain exceptions for income that otherwise would constitute FBCI:

(1) If the gross FBCI of a CFC for the taxable year is less than the lesser of five per cent of its total gross income or $1 million, then the CFC shall be considered to have no FBCI. Conversely, if the gross FBCI for the taxable year exceeds 70 per cent of the CFC's gross income, then all of its gross income less allocable deductions is considered FBCI.[25]

(2) FBCI does not include any item of income if the taxpayer (generally the US parent) can establish that the income was subject to an *effective* tax rate in a foreign country that was greater than the maximum *marginal* US corporate tax rate.[26]

7.2.4.2 Earnings invested in US property

The second major category of CFC income that Section 951(a)(1) subjects to current taxation to the US shareholders is the amount determined under Section 956, which, in general, refers to the earnings and profits of the CFC invested in US assets. Even if a CFC had no "subpart F income", it would be possible for it to avoid US taxation on its income but still make that income available to its US shareholders. For example, the CFC could loan its earnings to the US parent. There would be no US tax since the tax applies only to repatriated dividends; but the US parent would have the use of the funds in just the manner that

---

22. Sec. 954(f), 954(b)(7). For the order of computation of the categories, *see* Temp. Treas. Reg. Sec. 1.954-1T.
23. Sec. 954(g).
24. Sec. 954(b)(5).
25. Sec. 954(b)(3).
26. Sec. 954(b)(4). The provision applies only at the taxpayer's election. The purpose of the provision is to exclude from subpart F treatment situations where income may have been routed through a related corporation but no US tax advantage is gained thereby. Taxes paid to a foreign country are of course determined by its tax rules. But income is determined under US tax rules. The comparison of a foreign effective tax rate to the US marginal rate has obvious conceptual difficulties and, among other things, can have the effect of denying the benefit of the exclusion where a foreign country provides significant subsidies through its tax system rather than directly. Prior to the 1986 Act, the exception also had an "intent" test under which subpart F treatment could be avoided if the taxpayer could establish that the use of the foreign corporation was not motivated by a tax avoidance purpose.

would have been produced had a dividend in fact been paid. Unlike Section 951(a) income, however, Section 956 does not refer directly to an amount that would have been included as a dividend, but rather includes in the income of the US shareholder the lesser of

(1) the excess of
   (a) the shareholder's pro rata share of the average amount of US property held by the CFC (determined quarterly by reference to the property's tax basis) over
   (b) the shareholder's pro rata share of earnings and profits of the CFC which have previously been taxed under Sections 951 and 956,
   or
(2) the US shareholder's pro rata share of the "applicable earnings" of the CFC, i.e., the sum of its current and accumulated earnings and profits reduced by any distribution made during the year and by any earnings and profits previously taxed under Sections 951 or 956.[27]

In more straightforward language, the total earnings and profits of the CFC are reduced by amounts previously taxed under Sections 951 and 956. Then, if there has been any additional investment in US property, any remaining earnings and profits are deemed to have been used to make the investments.[28]

US "property" is defined to include, among other items, the following:

(1) tangible personal property located in the US (excluding certain oil and gas drilling rigs, certain transportation property and property intended for export from the US);[29]
(2) stock of a related US corporation (i.e. the corporation invested in is itself a shareholder of the CFC or US shareholders of the CFC own 25 per cent or more of the voting stock of the corporation in which the investment is made);[30]
(3) obligations of a US person (excluding debt of an unrelated corporation as determined in (2), money, bank deposits, obligations of the US government) and obligations arising in the ordinary course of trade or business;[31]

---

27. Sec. 956(a), (b).
28. Beginning in 1993, Sec. 956A also required current inclusion in a U.S. shareholder's income of earnings and profits invested in "excess passive assets," whether those assets were U.S. or foreign property. The provision was repealed in 1996, primarily because of its excessive complexity.
29. Sec. 956(c)(1)(A), (c)(2)(B), (D), and (G).
30. Sec. 956(c)(1)(B), (b)(2)(F). Investment in the stock of "unrelated" US corporations is thus excepted from the rule. However, by virtue of the attribution rules, stock owned by the CFC is attributed to the US shareholder. As a result, any 25 per cent investment by the CFC is automatically covered by Sec. 956.
31. Sec. 956(c)(1)(C), (c)(3)(A) and (C), (c)(3). *See Sherwood Properties, Inc. v. Commissioner,* 89 TC 651 (1987) (advance by CFC to related party not in ordinary course of the CFC"s business). Indirect transactions are also covered by Sec. 956. *See* Rev. Rul. 87-89, 1987-2 Cum. Bull. 195

(4) the right to use in the US patents, copyrights, secret processes, etc. acquired or developed by the CFC for use in the US.[32]

7.2.5 FOREIGN TAX CREDIT

Section 960 provides a foreign tax credit for income taxed to a US shareholder under the subpart F rules. For corporations, the rules correspond to those of Section 902 (6.5). The deemed foreign tax credit under Section 960 is available for taxes paid by subsidiaries as low as the sixth tier.[33] Section 78 applies the gross-up requirement to foreign tax credits allowed under Section 960.

The limitations of Section 904 apply to foreign tax credits available under Section 960. As discussed in 6.6.3.7, look-through rules are applied to a CFC to determine the appropriate limitation basket into which to place an actual dividend, i.e. the basket(s) into which the dividend is placed is determined by the types of underlying income out of which the dividend is deemed to be paid. Similarly, Section 951(a)(1)(A) income imputed to a US taxpayer is classified according to its character in the hands of the CFC, e.g. passive or shipping income.[34] Income inclusions that result from the application of Section 956 (earnings invested in US property) are subject to dividend rules applicable to CFCs since such inclusions are drawn from earnings and profits generally rather than from a specific source of income such as FBCI.[35]

Some special rules integrate the subpart F rules with the foreign tax credit limitation rules:

(1) If the de minimis rule discussed in 7.2.4.1 is applicable so that none of the CFC's income is FBCI, then interest, dividends, rents and royalties are placed in the general limitation income basket.[36]

(2) Income of a CFC which is not FBCI because of the foreign effective tax rate exception discussed in 7.2.4.1 is placed in the general limitation income basket rather than being subject to the look through rules.

(illustrating when Sec. 956 is applicable in situations when funds deposited by a CFC with an unrelated person then were loaned to the related party); Rev. Rul. 90-112, 1990-2 Cum. Bull. 186 (U.S. property owned by either a domestic or foreign partnership in which the CFC is a partner constitutes U.S. property of the CFC for purposes of Sec. 956); Treas. Reg. Sec. 1.956-1(e)(2) (pledges and guarantees); and Sec. 956(c)(3).

32. Section 956(c)(1)(D).
33. The computations necessary under Sec. 960 where there is an inclusion under Sec. 951(a) are illustrated in Treas. Reg. Sec. 1.960-1. The computations required where a US multinational corporation has both Sec. 902 and Sec. 960 foreign tax credits (because there is an actual distribution as well as a Sec. 951(a) inclusion) coupled with applying the Sec. 904 "basket" limitations to both, are truly staggering in their complexity. *See* Treas. Reg. Sec. 1.960-2. The necessary calculations are possible only with a sophisticated computer program.
34. Sec. 904(d)(3)(B); Treas. Reg. Sec. 1.904-5.
35. Treas. Reg. Sec. 1.904-5(c)(4).
36. Sec. 904(d)(3)(E); Treas. Reg. Sec. 1.904-5(d).

(3) If a CFC's gross FBCI for the year exceeds 70 per cent of its gross income so that all its gross income is FBCI, the actual non-subpart F income of the CFC which is required to be included in income is nonetheless placed in the appropriate basket for foreign tax credit limitation purposes rather than in the basket appropriate to the subpart F income.[37]

Individual US shareholders can obtain the benefits of the Section 960 credit by electing to be taxed at corporation rates on their income taxable under subpart F.[38]

7.2.6 DISTRIBUTIONS AND ADJUSTMENTS TO BASIS

Generally the basis in CFC stock is increased by the amount of income included under Section 951 (as if the dividend had been paid and then recontributed to the CFC) and reduced under Section 959 by amounts actually distributed that constitute previously taxed earnings (basis having previously been increased at the time the tax was imposed). Those distributions are correspondingly tax free.[39]

If the amount of previously taxed earnings received in a year exceeds basis, the excess is taxed as a capital gain.[40]

7.2.7 DENIAL OF DEFERRAL BENEFITS FOR BOYCOTT INCOME AND FOREIGN BRIBES AND TO ACHIEVE OTHER US FOREIGN POLICY OBJECTIVES

There are three additional categories of subpart F income. Under Section 952(a)(3), CFC earnings and profits attributable to participation in or cooperation with an international boycott are treated as subpart F income and are currently taxable to a US shareholder of the CFC.

Section 952(a)(4) includes in a CFC's subpart F income an amount equal to the sum of illegal bribes, kickbacks and other payments (as defined in Section 162(c)) that are paid by or on behalf of a foreign corporation directly or indirectly to any official, employee or agent of a foreign government. In addition, in computing the earnings and profits of a CFC, no reduction is allowed for such payments. Note that the amount of income that is taxable to the US shareholder under Section 952(a)(4) is not the income produced as a result of the bribe, but the amount of the bribe itself.

---

37. Treas. Reg. Sec. 1.904-5(e).
38. Sec. 962. Subsequent distributions of the income, however, are taxable.
39. Secs. 961(a), (b)(1); 959(a).
40. Sec. 961(b)(2).

Under Section 952(a)(5), a CFC's subpart F income includes income derived from any foreign country during any period in which Section 901(j)(6.8) is applicable. For example, income from a foreign country which the Secretary of State has designated as a country that supports terrorism constitutes subpart F income under this provision

The inclusion of these three items in subpart F income rests on policy bases quite different from those discussed in 7.2.4, above.

7.2.8 THE ROLE OF SUBPART F

The US subpart F rules were developed at a time when US tax rates were high and the US was a net exporter of capital. Those conditions had both changed by the mid-1980's. As a result the role of the subpart F rules significantly changed also. It is helpful to understand the background against which subpart F developed in order better to assess its present and future role.

As discussed in 6.3, the foreign tax credit is the mechanism adopted by the US to effect the proper application of its tax rules when US citizens or corporations derive income from other countries. One basic purpose of the credit is to achieve tax neutrality (so-called "capital export neutrality") in decisions by US taxpayers whether to invest in the US or abroad. For example, a US corporation that decides to expand into a new line of operations can do so through a US branch or division, a wholly-owned US subsidiary, a foreign branch, or a foreign subsidiary. The US tax system is neutral among the first three choices: a single US tax will be imposed on the profits of the operation if conducted through a US division or subsidiary (either because of the consolidated return rules or because of the dividends received deduction), and a single US tax will be imposed on the profits of the foreign branch. In all these cases, a foreign tax credit device generally insures that the US taxpayer's investment decision will not be influenced by taxes and the decision to invest at home or abroad can be based solely on economic considerations.[41]

---

41. As discussed in 6.9, capital export neutrality would theoretically require that the US grant a foreign tax credit even where the foreign tax rate exceeds the US tax rate. The US, however has been unwilling to extend the credit this far. Thus foreign taxes in excess of the United States rate represent an additional cost of doing business for foreign investment and to this extent the capital export neutrality standard is not followed. In addition, the existence of excess foreign tax credits may favor investment in low-tax foreign countries over domestic investment at the margin. There are also a number of explicit deviations from capital export neutrality in the form of various tax preferences granted solely to domestic investment, as discussed in 2.2.2.2. The point here is that, given the general principle of capital export neutrality, foreign earnings of US controlled subsidiaries should be taxed currently as a structural matter; it is then an independent decision as to whether tax (or direct) subsidies for investment should be extended to foreign investment.

If a foreign subsidiary is used, however, the situation changes. The US tax on the foreign earnings is only imposed when the earnings are repatriated to the US. At that time, they are included in income and, under the "deemed paid" credit provisions, a credit is given for the foreign taxes paid. Thus the foreign taxes are always creditable, but the US tax is deferred through the use of a foreign subsidiary until the profits are brought home. If the foreign tax rate is lower than the US rate, this deferral of tax gives a higher after-tax rate of return to operations undertaken through a foreign subsidiary than that available to the other forms of operation discussed above.

The tax deferral for operations conducted through foreign subsidiaries can be viewed as a subsidy granted by the US government to enable its corporations more effectively to compete abroad with local businesses and businesses controlled by foreign companies from countries that employ the exemption mechanism as their basic method of international tax accommodations. (*See* 6.3.) Such corporations will only be taxed in the country of operation. US companies over the years have successfully argued that they must be able to defer the US taxes on their foreign operations until repatriation in order to compete effectively in foreign markets. This deferral of tax is aimed at achieving "capital import (or competitive) neutrality" in the foreign market.[42]

The rules in subpart F which allow deferral in effect sacrifice capital export neutrality in the interest of capital import neutrality in the case of controlled foreign subsidiaries. From this perspective, the tax deferral allowed to the foreign subsidiaries functions as a subsidy device (in effect, an interest-free loan with no limitation on its term) operated through the tax system, when measured against the standard of capital export neutrality. The subpart F provisions, which eliminate deferral in certain situations, function as a part of this subsidy program. Their role is to limit deferral to those activities in which competitive neutrality is truly a factor. That is, in very general terms, the income and activities excluded from subpart F are those that the US wishes to include in its tax subsidy program. These primarily include the active income of CFCs which is generated in the country in which the CFC is actually located. In these situations the subsidy helps the CFC compete with foreign companies operating in the same country in which the CFC is conducting its business operation. But, if the CFC buys from its parent in one country and sells to a related corporation in another country, no competitive purpose is achieved if the US grants its subsidy to a CFC that is merely a conduit company. Thus the subpart F rules can be seen as defining the limits of the current US tax subsidy program.

There is still another perspective on Subpart F. The provision had its origins in part as a response to tax avoidance schemes using base companies to shift

---

42. See 6.3.

profits abroad. Thus, completely apart from considerations of capital export or import neutrality, the rules function to prevent the erosion of the domestic tax base through transactions which artificially shift profits outside the U.S.

The US subpart F rules were controversial from their inception. Indeed, they were the subject of criticism from other countries as well as from US corporations. But, in recent years, other industrial countries began to see that they also needed rules similar to subpart F to protect their own tax bases, especially given the proliferation of "tax havens." Provisions similar to subpart F accordingly have been adopted in a number of countries.[43]

Following the sharp reduction in US corporate tax rates in 1986 and the subsequent similar action by other industrialized countries, the subsidy element in the deferral allowed by subpart F plays a significantly diminished role. Most manufacturing operations conducted abroad by US corporations will incur foreign tax liabilities on foreign income equal to or somewhat in excess of the US tax on that income. Deferral obviously provides no financial benefit if the foreign tax is equal to or higher than the US; indeed, in some situations US taxpayers can obtain a preferable tax result by deliberately creating subpart F income!

The present role of subpart F appears limited to:

(1) Preventing the use of pure tax havens by US corporations seeking to reduce US tax on their active business income.

(2) Dealing with those situations in which a foreign country imposes a high nominal tax rate but on a tax base which is significantly narrower than that of the US.

(3) Preventing the artificial shifting of passive investment income to avoid current US tax.

Following the adoption of the subpart F rules in 1962, many tax theorists in the US favored the total repeal of tax deferral on income realized by CFCs on the grounds that the capital export neutrality principle should be followed rigorously and/or that the subsidy implicit on the deferral was unnecessary and should be repealed. Somewhat ironically, some of those same tax theorists now believe that deferral should be completely repealed because the extraordinarily complex structure of subpart F does not justify its current limited function in the US international tax system.

---

43. *See* Arnold, *The Taxation of Controlled Foreign Corporations: An International Comparison* (Canadian Tax Foundation, 1986), for an excellent and comprehensive study of the rules employed by six countries.

7.3 Formation, reorganization and liquidation of foreign corporations: Section 367

7.3.1 BACKGROUND

As discussed briefly in 2.2.6, under US law a number of transactions involving the formation and reorganization of corporations are tax-free to the shareholders and the corporations involved. In qualifying transactions, recognition of gain (or loss) is deferred and the taxpayer is taxed only when the stock or other property received in the transaction is disposed of at some subsequent date. Similarly, recognition of gain (or loss) on assets transferred to the corporation in such transactions is deferred until the assets are disposed of in a taxable transaction by the acquiring corporation. If it were possible to utilize one of these tax-free techniques to transfer appreciated property beyond the US taxing jurisdiction to a foreign corporation, US tax on the potential gain would be completely avoided. (On the other hand, taxpayers could always recognize losses by disposing of the depreciated assets in a taxable transaction.) In addition, a tax-free reorganization or liquidation involving a foreign corporation might eliminate or reduce foreign earnings on which US tax would potentially be applicable at the time of distribution.

To deal with these problems, Section 367 provides that certain transfers involving foreign corporations will not be accorded tax-free treatment or will be tax-free only if certain conditions are met.[44] Technically, Section 367 achieves this result by providing that unless various statutory requirements are met, a foreign corporation "shall not be considered to be a corporation" for purposes of the various sections providing for nonrecognition of gain. The basic rules governing the transactions to which Section 367 applies are described below.

7.3.1.1 Formation of corporation

Under Section 351, no gain or loss is recognized in a transaction in which property is transferred to a corporation in exchange for stock of the corporation if, after the transfer, the transferor owns at least 80 per cent of the voting stock of the corporation.

---

44. Prior to 1984, Sec. 367 required that the taxpayer obtain a ruling that the transaction involving the foreign corporation did not have a "tax avoidance" purpose. The 1984 changes in Sec. 367 eliminated the ruling requirement and the statute and Regulations now set forth the substantive rules under which tax-free treatment will or will not be granted.

7.3.1.2   Reorganizations

In general, the Internal Revenue Code permits certain corporate reorganizations to proceed on a tax-free basis both to the shareholders and the corporation involved. In addition, corporate tax "attributes" such as earnings and profits and net operating losses generally carry over in the reorganization transaction. Under the basic statutory patterns, six basic types of tax-free reorganizations are permitted. They are:

Type (A): A merger or consolidation in compliance with state law, as where Corporation X is merged into Corporation Y or Corporations X and Y consolidate into Corporation Z.

Type (B): The acquisition by one corporation of an 80 per cent interest in the voting stock of another corporation solely in exchange for the voting stock of the acquiring corporation. The shareholders of the acquired corporation thus become shareholders of the acquiring corporation.

Type (C): The acquisition by one corporation of substantially all of the assets of another corporation in exchange for the voting stock of the acquiring corporation. The acquired corporation which receives the stock must distribute the stock to its shareholders in liquidation and they then become shareholders of the acquiring corporation.[45]

Type (D): The creation of a new corporation to which are transferred some or all of the parent's assets with the shares of the new corporation distributed to the parent's shareholders.

Type (E): A change in the capital structure of an existing corporation, for example, the exchange of common stock for a new class of stock.

Type (F): A mere change in the identity, form or place of organization of the corporation.

In all of these transactions, Section 361 provides that the corporation transferring its assets or shares does not recognize gain or loss and Section 354 provides similar nonrecognition treatment for shareholders exchanging their shares in connection with the reorganization transaction.

7.3.1.3   Liquidations

Under Section 332, the liquidation of a subsidiary by a corporate parent owning at least 80 per cent of the voting stock of the subsidiary is tax-free to subsidiary and the parent corporation.

---

45. The type A, B, and C reorganizations thus provide a variety of techniques for undertaking corporate acquisitions on a tax-free basis. The provisions and their judicial interpretations are quite complex, but the basic principle behind the sections is that if the shareholders of the acquired corporation continue their investment in the form of stock in the acquiring corporation, the transaction should not be subject to current taxation. On the technical level the reorganization

7.3.2 Application of Section 367

7.3.2.1 General

In the context of the above transactions, Section 367 distinguishes between two types of transfers involving foreign corporations. First, for transfers involving property moving from the US transferor to the foreign corporation (so-called "outbound" transfers), Section 367(a) generally requires taxation of any accrued gain (but not losses) in the property at the time of the transfer but then goes on to specify certain transfers which can be made on a tax-free basis. For the types of transactions covered by the section but which do not involve the transfer of property outside the US taxing jurisdiction (for example, the reorganization of two foreign corporations controlled by a US parent), Section 367(b) controls. Section 367(b) grants broad regulatory authority to the fiscal authorities to promulgate Regulations setting forth the principles under which non-outbound transactions involving foreign corporations will be given tax-free treatment. The law in this area is governed almost exclusively by extensive and complex regulations issued under both Section 367(a) and (b).

7.3.2.2 "Outbound" transfers

Section 367(a)(1) states as a general rule that *all* transfers by US persons of appreciated property to a foreign corporation will result in recognition of gain.[46] Thus, the normally tax-free transactions described in 7.3.1 became taxable if carried out with a foreign corporation, unless an exception is applicable. The section then sets forth a series of exceptions and exceptions to the exceptions. In general, a transfer of property to be used in the active conduct of a foreign trade or business can qualify for non-recognition treatment.[47] Thus, for example, the transfer of machinery and equipment to a foreign subsidiary to be used

---

forms described in the text can also be undertaken through the use of subsidiaries of the acquiring corporation. Sec. 368(a)(2)(D) and Sec. 368(a)(2)(E) set forth certain additional requirements when subsidiaries are used as the acquiring vehicle but, in general, the principles remain the same.

46. The character and source of the gain are delineated as if the US transferor had sold the property to the foreign transferee. Temp. Treas. Reg. Sec. 1.367(a)-IT(b)(4).

   It is possible for Section 367(a) to apply to a transaction that appears to involve only U.S. corporations. Thus, if U.S. Corp. A merges into U.S. Corp. B, a subsidiary of Foreign Corp. F, in which the shareholder of A Corp. receives the stock of Foreign Corp. F, the transfer is treated as an "indirect transfer" subject to section 367(a). In effect, the transaction is treated as if A Corp. transferred its assets to F Corp. for F stock (an outbound transaction) and F Corp. transferred to assets to B Corp. See Temp. Treas. Reg. Sec. 1.367(a)-IT(c)(2) providing similar results for other types of reorganizations.

47. *See* Temp. Treas. Reg. § 1.367(a)-2T which defines each of the requisite statutory terms.

in manufacturing abroad can be done on a tax-free basis.[48] However, the active trade or business exception does not apply to transfers of inventory, foreign currency, installment obligations, or property leased to third persons.[49]

Section 367(d) provides a special rule for intangible property which makes most transfers of intangible assets taxable regardless of whether or not the intangibles are to be used in an active foreign business. The income deemed to be realized on the intangible transfer is calculated in accordance with the "super royalty" principles discussed at 8.3.4 and is treated as foreign source income.[50]

Special rules also apply to the transfer of stock to a foreign corporation. If the stock transferred is that of a foreign corporation, Section 367(a)(2) provides that the transfer will not be taxable under Section 367(a) if it is pursuant to a reorganization of the type described in 7.3.1.2.[51] If the stock transferred is that of a US corporation, the transfer may be tax-free if all US transferors have received 50 percent or less of the transferee corporation in the transaction and either the US transferors own 5 percent or less of the transferee or, if they own more, enter into an agreement with the IRS to recognize gain on the subsequent transfer of the US corporation stock by the transferee foreign corporation.[52]

Outbound transfers of stock of a subsidiary corporation pursuant to a "spin-off" transaction under Sec. 355 (a Type D reorganization described in 7.3.1.2) are fully taxable if the subsidiary is a foreign corporation but may be nontaxable if the subsidiary is a US corporation and the requisite gain recognition agreement is entered into.[53]

Outbound transfers of property to a foreign parent corporation on the liquidation

---

48. Temp. Treas. Reg. Sec. 1.367(a)-4T(b) provides that gain must be recognized to the extent that depreciation deductions have been taken on the property while the asset was used in the US. In addition, the active trade or business exception does not apply to the incorporation of a foreign branch to the extent that the branch has been operating at a loss in prior years. In effect the prior losses which have been deducted for US tax purposes must be "recaptured" on the incorporation of the branch. Sec. 367(a)(3)(C); Temp. Treas. Reg. Sec. 1.367(a)-6T.

49. Temp. Treas. Reg. Secs. 1,367(a)-5T and -4T(e) for detailed rules governing these exceptions to the trade or business exception.

50. See Temp. Reas. Reg. Sec. 1.367(d)-1T. Prior to 1997, the deemed income was treated as US source (resulting in no increase in the allowable foreign tax credit fraction, see 6.6); in practice that rule required US corporations to use an actual licensing agreement with the foreign corporation so as to generate foreign source income. The 1997 change applied the same foreign source rule to deemed and actual royalties. The 1997 legislation also empowered the Treasury to issue regulations applying the rules on transfer of intangibles to partnerships. Sec. 367(d)(3).

51. The conditions that must be satisfied to accord tax free treatment to such transfers are set forth in Notice 87-85, 1987-2 Cum. Bull. 385 and Prop. Treas. Reg. Sec. 1.367(a)-8 (1991).

52. The term of the gain recognition agreement is 5 years if US transferors in the aggregate own less than 50 percent of the stock of the foreign transferee corporation, 10 years if they own 50 percent or more. If a single US transferor owns more than 50 percent of the transferor foreign corporation, the gain is fully taxable under Sec. 367(a). The foreign transferee corporation must have been engaged in an active trade or business outside the US for the 36 months before the transfer. Temp. Treas. Reg. Sec. 1.367(a)-2T(b).

53. See Temp. Treas. Reg. Sec. 1.367(e)-1T.

of an 80% controlled US subsidiary corporation result in gain recognition regardless of the nature of the property transferred. Section 367(e)(2). (*See also* 11.10.)

7.3.2.3   Other transactions

All corporate formation, reorganization and liquidation transactions not involving an outbound transfer of property are dealt with by extensive Regulations issued under Section 367(b).[54] In general, the Regulations allow transactions to proceed on a tax-free basis as long as it is possible to insure that foreign earnings on which US tax has been deferred will ultimately be taxed to the US shareholders involved in the transaction. In some cases, this result is achieved by attributing the earnings of the corporation whose stock is exchanged to the stock received on the exchange. Where such attribution is not possible, the exchanging shareholder may have to recognize income to the extent of its share of the earnings as the price for having the rest of the transaction treated on a tax-free basis.[55] In order to qualify under the Regulations, the taxpayer must submit a notice of the transaction and specified information to the taxing authorities.[56]

The operation of Section 367(b) can be illustrated by two examples. First, suppose that US Corp owns all the stock of F Corp., a foreign corporation, and decides to liquidate F. Corp. Normally, the transaction would be tax-free under Section 332. At the time of liquidation, F Corp. has 100 of earnings and profits US Corp. has 200 of gain in the F Corp. stock. US Corp. must either include 100 in income in which case the balance of the transaction is tax free or it must recognize gain on the liquidation.[57]

Second, suppose US Corp. in addition owns all the stock of S Corp., a foreign corporation. S Corp. has 100 of earnings and profits and US Corp. has a 200 of gain in its S Corp. stock. S Corp. merges into F Corp. in a valid reorganization. US Corp. is not taxed on its gain in the S Corp. stock which it exchanges its F corp. stock in the merger. However, the 100 of S. Corp. earnings and profits attaches to the F Corp. stock owned by US Corp. and will be taxed as a dividend upon a subsequent sale of the F Stock.

7.3.3   OUTBOUND TRANSFERS TO OTHER ENTITIES

Prior to 1997, Section 1491 imposed a 35 per cent excise tax on the excess of the fair market value of property, tangible or intangible, over its tax basis when

---

54. Treas. Reg. Sec. 7.367(b)-1 to 13.
55. Treas. Reg. Sec. 7.367(b)-9.
56. Treas. Reg. Sec. 7.367(b)-1(c).
57. Treas. Reg. Sec. 7.367(b)-5(b). The 100 gain inherent in F Corp's assets is preserved by carrying over the basis of F Corp's assets to U.S. Corp. Sec. 334(b)(1).

the property was transferred by a US person to a foreign corporation as paid-in surplus or as a contribution to capital or to a foreign trust, a foreign estate or a foreign partnership. The provision applied, in the case of partnerships, trusts or estates, even though the US partners or beneficiaries remained fully taxed on the entity's foreign source income. Subsequent to the enactment of section 1491, US partnership rules were revised substantially so that shifting of un-taxed appreciation from a US to a foreign partner, for example, was severely limited. Similarly, rules regarding foreign trusts also had been tightened.

Accordingly, in 1997 Congress repealed Section 1491 and provided specific rules for the various entities covered by former Section 1491. First, under Section 684, gain is always recognized on the transfer of property by a US person to a foreign trust or estate. Second, the limited category of transfers to foreign corporations previously covered by Section 1491 were shifted to the regulatory regime of Section 367. Third, the Treasury was granted regulatory authority to tax the gain in property transferred to a foreign partnership in situations, presumably few, in which that gain could be shifted from the US transferor to a foreign partner.[58] Reporting requirements similar to that imposed on US shareholders of CFC's are imposed on US partners in foreign partnerships.[59]

7.4 Disposition of stock in a controlled foreign corporation: Section 1248

7.4.1 BACKGROUND

Under Section 1248, enacted in 1962 in connection with subpart F, a US shareholder's gain on the disposition of stock in a controlled foreign corporation which otherwise would be treated as capital gain must be reported as ordinary income to the extent of the shareholder's share of the foreign corporation's earnings and profits accumulated after 1962. At the time of the enactment of Section 1248, corporate capital gains were subject to a preferential tax rate. Section 1248 reflected the policy judgment that it was inappropriate for the US shareholder to receive the benefit of both deferral of US tax on the earnings of a controlled foreign corporation (to the extent permitted by subpart F) and also receive preferential capital gain treatment on the disposition of the foreign corporate stock. After the elimination of the preferential rate for capital gains for corporations in 1986, the provision lost its original purpose. Somewhat ironically, its principal role today is to ensure that US corporate shareholders can

---

58. Sec. 721(c).
59. Sec. 6038B.

obtain the indirect foreign tax credit on earnings which are taxed under Section 1248.[60]

7.4.2 SCOPE OF COVERAGE

Section 1248 applies to any sale or taxable exchange by a US person of stock in a controlled foreign corporation and to any corporate distribution to such person for which capital gain treatment is provided.[61] The foreign corporation must be a controlled foreign corporation as defined in the subpart F provisions and the US person selling or exchanging the stock must own at least a ten per cent interest in the voting stock of the corporation. For Section 1248 to apply, the corporation need not be a controlled foreign corporation at the time of the sale or other disposition as long as it was a controlled foreign corporation at any time during the five year period preceding the sale.

7.4.3 CALCULATION OF TAX

Under Section 1248, the gain recognized on the sale or exchange of stock in the controlled foreign corporation is included "as a dividend" in the income of the selling US shareholder to the extent of the shareholder's share of the earnings and profits of the foreign corporation accumulated after 31 December 1962 during the period that the stock sold was held by the selling shareholder. A US corporate shareholder otherwise entitled to a deemed paid credit under Section 902 may claim a credit for the foreign taxes paid on the earnings includible under Section 1248.[62] In calculating the earnings and profits of the foreign corpo-

---

60. Sec. 1248 can also be relevant in situations involving the acquisition of a United States corporation with foreign subsidiaries where the transaction is treated as a deemed sale of assets followed by a liquidation of the acquired corporation under Section 338. *See* Treas. Reg. Sec. 1.338-5.

61. That is, liquidations covered by Sec. 331 and redemption distributions which are given capital gain treatment under Sec. 302. As stated in 2.2.6, note 58, redemption of stock involving related persons can give rise to dividend treatment under Sec. 304. In the controlled foreign corporation context, this treatment can be beneficial in generating foreign tax credits to the US parent of CFCs. Sec. 304(b)(5), added in 1997, imposes limitations on the ability to achieve dividend treatment from transactions in which foreign corporations are involved.

62. Treas. Reg. Sec. 1.1248-1(d). Sec. 964(e) likewise includes as a dividend any gain realized by a CFC on the sale of stock in another foreign corporation to the same extent the gain would have been treated as a dividend to a U.S. shareholder under Sec. 1248 if the CFC were a US person.

   Sec. 1248(b) contains a limitation on the tax imposed on individuals who dispose of stock in a controlled foreign corporation in a transaction subject to Sec. 1248. Very generally, the US individual shareholder's tax liability is limited to the liability she would have incurred if (1) the foreign corporation had been taxed as a domestic corporation with an allowance for the foreign tax credit for foreign corporate taxes paid and (2) the shareholder was taxed at capital gains rates on the liquidation of the corporation.

ration, there are some special rules applicable only to Section 1248.[63] Section 1248 is coordinated with the subpart F rules by excluding from the earnings and profits subject to Section 1248 any earnings and profits previously included in the US taxpayer's income under subpart F.[64] Amounts included under Section 1248 are treated as previously taxed income under Section 959(e) and thus are not taxable again when actually distributed to a purchasing US shareholder.

7.5 Foreign investment activities by US persons utilizing foreign corporations

The US tax system contains a number of provisions dealing with investment activities of US persons which are carried on through foreign corporate form. Special rules apply to both closely held investment vehicles and publicly traded organizations like mutual funds. The provisions dealing with investment activities involving foreign corporations is complex, overlapping and in many ways illogical. The following material gives a brief overview of the most important aspects of the tax provisions.

7.5.1 FOREIGN PERSONAL HOLDING COMPANIES

7.5.1.1 Background

As discussed in 2.2.7.2, the personal holding company tax rules limit the ability to defer shareholder level US tax by carrying on investment activity through closely held corporations. A similar set of rules applies to closely held foreign investment corporations. Under the foreign personal holding company rules of Sections 551-557, a US shareholder in a closely held foreign corporation which realizes substantial amounts of passive income is taxed directly on the corporation's undistributed income.

7.5.1.2 Scope of coverage

For a foreign corporation to be classified as a foreign personal holding company, more than 50 per cent in value *or* in voting power of its outstanding stock

---

63. *See* Sec. 1248(d).
64. Sec. 1248(d)(1).

must be owned directly or indirectly by not more than five US individual citizens or residents.[65]

In addition, at least 60 per cent of the foreign corporation's gross income must be foreign personal holding company income, as defined.[66] Once the foreign corporation has been classified as a foreign personal holding company, the income percentage requirement drops to 50 per cent for subsequent years, subject to some qualifications. In determining the foreign corporation's gross income for purposes of the classification test, the gross income is computed as if the foreign corporation were a domestic corporation, i.e. income from foreign sources as well as US sources is included.[67] This provision is necessary to prevent US shareholders from sheltering foreign source income in a foreign personal holding company.

Foreign personal holding company income includes most kinds of passive investment-type income. In addition to including dividends, interest, royalties, and rents as foreign personal holding company income, gains from the sale or exchange of stock or securities and gains on commodity transactions are also covered.[68]

Foreign personal holding company income also includes the undistributed foreign personal holding company income of any subsidiary foreign personal holding company in which the first tier foreign personal holding company is a shareholder. The income attributed to the parent foreign personal holding company is then taken into account in calculating its income for purposes of the gross income tests.[69]

7.5.1.3   Calculation of the tax

Assuming that the share ownership and income requirements are met, each US shareholder must include currently in his income his share of the undistributed

---

65. Sec. 554. The rules are similar in scope, though not in detail, to the constructive ownership rules applicable under subpart F in Sec. 958. A special problem in the foreign personal holding company area involves the attribution of stock of nonresidents to US shareholders in determining the status of the corporation as a foreign personal holding company. While the statute would appear to require such attribution, the Tax Court in *Estate of Miller v. Commissioner,* 43 TC 760 (1965), refused to apply the rules in a situation in which the US shareholder to whom the stock was attributed had no direct interest in the foreign corporation and the effect of the attribution rules was to make the minority US shareholder subject to the foreign personal holding company tax.

66. Sec. 552(a)(1).

67. Sec. 555(a).

68. Sec. 553(a)(2)-(3).

69. Sec. 555(b). This technique of attributing the income of the subsidiary to the foreign parent corporation is to be contrasted to the so-called "hopscotch" principle used in the subpart F provisions under which the income of the foreign subsidiary is attributed outside the chain of foreign ownership directly to the US shareholder. *See* Sec. 951(a).

foreign personal holding company income of the foreign corporation.[70] The calculation of the amount subject to tax begins with the foreign corporation's taxable income with adjustments downward for items such as taxes paid and charitable contributions and adjustments upward for certain deductions such as the dividends received deduction. The US shareholder includes in income the amount which he would have received had the foreign personal holding company distributed its undistributed foreign personal company income as a dividend on the last day of its taxable year. Thus, under the literal language of the statute, if the US shareholder acquired the stock on the last day of the corporation's taxable year he would be subject to tax on his share of the undistributed foreign personal holding company income for the entire year.[71]

Where the US shareholder is taxed on the undistributed foreign personal holding company income of the foreign corporation, appropriate adjustments are made in the foreign corporation's earnings and profits and in the US shareholder's basis in the shares of the foreign corporation.[72]

7.5.2 PASSIVE FOREIGN INVESTMENT COMPANIES

7.5.2.1 Background

Subpart F and the foreign personal holding company rules only deal with the taxation of investment income earned by US shareholders through foreign corporations when, broadly speaking, the US ownership is concentrated and closely held. Thus these provisions do not limit the deferral of US shareholder level tax available through investment in widely held foreign investment companies, for example, foreign mutual funds. Here, absent any special rules, the US investor's earnings could accumulate abroad free from US tax until distributed or realized indirectly through sale of the shares. Section 1246 was initially aimed at this problem and denies US shareholders capital gain treatment on the disposition of shares in a foreign investment company, as defined. But this provision did nothing, of course, to offset the benefit of deferral of tax. Congress

---

70. For purposes of the foreign personal holding company provisions, in general the US shareholder subject to tax must actually own the shares of the foreign corporation. The rules of constructive ownership apply only to determine whether or not the foreign corporation is to be treated as a foreign personal holding company. However, under Sec. 551(f), a US person is taxed directly on his share of the income of a foreign personal holding company owned by a foreign corporation, foreign partnership, or foreign trust in which the US person has an interest.

71. Several courts have refused to apply this rule where the US shareholder was a nonresident alien for some portion of the tax year in question. See *Marsman v. Commissioner*, 205 F.2d 335 (4th Cir. 1953); *Gutierrex v. Commissioner*, 72-1 USTC Par. 9121 (D.C. Cir. 1971). Sec. 551(b) itself provides for an allocation if the US shareholder group is not in existence at the end of the corporation's taxable year.

72. Sec. 551(d)-(e).

responded to the situation in 1986 by enacting the passive foreign investment company (PFIC) rules. While the rules are directed at US investment in foreign mutual funds, their scope is much broader and they are potentially applicable to a wide range of situations.

7.5.2.2   Definition of passive foreign investment company (PFIC)

Under Section 1296(a), a foreign corporation is a PFIC if (1) 75 per cent or more of its gross income is "passive"[73] *or* (2) 50 per cent or more of the value of its assets generate passive income. Unlike the subpart F or foreign personal holding company rules, there are no minimum shareholder ownership requirements and no de minimis rules.[74] In applying the income and assets tests, there is a "look through" to the income and assets of any foreign corporation in which the potential PFIC owns 25 per cent or more of the stock. If the combined income and assets (disregarding the 25 per cent stock interest as an asset and any dividends paid on the stock as income) do not meet the threshold tests, then the corporation will not be classified as a PFIC.[75] Special rules provide an exception from PFIC status if the foreign corporation meets the tests only temporarily, as in a start up or change of business situation where the concentration of passive income or assets is atypical.

Once a corporation is classified as a PFIC while a US person is a shareholder in the corporation, it remains a PFIC for later years as to that shareholder, even if it does not meet the definitional tests in those years.[76]

7.5.2.3   Taxation of US shareholders of an "interest charge" PFIC

Unlike subpart F and the foreign personal holding company rules, the PFIC provisions do not tax the US shareholder currently on his share of PFIC in-

---

73. The definition of "passive" is that of Sec. 954(c) (*see* 7.2.4.1) with certain modifications.

74. Sec. 1297(a) has a set of attribution rules which attribute PFIC stock to US shareholders through intervening entities.

75. For an application of the look-through rule, *see* Rev. Rul. 87-90,1987-1 Cum. Bull. 216. The look-through rule only affects the status of the top tier foreign holding company. If the subsidiary corporation, tested solely on the basis of its own income and assets, meets the PFIC tests it will be classified as a PFIC with the result that, under the attribution rules of Section 1297, the US shareholder will be treated as a shareholder in a PFIC.

76. This "once a PFIC, always a PFIC" rule does not apply in the case of qualified electing funds discussed at 7.5.2.4. In addition, the US shareholder can purge his stock of its PFIC "taint" by electing to realize gain on the PFIC shares as if they had been disposed of on the last day of the last year in which the corporation qualified as a PFIC, thus avoiding PFIC status for future years.

come.[77] Rather, recognizing that the deferral of US tax on the PFIC income is in effect a loan from the US government to the shareholder in the amount of the deferred tax liability, the PFIC rules impose an interest charge on the deferred taxes.[78]

More technically, Section 1291 provides for the computation of a "deferred tax amount" when a PFIC makes an "excess distribution." An "excess distribution" is the amount of any current distribution which exceeds the "normal" level of the PFIC's distributions.[79] This amount is treated as having been received *ratably* over the period which the US shareholder has held the stock and is taxed at the highest marginal rates applicable for those years. An interest charge (based on the interest rate applicable to income tax deficiencies) is then imposed on the amount of tax attributable to each year, with the amount of interest a function of the number of years between the year to which the distribution is allocated and the year of actual distribution.[80]

For example, assume that a PFIC earns a total of 500 over a five year period during which it makes no dividend distributions. At the end of year 5, the entire 500 is distributed. Since the corporation has made no distributions in the past, the entire 500 is an excess distribution. A ratable amount (100) of the distribution is allocated to each of the five years involved (regardless of the years in which the income was actually earned). For the income allocated to year 5, no special rules apply since that income is being taxed currently. However, for the 100 allocated to each of the preceding four years, a tentative tax is calculated based on the highest marginal rates of tax applicable in each of those years. This tax for each year is then increased by an interest charge based on the length of time that the tax has been deferred. Thus, for the amount allocated to Year 1, the tax would be increased by four years of compound interest. The sum of the deferred taxes plus interest for each year is payable as an additional tax liability for the year of distribution.[81]

The same interest charge principles apply under Section 1291 to gain on the sale of stock in a PFIC. Thus, if in the above example, the corporation had made no distributions and the taxpayer sold the PFIC stock in year 5 for 750 gain (the additional 250 of gain being attributable to unrealized appreciation in

---

77. Since the PFIC rules apply regardless of the level of US ownership, it was thought unfair to tax the US shareholders in the PFIC directly when they might have only a minority interest which could not influence distribution policy.

78. This interest charge technique is also used in connection with accumulation distributions from foreign trusts. *See* 7.6.3.

79. "Excess distribution" is defined in Sec. 1291(b)(2) as a distribution in excess of 125 per cent of the corporation's average distributions for the past three years. Excess distributions from past years are not included in the 125 per cent base.

80. The interest is measured from the due date of the tax return for the year to which the income is allocated to the due date for the year of actual distribution.

81. Sec. 1291(a)(1)(C).

the PFIC assets) 600 of the gain (that portion not allocated to year 5) would be "thrown back" ratably to prior years and subject to tax at prior years' rates together with the interest charge.[82]

If PFIC stock is held by an intervening entity and is attributed to a US shareholder under the PFIC attribution rules, then the sale by the entity of the PFIC stock will result in the application of the PFIC provisions to the US shareholder. This means, for example, that the sale by a foreign holding company of the stock of a subsidiary which qualified as a PFIC could be directly taxable to the US shareholder in the holding company and would be subject to the interest charge.[83]

7.5.2.4   Qualified electing funds

The US shareholder can elect to have the PFIC treated as a "qualified electing fund." The election can be made on a shareholder-by-shareholder basis and the election by one US shareholder does not affect any other shareholder.[84] The effect of the election is that the electing shareholder must include in income currently his share of the PFIC's ordinary income and capital gain.[85] Because the current inclusion eliminates the deferral advantage, later distributions by the qualifying electing fund are not subject to the interest charge rules of Section 1291.[86] In addition, gain on the disposition the PFIC stock is exempted from Section 1291 if the PFIC has been a qualified electing fund at all times. The gain is simply taxed at the shareholder's current rates and no interest charge is imposed. The shareholder in a qualified electing fund can elect to defer his tax liability on undistributed PFIC income (with interest) until a distribution is actually made and he has cash to pay the tax.[87]

---

82. As the example indicates, the interest charge can apply to gain attributable to unrealized appreciation in the PFIC assets and thus goes beyond simply imposing a deferral charge on realized but undistributed earnings.

83. Sec. 1297(b)(5). This rule is only applicable to the extent set forth in Regulations which have not yet been issued. It is not applicable to a PFIC which at all times has been a qualified electing fund. The section also treats distributions to the intervening entity as distributions made to the US person.

84. Sec. 1295. The procedures for making the election are set forth in Notice 88-125, 1988-2 Cum. Bull. 535. In general, the PFIC must agree to provide to the electing shareholder the books and records necessary for the shareholder to establish his share of the PFIC's income. Legislation enacted in 1988 made the election available on a shareholder-by-shareholder basis. Under the original 1986 legislation, the election was made by the corporation and was binding on all shareholders. A somewhat more simple electing procedure would be implemented by Prop. Treas. Reg. Sec. 1.1295-2 (1996).

85. Sec. 1293.

86. Sec. 1293(d) allows the shareholder to increase his basis in the PFIC shares by the amount of the inclusion and, under Sec. 1293(c), distributions of previously taxed income are tax-free (with a corresponding reduction in basis).

87. Sec. 1294. Unlike taxation under Sec. 1291, the qualified electing fund inclusion is taxed at the actual rates applicable to the taxpayer.

7.5.2.5 Mark-to-market election

Under Section 1296, a U.S. shareholder in a PFIC may avoid the rules of Section 1291 by making an election to mark his PFIC stock to market at the close of each taxable year. The election is available only with respect to stock that is "marketable," generally stock that is regularly traded on a national securities exchange or stock of a mutual fund that is always redeemable at its net asset value. An electing shareholder recognizes gain or loss equal to the difference between his adjusted basis in the PFIC stock at the beginning of the taxable year and its fair market value at the end of the taxable year. The deductibility of a mark-to-market loss in a stock is limited to any mark-to-market gains realized by the shareholder in prior years with respect to the same stock. The shareholder's adjusted basis in the PFIC stock is adjusted upward or downward to reflect included gain or deducted losses resulting from the election. Gains or losses realized pursuant to the election are ordinary rather than capital and are sourced in the same manner as if the PFIC stock had been sold.

7.5.3 RELATIONSHIP OF PROVISIONS DEALING WITH CORPORATIONS USED TO AVOID OR DEFER US TAX

As the previous material indicates, the US tax system contains a number of overlapping provisions which deal in one way or another with the problem of deferral of US tax by US investors utilizing foreign corporations. The provisions have been introduced at various times in the development of the tax laws with little attention to their interaction.[88] The different sets of rules abound with technical distinctions. For example, under the foreign personal holding company tax rules, the required shareholder ownership is tested in terms of voting power or the value of the stock interest held by any US person in the US group. On the other hand, in the controlled foreign corporation provisions, while the test is also in terms of either voting power or value, only US voting interests of ten per cent or more are considered.

The definition of the type of income reached by the provisions also varies among controlled foreign corporations, foreign personal holding companies, personal holding companies and PFICs. The methods of taxation likewise overlap.

Legislation in 1997 provided greater coordination among the various antideferral regimes than had previously existed. In general, income includible by the US shareholder under both subpart F and the foreign personal company provisions is covered only by the former. A "U.S. shareholder" with stock in a

---

88. For a more coordinated approach to the issues involved *see* American Law Institute, *International Aspects of United States Income Taxation* (1987), pp. 168-306.

CFC that is also a PFIC is taxed only under subpart F.[89] However, a less than 10 percent U.S. shareholder in the same corporation remains subject to the PFIC regime. Regulations are to be provided to exempt from the interest charge regime of the PFIC rules distributions of income previously taxed under subpart F, the personal holding company rules or the qualified electing fund rules.[90]

7.6 Investment through foreign trusts

7.6.1 BACKGROUND

In most respects, the basic rules governing taxation of US trusts apply to foreign trusts.[91] Special rules apply, however, to prevent avoidance or deferral of US tax through the use of foreign trusts where US persons are involved. Thus tax is imposed on transfers of appreciated property to foreign trusts, as discussed in 7.3.3

7.6.2 FOREIGN GRANTOR TRUSTS

Section 679 subjects to the grantor trust rules a US grantor who transfers property to a foreign trust that has a US beneficiary. As a result, the US grantor will be taxed currently on all income earned by the trust, whether distributed or accumulated, that is attributable to the property he transferred to the trust.

Section 679 applies to all grantors who are US "persons," thus including individuals, corporations, partnerships, trusts, and estates. The section does not apply to (1) testamentary transfers or (2) property transferred to the trust in a sale or exchange where the transferor receives full fair market value consideration for the property transferred.[92]

In 1996, the grantor trust rules were tightened to curtail still further the use of foreign grantor trusts to avoid U.S. income tax. Thus, a special rule provides that if a nonresident alien transfers property to a foreign trust and, within 5 years thereafter, becomes a U.S. resident, the individual is treated as having created a grantor trust on the residency starting date and therefore is subject to the rules of Section 679.[93] Conversely, if a U.S. individual creates a U.S. trust

---

89. Sec. 951(d), (f); 1291(b)(3)(F); Sec. 1297(e).
90. See Prop. Treas. Reg. Sec. 1.1291-2(b)(2) (1992).
91. See 2.3.5 and 5.7.1.
92. Sec. 679(a)(2)(B). Sec. 679(a)(3) provides that any note issued for the property by the trust, the grantor, a beneficiary or any person related to the grantor or beneficiary is disregaded in determining the amount of consideration paid for the transferred property.
93. Sec. 679(a)(4).

which then becomes a foreign trust, the individual is treated as having created a foreign grantor trust on the date the trust became a foreign trust.[94]

Section 679 covers indirect as well as direct transfers by US persons. Thus, if a US individual transfers property to a foreign entity which in turn transfers property to a trust with a US beneficiary, the US individual will generally be treated as the grantor of the trust under Section 679.[95]

A foreign trust is treated as having a US beneficiary unless (1) under the terms of the trust no part of the trust income can be paid to or accumulated for the benefit of a US person, and (2) if the trust were to terminate during the taxable year, no part of the income or corpus of the trust could be paid to or for the benefit of a US person. Attribution rules are applied so that a US beneficiary is present if amounts are paid to or accumulated for the benefit of a controlled foreign corporation, a foreign partnership with a US partner, or another foreign trust with a US beneficiary.[96]

At the time a US person transfers property to a foreign trust it may have no US beneficiary. However, if a US person subsequently becomes a beneficiary of the trust, Section 679 is triggered. In such a case, the US grantor is then treated as the owner of a trust and is taxable on the income attributable to the property originally transferred. Moreover, the trust may have accumulated income which would be taxable to the new US beneficiary if distributed. The grantor must include this accumulated income (attributable to the property he transferred) in his own income in the taxable year a US person becomes a beneficiary, unless the trust distributed all accumulated income before the end of the prior taxable year.[97]

7.6.3 FOREIGN ACCUMULATION TRUSTS

In cases where the grantor trust rules do not apply, e.g. testamentary trusts or trusts created by foreign grantors, Section 668 imposes an interest charge on the tax deferral resulting from any accumulation of trust income. The compound interest rate is that specified each month for underpayments of tax (nondeductible) per each year the income has been accumulated applied to the tax paid by the beneficiary on the accumulated distribution (net of the credits for foreign taxes paid by the trust).[98] The interest charge is added to the tax, but the total amount due cannot exceed the amount actually distributed by the trust to the beneficiary.

---

94. Sec. 679(a)(5).
95. Sec. 679(a)(5).
96. Sec. 679(c). A beneficiary who became a U.S. person more than 5 years after the initial transfer in trust is not a U.S. beneficiary.
97. Sec. 679(b).
98. Sec. 668(c).

7.6.4 PROCEDURAL ASPECTS

Compliance with US rules regarding investment and doing business through foreign entities is generally enforced through the filing of information returns. Thus, any US person who is an officer, director or ten per cent shareholder of a foreign personal holding company must file an annual return which includes information concerning the income and shareholder composition of the corporation.[99] A similar return must be filed by any US person who controls (10 per cent) a foreign corporation or a foreign partnership.[100] Notices and returns must also be filed by any US person who is a transferor of property to a foreign partnership or in a corporate transaction such as those discussed in 7.3, e.g. a corporate reorganization, and/or who are officers, directors, or ten per cent shareholders of foreign corporations involved in such transactions.[101] Transfers by US persons to foreign trusts must also be reported.[102] Penalties are imposed for failure to file the various information returns at the time and in the manner prescribed.[103]

---

99. Sec. 6035.
100. Sec. 6038.
101. Sec. 6038B, 6046.
102. Sec. 6048.
103. Sec. 6652, 6677, 6679.

Chapter 8
Transfer pricing

8.1. Background

Section 482 authorizes the fiscal authorities to allocate gross income, deductions, and credits between related taxpayers to the extent necessary to prevent evasion of taxes or clearly to reflect the income of related taxpayers.[1] The section has a very broad scope. It applies to domestic as well as international transactions and does not require a finding of a tax avoidance purpose on the part of the parties involved for a reallocation of income to be undertaken. Detailed Regulations have been issued under the section.[2] The Regulations are based in general on the principle that transactions between related parties should take place on an arm's length basis.[3]

The section performs two related but distinct functions in the US tax system. In the first place, it prevents a shifting of income or deductions among taxpayers in order to take advantage of differentials in rate brackets, whether in the domestic or international context. In the international setting, however, the section plays an additional role. Even if intercompany transactions result in no overall reduction in tax burden on the controlled group when US and foreign

---

1. A version of Sec. 482 has appeared in the United States Internal Revenue provisions since 1921.
2. The Regulations were first issued in their present detailed form in 1968. In 1988, pursuant to Congressional instructions, the Internal Revenue Service prepared a comprehensive study of intercompany pricing rules and in particular the rules dealing with the transfer of intangibles. The study contains an extensive discussion of the history of Section 482 and its application to various types of transactions. Treasury Department and Internal Revenue Service, *Study of Intercompany Pricing* (18 October 1988). The "White Paper" study was followed by proposed and temporary Regulations in 1992 and 1993 which followed some aspects of the method of analysis used in the White Paper, particularly the "comparative profits" approach. Final Regulations were issued in 1994.
3. The arm's length standard is not contained in the statute itself which speaks only of the need clearly to reflect the income of related parties. The Regulations interpret the statutory requirement that income be clearly reflected in terms of the necessity of arm's length dealings between related parties. Treas. Reg. Sec. 1.482-1(b)(1). However, while the arm's length standard is nominally required, the use of profit splitting and comparable profits methods which are allowed under the 1994 Regulations moves some ways in the direction of a more formulary approach to transfer pricing. *See, e.g.*, Notice 94-40, 1994-1 Cum.Bull. 351, dealing with the allocation of profits arising in connection with "global trading" activities. The Notice describes a "profit split" method which focuses on factors such as value of assets, risk and activity in each trading location. In addition, the Regulations contain a number of "safe haven" rules which are not consistent with the arm's length principle.

taxes are taken into account, it is still necessary that the US protect its appropriate share of tax revenues in international transactions. Thus the arm's length standard of Section 482 is invoked to allocate income to the US even where there has been no reduction in overall tax burden on the group because of the non-arm's length intercompany pricing practices in the group.

The following discussion views the operation of Section 482 primarily from the perspective of transactions between a US parent and its foreign subsidiary. But it must be kept in mind that the section is equally applicable to transactions between a foreign parent and its US subsidiary and between commonly controlled "brother-sister"companies.

8.2. Scope of coverage

The allocation of income and deductions under Section 482 is only available to the fiscal authorities; the section may not be invoked by the taxpayer.[4] The section applies in any case where two taxpayers are "owned or controlled directly or indirectly by the same interests." The Regulations interpret the "controlled" requirement quite broadly and look to the realities of the situation and not to the presence of formal legal control.[5] There was initially some question whether the section could be used to create income as well as simply to allocate income between related parties. But the court decisions in general have upheld the authority of the Commissioner of Internal Revenue to create income in such transactions. For example, in the case of interest free loans between parent and subsidiary, the Commissioner has successfully imposed an arm's length interest charge under Section 482.[6]

8.3. General approach

The Regulations provide specific methods (discussed in 8.4 below) to be used to determine whether transactions between related parties conform to the arm's

---

4. Treas. Reg. Sec. 1.482-1(a)(3). The taxpayer may report (on timely filed returns) income based on prices other than those actually charged in order to reflect true income. In addition, under Sec. 1059A(a), in the case of imported goods, the costs on which the income determination is based may not exceed the amount used in customs valuation.

5. Treas. Reg. Sec. 1.482-1(i)(4).

6. *B. Forman Co. v. Commissioner*, 453 F.2d 1144 (2d Cir. 1972); *Kahler Corp. v. Commissioner*, 486 F.2d 1 (8th Cir. 1973); *Fitzgerald Motor Co. v. Commissioner*, 508 F.2d 1096 (5th Cir. 1975); *Likins-Foster Honolulu Corp. v. Commissioner*, 840 F.2d 642 (9th Cir. 1988). Sec. 7872 now specifically deals with the treatment of such interest free loans. *See also Central de Gas de Chihuahua, S.A. v. Commissioner*, 102 TC 515 (1994)(rent imputed on equipment used with no charge).

length standard. If different types of transactions are interrelated, a different method may be applied to each aspect of the transaction. In selecting the method to be used, the taxpayer is instructed to apply the "best method", that is, "the method that, under the facts and circumstances provides the most reliable measure of an arm's length result."[7] Thus, there is no specified hierarchy of methods and "no method will invariably be considered to be more reliable than others."[8] In selecting the "best method," the Regulations focus on the degree of comparability between the related party transaction in question and the uncontrolled transaction and the "quality of the data and assumptions used in the analysis."[9] Thus, for example, if there are relatively poor data with regard to a comparable uncontrolled price but good data as to a profit split method, the latter would be the "best" method even though not based on the prices in an uncontrolled transaction.

8.3.1 DETERMINING COMPARABILITY

The various specific methods all depend on establishing comparable prices or profits of third parties dealing at arm's length ("uncontrolled" transactions) and all factors which could influence prices or profits have to be taken into account in determining the relation between the related party transaction under analysis and the uncontrolled transaction. This requires a consideration of the functions being performed by the parties, the terms and conditions of contractual arrangements, the risks being borne by each party and the general economic conditions under which the transactions have taken place.[10] For example, if a comparable uncontrolled price is being determined in a different geographical market from that in which the related party transaction took place, adjustments must be made to account for the differences in the two markets. "Market share strategy" involving temporarily reduced prices to increase market share can be used to justified a lower related party price. The taxpayer must show, however, that an uncontrolled taxpayer engaged in a similar strategy and that the reduced prices are only used for a "reasonable" period of time.[11]

Similarily, the extent to which a party assumes a market or financial risk is a factor which will affect the determination of the degree of comparability of related and controlled transactions. For example, the price charged to a distributor by a manufacturer will be affected by the allocation of the risk of product

---

7. Treas. Reg. Sec. 1.482-1(c)(1).

8. Id.

9. Treas. Reg. Sec. 1.482-1(c)(2).

10. Treas. Reg. Sec. 1.482-1(d). The Regulations provide an extensive analysis of the factors to be considered and the adjustments needed to arrive at comparability.

11. Treas. Reg. Sec. 1.482-1(d)(4)(i).

liability for product defects. However, for the allocation of risk between related parties to be respected, the party bearing the risk must have sufficient financial capacity to absorb the loss should it occur.[12]

8.3.2 ARM'S LENGTH RANGES

The Regulations recognize that the application of a method may not produce a single "correct" arm's length amount. Accordingly, the taxpayer is authorized to establish a "range" of results derived by applying the selected method to more than one set of adjusted comparable uncontrolled transactions. Statistical methods are used to insure the reliability of the range, excluding results at both ends of the range. If the result shown in the related party transaction falls within the "arm's length range", no adjustment will be made. If the taxpayer reported a result which falls outside the range, the IRS adjustment can be based on any value within the range.[13]

8.3.3. DETERMINING "THE TRANSACTION"

In principle, the "true taxable income" from the related party transactions should be determined on the basis of the data involved in each individual transaction. However, the Regulations allow the taxpayer to apply the pricing methods to product lines or similar groups of products and to use sampling and other statistical techniques. In addition, interrelated transactions may be aggregated and data may be based on multiple years to reduce the effects of short term variations which might distort prices or profits.[14]

8.4 Specific transactions

8.4.1. SALES OF GOODS

The Regulations set forth five pricing methods to be used in determining the income from the sale of tangible property between related parties. They are the comparable uncontrolled price ("CUP") method, the resale price method, the cost plus method, the comparable profits method and the profit split method.[15]

---

12. Treas. Reg. Sec. 1.482-(d)(3)(iii).
13. Treas. Reg. Sec. 1.482-1(e),(e)(3).
14. Treas. Reg. Sec. 1.482-1(f)(2).
15. Treas. Reg. Sec. 1.482-3(a). The Regulations also allow the use of an "unspecified method." However, if the taxpayer uses an "unspecified" method and the results are ultimately determined not to conform to the arm's length standard, it is more likely to be subject to penalties than if a "specified" method had been used. Treas. Reg. Sec. 1.482-3(e)(1).

The latter two methods are also used in connection with intangibles, discussed in 8.4. As indicated, there is no order of preference and the various methods are subject to the "best method" rule discussed in 8.3.

8.4.1.1 Comparable uncontrolled price method

Under the comparable uncontrolled price method, the price is determined on the basis of "uncontrolled sales" made to buyers which are not members of the same controlled group. Such comparable sales include sales made by a member of the group to an unrelated party and sales of the same product made between parties which are not members of the controlled group and are unrelated. In determining the basis for comparability, differences in the properties of the product sold and the circumstances surrounding the sale are taken into account under the principles discussed in 8.3.1. In determining comparability, the most important factor is the similarity of the products.[16] Where trademarked goods are involved, for example, the effect of the trademark on price must be taken into account and may prevent an uncontrolled price from being appropriately adjusted, thus requiring the use of some other method under the "best method"rule.[17]

8.4.1.2 Resale price method

The resale price method bases the determination of arm's length price on the gross profit margin of sales in uncontrolled transactions. That margin is subtracted from the resale price involved in the related party transaction to establish the transfer price on the related party sale.[18] Assume, for example, that property is manufactured by the parent corporation, sold to a distribution subsidiary and then is sold outside the group by the distributor subsidiary in an uncontrolled sale for a price of 100. An examination of comparable uncontrolled sales establishes a gross profit margin of 20 per cent. The arm's length price for the sale within the group from the manufacturing parent to the distributor subsidiary would thus be 80 (100 minus 20% × 100). Comparability is determined principally on functions performed and risks borne.[19] The resale price method is generally appropriate when the reseller does not add substantial value to the product and is functioning primarily as a distributor.

---

16. Treas. Reg. Sec. 1.482-3(b)(2)(i). Despite the "best method" approach,the Regulations state that "generally" the results from applying the CUP method will be the most direct and reliable measure of an arm's length price.
17. Treas. Reg. Sec. 1.482-3(2)(b)(4)Ex.1.
18. Treas. Reg. Sec. 1.482-3(c).
19. Treas. Reg. Sec. 1.482-3(c)(3)(ii).

8.4.1.3   Cost plus method

Under the cost plus method, the cost of goods sold of the company selling to the related party is determined under normal accounting principles and then an appropriate "gross profit markup" derived from an analysis of uncontrolled transactions is applied. The cost plus method is usually used in situations involving the production or manufacture of products which are then sold to related parties.[20]

8.4.1.4   Comparable profits method

The most radical change in the 1994 Regulations is the introduction of the comparable profits method ("CPM"). Rather than looking at prices or gross profit margins in uncontrolled transactions, the CPM looks at the profit level indicators of uncontrolled parties and in effect adjusts the related party transfer prices so that an equivalent profit is made by the controlled party. The 1992 Proposed Regulations would have made CPM a more general standard and would have required the results reached under other methods to be tested against the CPM in many circumstances. The final Regulations downplay the CPM considerably though it is still one of the "approved"methods.[21]

8.4.1.4.1   Profit level indicators

The first step in applying the CPM is to establish appropriate measures of profitability, "profit level indicators", based on data of uncontrolled parties. Profit level indicators are ratios which measure the relation between expenditures and profits or rates of return. Thus the rate of return on operating assets, the ratio of operating profits to sales and the ratio of gross profit to operating expenses are all given as examples of profit level indicators.[22] As with all the methods, the comparability of the external data is a key factor in the CPM though the Regulations give little guidance beyond a reference to general factors such as the lines of business, asset composition, size and scope of operations and the stage

---

20. Treas. Reg. Sec. 1.482-3(d(1).
21. Despite the "best method" rule, which would involve the CPM if the data for that method were the most reliable, there seems to be some tendency to restrict the role of the CPM, in part perhaps to allay taxpayer fears of indiscriminate use of the CPM by IRS agents on audit. Thus the Treasury Decision announcing the new Regulations stated that, given the general availability of data on price and margins, the CPM "generally would be considered a method of last resort." T.D. 8852, 1994-2 Cum. Bull.93.
      The conceptual basis for the CPM is outlined in the White Paper cited in footnote 2.
22. Treas. Reg. Sec. 1.482-5(b)(4). Other measures can also be used as long as they are based on "objective" data.

in a business or product cycle.[23] Profit level indicators must be established for several years to reasonably measure the returns being realized by third parties in comparable activities.

8.4.1.4.2 Calculating operating profit

After the profit level indicators have been established, they are applied to the financial data of the "tested" related party. This is generally the related party which has the least complex business and for which it would be most possible to isolate the relevant business activities. The "comparable operating profit" calculated in this manner is then compared to the reported operating profit to determine if the related parties have been dealing at arm's length.

Assume, for example, that US parent company M manufactures a consumer product which it sells through a foreign distributor subsidiary FD. There are no sales to uncontrolled parties and there are no comparable uncontrolled prices of similar products. Thus CPM would generally be the "best method" for establishing arm's length results. FD would be the tested party, since it is engaged in less complex activities than M. Based on data from independent distributors in the same industry segment, the average ratio of operating profits to sales is 3%. FD's sales for the relevant period were 10,000 and its reported operating profit 350. Under the CPM, its profits would be decreased to 300 and a corresponding increase would be made to the income of M to reflect the results of the CPM analysis.

8.4.1.5 *Profit split*

The "profit split"method, though not formally recognized in the 1968 version of the Regulations, was followed in a number of court cases[24] and is one of the accepted methods in the 1994 Regulations. The profit split method examines the "combined operating profit or loss" in a related party transaction and allocates that amount based on the relative value of the contributions to the generation of the profit made by each member of the related party group.[25] Under the profit split method, the profit allocated to one member is not limited to the combined operating profit of the group; in a given year one member may have a profit while another has a loss.[26] The Regulations provide for two types of profit splits, a "comparable profit split" and a "residual profit split."

In a comparable profit split, the split is determined by looking at the division of operating profits among uncontrolled taxpayers performing similar activities

---

23. Treas. Reg. Sec. 1.482-5(c)(2).
24. *See, e.g., Eli Lilly & Co. v. Commissioner*, 856 F2d 855 (7th Cir. 1988).
25. Treas. Reg. Sec. 1.482-6(a).
26. Treas. Reg. Sec. 1.482-6(b).

under similar circumstances. The contractual allocation of risks and functions in the uncontrolled situation are particularly important in determining comparability. The residual profit split attributes normal market returns to the routine contributions made by each party. Then any residual profits are allocated to the intangibles owned by each of the related parties, based on the fair market values of those intangibles if those can be determined, or on some estimated value based on the capitalized costs of developing the intangibles.[27] These are obviously daunting valuation issues but in appropriate circumstances the residual profit split will nonetheless be the "best method."[28]

8.4.2. INTANGIBLES

Developing appropriate transfer pricing methods to deal with intangibles is one of the most difficult tasks in the transfer pricing area. Many intangibles are unique and it is impossible to find a comparable transaction in order to establish an arm's length price or royalty. The 1968 Regulations simply listed various factors to be taken into account but gave no indication of the weight each factor was to be given. In response to these difficulties, Congress in 1986 amended Section 482 as it applies to intangibles by specifically providing that in the case of a transfer or license of an intangible "the income with respect to such transfer or license shall be commensurate with the income attributable to the intangible". This amendment had two functions. In the first place, it required periodic reviews of the relation between the consideration paid for the intangible and the income which the intangible in fact generated. Under the "commensurate with income" standard it would not be possible to license an intangible at a low royalty rate when the possible success of the intangible was unknown and then keep that rate if in fact it turned out that the intangible was successful. The royalty would have to be adjusted periodically to reflect the success of the intangible.[29] The requirement of periodic adjustments is justified as consistent with the arm's length standard on the ground that unrelated parties would not enter into long term contracts fixing the rate of return but would instead require periodic renegotiations.[30] The 1986 addition of the "commen-

---

27. Treas. Reg. Sec. 1.482-6(c)(3)(i)(B).
28. *See* Treas. Reg. Sec. 1.482-8 Ex. 8 for an example of the conditions necessary to apply the residual profit split as the "best method."
29. Treas. Reg. Sec. 1.482-4(f)(5). Adjustment is required regardless of the form that the consideration for the transfer takes. Thus if the transfer involves a lump sum payment, the payment is converted into a series of payments over the life of the agreement based on present value principles and the amount of that deemed payment is compared with the subsequently determined arm's length amount in future years.
30. *See* Notice 88-123, 1988-2 Cum. Bull. 458, 477; Treas. Reg. Sec. 1.482-4(f)(2). The taxpayer is not required to make a periodic adjustment if it can establish a comparable uncontrolled agreement which does not call for readjustment.

surate with income" requirement also shifted the inquiry in the intangibles area more directly on profits-based methods such as the profit split method and comparative profits approach.[31] See 8.3.4 and 8.3.5.

8.4.2.1. Comparable uncontrolled transaction

The Regulations provide one method for the determination of an arm's length result in the case of intangibles, the "comparable uncontrolled transaction"("CUT") method. Like the corresponding CUP method for tangible property, the CUT method attempts to establish the arm's length charge for the transfer or license of an intangible based on comparable uncontrolled transactions.[32] Substantial guidance is given with respect to the factors to be taken into account in determining comparability of uncontrolled transactions involving intangibles. The intangibles must be used in connection with similar products in the same general industry, they must have the same "profit potential" expressed in terms of the net present value of the of the anticipated returns, and the transfer must be made in similar circumstances, including the extent of the rights granted and the duration of the license.[33] Under the "best method" rule, the CUT method will only be applied when the data and assumptions used for that method are superior to the other methods. Thus, it is likely that in most situations involving intangibles, the profit split or CPM will be applicable. See 8.3.4 and 8.3.5.

8.4.2.2. Cost sharing agreements

The Regulations have special rules for so-called "qualified cost sharing" arrangements between related parties which provide for the sharing of costs and risks in developing an intangible. The costs are allocated in proportion to the reasonably expected benefits assigned to the parties under the agreement.[34] When such cost sharing arrangements are present, no charge need be made between related parties for intangible property developed under the agreement. Thus, for example, assume a US parent company and its foreign subsidiary enter into a cost sharing agreement to develop an intangible which the parent company will exploit in the US market and the subsidiary will exploit in the rest of the world. The costs would be allocated on the basis of the anticipated

---

31. The Section 482 White Paper discussed in footnote 2 contains an extensive analysis of the issues involved in developing the commensurate with income standard and many of the positions taken there were ultimately be adopted in the Regulations, especially as concerns profit-based methods.
32. Treas. Reg. Sec. 1.482-4(c)(1).
33. Treas. Reg. Sec. 1.482-4(c)(2)(iii).
34. Treas. Reg. Sec. 1.482-7(a)(1).

sales in the relevant markets, with reimbursements required where one party incurs more than its share of costs. In this case, adjustments would be required under Sec. 482 only to the extent necessary to insure that each party bears its appropriate share of the costs. Since after the intangible has been developed each party will be an owner of the intangible, no additional charge or royalty need be paid to exploit the property.[35] If a new participant enters into a preexisting cost sharing agreement, it must compensate the existing participants on an arm's length basis; similarily if a participant relinquishes its interest, it must be compensated by the participants whose interest increases.[36]

8.4.3 SERVICES

An arm's length charge for services undertaken for or on behalf of a related party is generally deemed to equal the costs or deductions incurred with respect to such services by the related party rendering the services. Thus the Regulations do not in general require that a profit be made on the charge for services between related parties.

If the services are an "integral part" of the business activity of the providing party, however, then the arm's length charge is the amount which would have been charged for the same or similar services to an independent party; in other words, some sort of profit factor must be included.[37]

In general, a charge for services need not be made if the probable benefits to the related members are remote or indirect. For example, no charge must be made for services which duplicate services that the related party is performing independently.[38]

8.4.4 LOANS

Loans between related parties in general must be made at an arm's length interest rate. In general, the interest rate prevailing at the situs of the lender or creditor is the standard. However, if the loan represents the proceeds of a borrowing by the lender undertaken at the situs of the related party-borrower, that rate may be used.[39]

The Regulations also provide a range of "safe haven" rates within which the actual rate of interest will not be challenged. The safe haven rates are based on

---

35. Treas. Reg. Sec. 1.482-7(f)(3)(iii)(E) Ex. 5; Treas. Reg. Sec. 1.482-7(a)(2).
36. Treas. Reg. Sec. 1.482-7(g)(3).
37. Treas. Reg. Sec. 1.482-2(b)(3). For a case in which the taxpayer was able to establish an arm's length charge for services based on services performed for unrelated third parties despite the fact that the income from unrelated parties was only a small percentage of the taxpayer's total income, *see US Steel Corp. v. Commissioner*, 617 F.2d 942 (2d Cir. 1980).
33. Treas. Reg. Sec. 1.482-2(b)(3).
39. Treas. Reg. Sec. 1.482-2(a)(2)(ii).

the so-called "applicable Federal rate," i.e. the rate paid by the Federal government on similar obligations at the time the related party loan is made. If the related party loan bears an interest rate which is at least 100 per cent and not
more than 130 per cent of the applicable Federal rate, the safe haven test will
be met and no adjustment will be made under Section 482. Thus if the applicable Federal rate is ten per cent any interest rate between ten and thirteen per
cent would be acceptable. If less than ten per cent interest were charged, the interest rate would be adjusted up to ten per cent unless the taxpayer could establish that the lower rate was in fact an arm's length rate. Similarly, if the
interest charged was above thirteen per cent, the rate would be adjusted down
to thirteen per cent, again unless the taxpayer could establish a different arm's
length rate.[40]

Special rules for intercompany trade receivables allow an "interest free period" before which interest will be imputed under Section 482.[41] The Section
482 rules are coordinated with the rules governing original issue discount and
shareholder-corporation below market or interest free loans. In general terms,
the latter rules apply first to establish the interest rate and that rate is then adjusted under the Section 482 rules.[42]

8.5. Other aspects of Section 482 allocations

8.5.1. SET OFFS

The Regulations provide that in making allocations under Section 482, the fiscal authorities must consider the effect of any other non-arm's length transactions between the parties in the taxable year in question. For example, if one
party performs services without an arm's length charge for a related party
which in turn sells products to the first party at a discount, the value of the services received without charge would be set off against the allocation which otherwise would be made under Section 482 as to the discount.[43]

8.5.2. CORRELATIVE ADJUSTMENTS

The Regulations require that where the fiscal authorities make an adjustment to
the income of one member of a group under Section 482 a corresponding adjustment ("correlative allocation") must be made in the income or deductions

---

40. Treas. Reg. Sec. 1.482-2(a)(2)(iii)(B). The safe haven rules only apply to loans made in US dollars. Treas. Reg. Sec. 1.482-2(a)(2)(iii)(E).
41. Treas. Reg. Sec. 1.482-2(a)(1)(iii).
42. See 2.7 for a discussion of Sec. 1274 and 7872. Treas. Reg. Sec. 1.482-2(a)(3).
43. Treas. Reg. Sec. 1.482-1(g)(4).

149

of the related party.[44] For example, in a situation in which inadequate interest is charged on a related party loan, imputation of interest income to the lending party results in a corresponding interest deduction to the borrowing party. In a purely domestic context, this could result in a reduction of income tax liability for the related party or perhaps in an increased net operating loss carryover.

In the international context, where the related party is not subject to US tax jurisdiction, no such direct correlative adjustment can be made. However, if it later becomes necessary to determine the income of the related party, for example, in connection with the foreign tax credit, the earnings and profits of the related party will be computed as if the correlative adjustment had been made.

8.5.3. ADJUSTMENTS OF ACCOUNTS AFTER SECTION 482 ALLOCATION

When a Section 482 allocation has been made, the income of one of the related parties will be increased. However, the actual funds representing that allocation will still remain with the other party. If no special rules were applicable, when those funds were subsequently transferred to the related party, for example, as a dividend distribution by a subsidiary to its parent, an additional tax would be incurred. To solve this problem the Internal Revenue Service has issued administrative guidelines which provide that the taxpayer to whom income is allocated under Section 482 may receive a dividend payment from the related party in the year in which the allocation has been made which it can exclude from its US income. If such a dividend is not paid, the taxpayer has the alternative of setting up an account receivable on its books reflecting the amount of the Section 482 adjustment which can then be paid over to it by the related party with no further tax consequences. These relief procedures, however, apply only in the case that the arrangements of transactions giving rise to the Section 482 allocation did not have as one of their principal purposes the avoidance of federal income tax.[45]

8.6. International aspects

8.6.1. TREATIES

Most US income tax treaties contain an article which allows the US to determine the income of persons subject to its taxing jurisdiction on the basis of an

---

44. Treas. Reg. Sec. 1.482-1(g)(2).
45. Rev. Proc. 65-17, 1965-1 Cum. Bull. 833.

arm's length principle in any situation in which arrangements or conditions in transactions between related parties do not conform to the arm's length standard.[46] In general, the tests applied under Section 482 are also relevant under the treaties. Under recent treaties, where a reallocation of income has been made by one country, the other country agrees to make corresponding adjustments to the extent that it agrees with such a redetermination of income. To the extent that the other country does not agree with the redetermination, the two countries endeavor to reach a compromise under the general mutual agreement procedures contained in the treaty.[47] If no such compromise can be reached, the taxpayer is faced with possible international double taxation as a result of the countries' disagreement on the proper allocation of the income or deductions in question.

8.6.2. FOREIGN TAX CREDIT

Under the US foreign tax credit provision discussed in Chapter 6, the amount of foreign tax credit available is determined in part by the US taxpayer's foreign source income. Thus a Section 482 allocation which, coupled with the source rules, has the effect of increasing the US taxpayer's US source income and correspondingly decreasing the income of a foreign related party can have an effect on the available foreign tax credit. For example, suppose a US parent corporation receives a dividend from its foreign subsidiary and claims the deemed paid foreign tax credit under Section 902 for the taxes paid by the subsidiary. In a subsequent year, a Section 482 adjustment is made allocating income, which was reported initially by the foreign subsidiary, to the US parent corporation. Under the correlative adjustment principle, the foreign subsidiary's income will be reduced correspondingly and the foreign tax credit calculation, which under Section 902 is based in part on the subsidiary's income in the year in question, will be changed. To claim the foreign tax credit for the foreign taxes imposed on the items of income allocated under Section 482 from a foreign subsidiary to the US parent, the taxpayer must establish that the foreign subsidiary has exhausted its administrative remedies under foreign law in seeking a refund of the foreign taxes paid on the income so reallocated. Otherwise, it is presumed that the foreign taxes paid were in fact a voluntary contribution to the foreign government not qualifying for the foreign tax credit. In addition, if the allocation under Section 482 is made in connection with a

---

46. *See, e.g.*, US Model Treaty, Art. 9.
47. In order for Rev. Proc. 65-17 relief to be available in these circumstances, the taxpayer must request assistance under the mutual agreement procedure. *See* Rev. Proc. 91-24, 1991-1 Cum. Bull. 542; Rev. Proc. 96-13, 1996-1 Cum. Bull. 616; Rev. Proc. 96-14, 1996-1 Cum. Bull. 626.

foreign subsidiary in a country with which the US has an income tax treaty, the parent must demonstrate that it exhausted its rights under the competent authority provision of the treaty.[48]

Thus the US insures that, if at all possible, the increase in revenue under the Section 482 allocation will not simply be offset by an increased foreign tax credit resulting from a failure to adjust the taxes paid in the foreign country to reflect the Section 482 adjustment.

8.6.3. BLOCKED INCOME

If a payment between related parties is prevented because of currency or other restrictions under the laws of a foreign country and a Section 482 allocation is made, the taxpayer may defer the reporting of the Section 482 allocation under the general method for accounting for income subject to currency restrictions. The taxpayer is not forced to pay current tax on an income allocation which it in fact cannot receive because of the foreign law restrictions.[49]

8.7 Advance Pricing Agreements

Beginning in 1990, the IRS established procedures which allow taxpayers to obtain "advance pricing agreements" ("APA's")with respect to proposed transactions involving intercompany pricing issues. Under the procedure,the taxpayer submits a request for an advance ruling with respect to the transfer pricing methodology it proposes to use in anticipated transactions. The request must be accompanied with the kind of data on comparability required by the Regulations for a particular method.[50] In an interesting twist, the taxpayer can be required to bear the costs of an "independent expert", approved by the IRS, to give an opinion concerning the taxpayer's request. Where international transactions are involved, the APA request may involve obtaining the agreement of foreign revenue officials under the competent authority provisions of a tax treaty. Thus the taxpayer can be assured that the same pricing methodology will be acceptable in the two (or more) countries involved.[51] Information sub-

---

48. Rev. Rul. 74-158, 1974-1 Cum. Bull. 182; Rev. Rul. 92-75, 1992-2 Cum. Bull. 197.
49. Treas. Reg. Sec. 1.482-1(h)(2). The principle was established by the Supreme Court in *Commissioner v. First Security Bank of Utah*, 405 US 394 (1972). The IRS has attempted to limit the scope of the holding of *First Security*, with little success. *See Proctor & Gamble Co v. Commissioner*, 95 TC 323, aff'd,961 F.2d 1255 (6th Cir. 1992). The Regulations set forth a number of conditions which must be fulfilled before the blocked income rule can be invoked. Treas. Reg. Sec. 1.482-1(h)(2)(ii).
50. Rev. Proc. 96-53, 1996-2 Cum. Bull. 375.
51. The first widely publicized APA involved Apple Computer's activities in Australia.

mitted in connection with an APA request is confidential and the agreement itself is not made public[52] but the IRS will publish information as to basic approaches taken in the APA's which have been issued.[53] After some initial reluctance on the part of taxpayers to participate in the APA program, the number of requests has increased substantially. Both the government and the taxpayer are better off if the wasteful, costly and protracted litigation associated with transfer pricing cases can be avoided.

8.8   Accuracy-related penalties

In addition to the "carrot" of the APA procedures and the wide range in choice of methods under the new Regulations, Congress has also equipped the tax authorities with the "stick" of the accuracy-related penalties of Section 6662. These penalties, extended to transfer pricing cases in 1990 and further strengthened in 1993, impose a 20 per cent or 40 per cent penalty where the taxpayer's transfer pricing methodology resulted in reported income substantially less than that ultimately determined to be due. The 20 per cent penalty is imposed if there is a "substantial valuation misstatement" in the amount reported by the taxpayer with respect to a related party transaction. A substantial valuation misstatement is present if the price reported is more than 200 per cent higher or 50 per cent lower than the amount determined to be correct under Section 482 (the "transactional" penalty). In addition, there is a substantial valuation misstatement if the total transfer pricing adjustment exceeds the lesser of $5,000,000 or 10 per cent of the taxpayer's gross receipts (the "net adjustment" penalty).[54] The penalty is increased to 40 per cent in the case of a "gross valuation misstatement" which applies if the transactional misstatement on prices is 400 per cent too high or 25 per cent too low or the total adjustment is the lesser of $20,000,000 or 20 per cent of the taxpayer's gross receipts.[55] The penalties can be avoided if the taxpayer acted in "good faith" and had "reasonable cause" for the misstatement.[56] The Regulations spell out some of the factors relevant in establishing "reasonable cause" including when reliance on the advice of experts can be exculpatory.[57] In addition, the net adjustment penalty can be

---

52. A private publisher has sued the IRS to require it to make redacted versions of APA's public. *Bureau of National Affairs, Inc. v. Commissioner*, No. 96-CV376 (DC DC), filed on February 27, 1996, as reported in BNA Daily Tax Report GG-1 (Feb. 28, 1996).
53. *See, e.g.*, Notice 94-40, 1994-1 Cum.Bull. 351, dealing with global trading.
54. Sec. 6662(e)(1)(B).
55. Sec. 6662(h).
56. Sec. 6664(c).
57. Treas. Reg. Sec. 1.6664-4(c)(1).

avoided if the taxpayer "reasonably" (though wrongly) used one of the stipulated methods and has contemporaneous documentation supporting the method chosen and why such method was reasonable.[58] The requirement of contemporaneous documentation is especially important and the required documents are spelled out in detail and must be available at the time of the filing of the US return.[59]

---

58. Sec. 6662(e)(3)(B).
59. Treas. Reg. Sec. 1.6662-6(d)(2)(iii). The emphasis on documentation is a result of the belief (or suspicion) by the IRS that taxpayers were "making it up as they went along" in many transfer pricing situations. On the other hand, some foreign taxpayers (and foreign governmental officials) view the Sec.6662 penalties as an attempt by the US to insure that foreign taxpayers will bend over backwards to allocate income to the US to avoid any suggestion that the penalties would apply, all to the detriment of the foreign fisc.

Chapter 9
Special treatment of foreign income

9.1 General

Generally, under US tax principles considered thus far, no special treatment is provided for foreign income of US taxpayers by virtue of the type of income involved, the activity that generates it, the geographical source of the income, or the personal circumstances of an individual income earner. If, under the source rules discussed in Chapter 4, the income is foreign source and attracts a foreign tax, the foreign tax credit mechanism is available; if it is US source income, it is simply subject to US tax.[1]

In some situations, however, the US has adopted preferential treatment for foreign income to achieve two different non-tax policy objectives: (1) to provide incentives for increased exports of US-produced goods; and (2) prior to 1996, to provide economic assistance to US possessions.

9.2 Incentives to increase US exports

9.2.1 BACKGROUND

In 1971, concern over the level of US exports led Congress to adopt a tax subsidy for export income. It enacted the Domestic International Sales Corporation (DISC) provisions to provide a tax incentive for US companies to engage in export activities. The subsidy took the form of a deferral of US tax on a portion of export income channeled through a DISC, in effect an interest-free loan from the Treasury to US exporters. In 1976, however, a GATT panel found that the DISC rules violated the GATT provisions on export subsidies and the DISC rules also appeared to constitute prohibited "export subsidies" under the agreements reached in the Tokyo Round of Multilateral Trade Negotiations.

In the face of pressure from its GATT trading partners to repeal DISC, Congress in 1984 adopted a new type of tax-preferred corporation, a Foreign Sales Corporation (FSC), which was designed to encourage exports and to try to

---

1. Two notable exceptions to these general statements are the tax treatment of income earned through controlled foreign corporations, (7.1.) and the source rules for US exports (4.3.2).

eliminate the aspects of DISC which had caused it to be a prohibited export subsidy. The DISC provisions were retained but an interest charge equal to the US Treasury borrowing rate was imposed on the tax deferral.

Another special provision allows US citizens or residents who work abroad to exclude a certain amount of earned income from gross income. This preferential provision is also defended on the ground that it helps increase US exports by increasing the likelihood that foreign companies — controlled or uncontrolled — will acquire their products or services from US companies.

9.2.2 THE FOREIGN SALES CORPORATION (FSC)

9.2.2.1 Background

As Congress interpreted the GATT rules, an exemption from tax on export income is permissible if the economic processes that generate the income take place outside the country of export. Thus, many of the FSC rules can be understood in light of this interpretation, particularly those provisions that nominally require an FSC to have a foreign presence, economic substance and perform income producing activities outside the US.

9.2.2.2 Summary

The following outlines the FSC regime:

The taxpayer first determines the amount of "foreign trading company gross receipts" of the FSC, the "transfer pricing method" to be employed, and the "foreign trade gross income" of the FSC. The amount of foreign trade income that is exempt from US taxation is then equal to either (1) 30 per cent of foreign trade income from transactions in which the arm's length transfer pricing method is employed or (2) 15/23 (65.21739 per cent) of the foreign trade income from transactions in which one of the available administrative transfer pricing methods is employed. If the arm's length transfer pricing method is used, a shareholder of an FSC is subject to US tax under the rules described in Chapter 7 on that portion of the FSC's income which is not exempt from US tax under the FSC rules; a foreign tax credit is available, although such income is placed in one of the separate limitation income baskets. If an administrative transfer pricing method is used, the FSC is taxed currently on the amount in excess of the amount exempt under the FSC rules; no foreign tax credit is allowed. For purposes of determining an FSC's taxable income, deductions must be allocated between exempt and nonexempt foreign trade income, with those allocable to the exempt income being disallowed.

Behind this highly simplified outline are a host of definitions, special rules and requirements of substantial complexity. The following material highlights the main elements of the FSC legislation.

9.2.2.3 Requirements to qualify as an FSC

The eligibility requirements which must be satisfied before a foreign corporation can elect to be treated as an FSC are intended to establish at least nominally that the FSC has a "foreign presence." An FSC must:
1. be created under the laws of a foreign country or US possession (other than Puerto Rico);[2]
2. have fewer than 25 shareholders;[3]
3. not have any preferred stock outstanding;[4]
4. maintain an office in the foreign country or possession in which a permanent set of books is maintained and maintain within the US the books and records required to be kept by all taxpayers for income tax purposes;[5]
5. have one member of its board of directors who is not a US resident (though that director may be a US citizen);[6]
6. not be a member of a controlled group of corporations which includes a DISC.[7]

Usually, an FSC is a wholly-owned subsidiary of a US corporation. The following discussion assumes that this structure is employed unless otherwise noted.

9.2.2.4 Treatment of foreign trade income

9.2.2.4.1 Determination of the exempt amount

As noted above, a portion of an FSC's "foreign trade income" is exempt from US tax. The amount of income that is exempt depends on the transfer price mechanism used to determine the foreign trade income of the FSC (see 9.2.2.5, below). The exempt amount is:
1. 30 per cent of the foreign trade income derived from a qualifying transaction if the taxable income realized from the transaction is determined

---

2. Sec. 922(a)(1)(A). Only a foreign country which has concluded an exchange of information agreement with the US or which has concluded a tax treaty with the US which the Treasury has certified contains an adequate information exchange provision can qualify as a host country for an FSC. Sec. 927(e)(3). The Treasury periodically publishes a list of qualifying countries.
3. Sec. 922(a)(1)(B).
4. Sec. 922(a)(1)(C). This requirement apparently was put in to prevent the FSC from being able to direct nontaxable dividends to shareholders with taxable income and taxable dividends to shareholders with net operating loss carryovers.
5. Sec. 922(a)(1)(D).
6. Sec. 922(a)(1)(E).
7. Sec. 922(a)(1)(F).

on the basis of arm's length pricing between unrelated parties or between related parties under the rules of section 482;[8] or

2. 15/23 of the foreign trade income derived from a qualifying transaction if the taxable income realized from the transaction is determined under one of two administrative pricing formulas.[9]

The resulting amount is "exempt foreign trade income."

A simplified example at this point illustrates the computation of "exempt foreign trade income." Assume US Corporation X owns all the stock of foreign Corporation Y, a Y country corporation, which is an FSC. Y realizes 600 in foreign trading company gross receipts from the sale of goods produced by its US parent and sold for use outside of Country Y. Its cost of goods sold, determined under an arm's length method, is 400 and it has other expenses of 60. Y's foreign trade income is 200. Its exempt foreign trade income is 60 (30% × 200); 18 of the expenses must be allocated to the exempt income (60/200 × 60) and are not deductible.

9.2.2.4.2 Taxation of the nonexempt amount

Foreign trade income other than exempt foreign trade income is denominated "nonexempt foreign trade income." The US tax treatment of the nonexempt income is determined by the transfer pricing method employed. If one of the administrative pricing methods is used, the nonexempt income is treated as US source income effectively connected with the conduct of a trade or business through a permanent establishment of the FSC within the US.[10] Thus, in this case, nonexempt foreign trade income is taxed currently in the US and, e.g. constitutes US source income for purposes of calculating the limits on the foreign tax credit under Section 904. On the other hand, if an arm's length transfer price system is employed, the source and taxation of the nonexempt income is determined apart from the FSC rules, e.g. subpart F rules may apply to tax income currently to the US parent.

To return to the above example, the nonexempt foreign trade income of Corporation Y is 140 (200 – 60); 42 of the expenses must be allocated to such income; and the nonexempt taxable income of Corporation Y is 98. Since the arm's length transfer price method was employed, the taxation of the 98 depends on rules generally applicable to foreign corporations controlled by a US shareholder. As discussed in 7.2, this income would be taxed currently to Cor-

---

8. Sec. 923(a)(2). The statutory provision specifies 32 per cent but that figure is applicable only where individual shareholders are involved. For corporate shareholders the 32 per cent figure is reduced to 30 per cent by virtue of Sec. 291(a)(4).

9. Sec. 923(a)(3). The statutory numerator is sixteen but that figure is applicable only to individual shareholders. For corporate shareholders the numerator is reduced to fifteen by virtue of Sec. 291(a)(4).

10. Sec. 921(d).

poration X under subpart F since the goods were sold for use outside Country Y. Under Section 960 a credit would be given for foreign taxes paid, if any. Under these circumstances Corporation X would account currently for the 98 of nonexempt income; Corporation Y would have no US liability. However, if Corporation X's products were sold by Corporation Y in Country Y, thus avoiding the application of subpart F, US tax on the Country Y income would be deferred until repatriated to the US. Here neither Corporation X nor Corporation Y would have any current US tax liability. By contrast, if one of the administrative transfer pricing methods had been employed, Corporation Y (and not Corporation X) would be subject to current US taxation on its nonexempt income as determined under the transfer pricing method employed.

Generally, an FSC will not be entitled to a foreign tax credit with respect to its currently exempt or nonexempt income (except as noted above). Its US shareholder also will not be eligible for a foreign tax credit with respect to any withholding tax imposed on a dividend attributable to exempt foreign trade income since, in effect, the US has adopted a territorial system for such portion. With respect to the nonexempt portion, if the arm's length pricing rules are met and the income is not treated as US source, a foreign tax credit is available.[11]

9.2.2.4.3 Definition of foreign trade income

Foreign trade income is gross income of an FSC attributable to "foreign trading gross receipts.'[12] These receipts arise in such transactions as the sale of export property, the lease of property for use outside the US, or the performance of services with respect to either sale or lease transactions.[13]

In order for an FSC to have "foreign trading gross receipts" (and hence foreign trade income), it must satisfy two requirements which are intended to assure that significant economic activities with respect to exports take place outside the US.[14]

The *foreign management* requirement is satisfied if directors and shareholders meetings are held outside the US, the principal bank account of the FSC is main-

---

11. Temp. Treas. Reg. Sec. 1.921-3T(d)(2). The income is placed in a separate limitation basket. *See* 6.6.3.6.
12. Sec. 923(b).
13. Sec. 924(a); Temp. Treas. Reg. Sec. 1.924(a)-1T. The types of property that qualify as export property are defined in Sec. 927(a). The critical elements are that the property be manufactured or produced in the US for sale by or to an FSC and that not more than 50 per cent of the value of the property be attributable to articles imported into the US. Intangible property, such as patents and trademarks, is specifically excluded from the definition of "export property" but, reflecting the expanding role of technology, income from the licensing of computer software to foreign licensees does qualify.
14. The two requirements are intended to satisfy EU objections to the DISC provisions under GATT. However, a "small FSC," i.e. one with $5 million or less of foreign trading gross receipts for the year, does not have to satisfy either requirement.

tained outside the US, and all dividends, legal and accounting fees, salaries and directors fees are disbursed out of bank accounts maintained outside the US.[15]

The *foreign economic processes* requirement is composed of two elements. The first element is satisfied if the FSC has participated outside the US in the solicitation, negotiation or the making of a contract with respect to an export transaction. This element of the requirement can be satisfied by a contract between the FSC and its US parent (or other domestic or foreign subsidiary) pursuant to which all of the export activities are performed by the related party and none by the FSC as such. The second element requires that the direct costs incurred by the FSC in an export transaction equal specified percentages of the total direct costs attributable to the transaction. Again, the direct costs test can be satisfied if the FSC pays its parent (or other related party) for performing the activities which generate the direct costs.[16]

Although elaborate and detailed Regulations set forth how the foreign economic processes requirement is to be satisfied, in fact the FSC need be little more than a foreign bank account in which proceeds from export transactions are deposited and from which the proceeds are immediately wired to the bank account of its US parent (or related corporation) which has carried out the actual export transaction pursuant to a contract (oral or written!) with the FSC.

9.2.2.5   Transfer pricing rules

The taxable income of an FSC must be determined either under the arm's length transfer pricing rules of Section 482 or under one of two "administrative transfer pricing" formulae which are asserted to approximate the results under Section 482 but which in fact are much more generous.

In order to be able to take advantage of one of the administrative transfer pricing formulas the FSC must perform (1) the economic processes that are the same as must be performed to satisfy the "foreign economic processes" test discussed in 9.2.2.4.3; and (2) all the activities relating to the solicitation negotiation, and making of the sales contract.[17] It is not necessary that any of the activities be performed outside the US. While these requirements nominally indicate substantial economic activities by the FSC, none of them actually have to be performed by the FSC; they can all be performed by the US parent (or related party) pursuant to an agency contract with the FSC.

---

15. Sec. 924(c). No actual meetings need take place outside the US if local law does not require the physical presence of officers or directors but, for example, allows them to act by written consent without a meeting. Treas. Reg. Sec. 1.924(c)-1(b). The Regulations take a similarly relaxed view of how the other requirements may be satisfied, permitting, for example, the satisfaction of the dividend payment requirement by book entries that offset payments owed to the FSC by its US parent.
16. Sec. 924(d)-(e); Treas. Reg. Sec. 1.924(d), (e).
17. Sec. 925(c); Temp. Treas. Reg. Sec. 1.925(a)-1T(a) and (b).

Assuming that the FSC satisfies the requirements for use of an administrative transfer price method, the taxable income of the FSC is computed by utilizing that one of the following rules that produces the *greatest* profit to the FSC: (1) An amount which would give the FSC a profit of 1.83 per cent of the foreign trading gross receipts of the FSC on its resale of the product; (2) an amount which would give the FSC a profit from the sale of a product equal to 23 per cent of the combined taxable income of the FSC and its parent attributable to the sale; or (3) the transfer price actually charged if it satisfies the rules of Section 482.[18] These three methods are available on a sale-by-sale basis; accordingly, in a given taxable year, all three methods could be applied to sales through the FSC.

The determination of the appropriate transfer price paid by the FSC to its US parent is also used in computing the parent's taxable income for US tax purposes.

9.2.2.6 Distributions to shareholders

Distributions by an FSC are deemed to be made first out of earnings and profits attributable to foreign trade income and then out of any other earnings and profits (e.g. resulting from investment income). If there is a nonresident alien or foreign corporate shareholder of the FSC, a distribution out of earnings and profits attributable to foreign trade income of the FSC is treated as US source income effectively connected with the conduct of a trade or business through a permanent establishment in the US.[19]

A US corporation that receives a dividend distribution out of earnings and profits attributable to foreign trade income is entitled to a 100 per cent dividends received deduction.[20] As a result, there will be no US corporate level tax on the exempt foreign trade income and a single US corporate level tax on nonexempt foreign trade income imposed on the FSC level. No dividends received deduction is available to the extent the distribution is out of earnings and profits attributable to other income of the FSC.

9.2.2.7 Evaluation

As stated at the outset, the FSC rules ostensibly were intended to satisfy GATT objections to the US export subsidy provided through the DISC mechanism. As has been seen, however, the economic presence of the FSC abroad is one which may be established on paper only since all critical elements of the foreign export sales can be carried out in the US by its parent under an agency contract. Indeed, a "small FSC" need not even bother with the paperwork requirements.

---

18. Sec. 925(a); Temp. Treas. Reg. Sec. 1.925(a)-1T(c).
19. Sec. 926(a)-(b); Temp. Treas. Reg. Sec. 1.926(a)-1T provide detailed ordering rules.
20. Sec. 245(c).

In addition, the taxpayer is given the option to choose from among three transfer pricing methods depending on which will provide the greatest exempt profit from a given transaction. The European Commission filed a complaint in 1997 challenging the FSC legislation under World Trade Organization rules and procedures.

9.2.3 THE DOMESTIC INTERNATIONAL SALES CORPORATION (DISC)

A DISC is not a taxable entity as such. Instead, the DISC income is taxed to its shareholder when actually or deemed distributed.[21] In general, a distribution is deemed to occur each year to the extent of 1/17 of the DISC's taxable income. The tax on the balance may be deferred until distributed. As the price for deferral of the tax, the DISC shareholder must pay an interest charge each year on the amount of tax deferred. The interest charge thus converts interest-free loans formerly available to a DISC into an interesting-bearing loan, thus removing the major element of the subsidy that had been found to violate GATT. In addition, only $10 million or less of qualified export receipts of a DISC can qualify for tax deferral.

In general, to qualify as a DISC, at least 95 per cent of a corporation's assets must be related to export activities and 95 per cent of its gross income must be derived from export sale or lease transactions and certain other export-related activities. Under the DISC rules, the gross income that qualifies will normally result from the sale of inventory items, manufactured or produced by a related corporation, which are to be used or consumed outside the US. The DISC rules contemplate that the DISC will be little more than a paper corporation through which the export activities of its parent will be booked for tax purposes.[22] To facilitate this mode of operation, the Section 482 intercompany pricing rules are drastically relaxed in order to permit a larger than normal profit to be allocated to the DISC (and hence to qualify for the tax deferral and the resulting interest-bearing loan). When a DISC is sold or otherwise disposed of, or ceases to qualify, then the amounts previously deferred are recaptured and included in the income of the shareholders.

9.2.4 TREATMENT OF INCOME EARNED ABROAD

9.2.4.1 General

For many years, a US citizen who works in and is a resident of a foreign country has been granted preferential tax treatment for foreign source earned in-

---

21. The DISC rules are set forth in Sec. 991-998.
22. Rev. Rul. 72-166, 1972-1 Cum. Bull. 220 (only activities of qualified DISC were bookkeeping to identify DISC profits).

come in the form of an exclusion from tax of a specific amount of such income. The exclusion has been the subject of much controversy and numerous legislative changes.

While the tax preference is granted to individuals, its financial benefits may be captured in whole or in part by employers of the individuals in the form of lower salaries than they would have been required to pay in the absence of the exclusion. The employers defend the special tax benefit on the ground that it enables them to employ US citizens in the foreign operation rather than lower-paid foreign nationals; the US citizens will be more likely to purchase needed goods and services from US providers than would non-US employees; therefore, it is asserted, the exclusion helps ensure higher levels of US exports. The validity of this argument is contested by opponents who argue that the subsidy either provides a windfall to US multinationals for doing what they would have done in the absence of the tax subsidy or is an inefficient mechanism by which to attempt to achieve greater US exports when compared with more targeted subsidies. The frequent legislative changes in the exclusion reflect the ebb and flow of views in Congress regarding export subsidies and revenue needs.

In general, Section 911(a) permits a qualified US citizen or resident who works abroad to elect to exclude from US gross income $70,000 (rising to $80,000 by $2,000 per year increments between 1998 and 2003) of foreign earned income plus a portion of the employer-provided housing costs (an alternative deduction is available if the individual's employer does not provide or pay for the housing).[23]

9.2.4.2 Eligibility for the exclusion

An individual can qualify for the exclusion if the individual's "tax home" is in a foreign country and one of two additional conditions is satisfied: (1) A US *citizen* establishes that he or she has been a *bona fide* resident of the foreign country for the entire taxable year; or (2) a US *citizen* or *resident* is physically present in the foreign country for 330 full days out of any twelve consecutive months period.[24] The maximum exclusion (plus alternative deduction) may not exceed the individual's foreign earned income for the year.[25]

The "tax home" of an individual is determined under the principles established by the Internal Revenue Service and the courts under Section 162(a)(2).

---

23. A separate exclusion is provided in Section 119(c) for the value of meals and lodging provided by an employer in a "camp" located in a foreign country. A "camp" is "lodging" which is (1) provided by the employer for the employer's convenience because the place of work is in a remote area where satisfactory housing is unavailable, (2) located as near as practicable to the place of work, and (3) a common living area, not open to the public, accommodating ten or more employees. The definition is designed to benefit primarily construction firms and oil companies.

24. Sec. 911(d)(1).

25. Sec. 911(d)(7).

That Section permits deductions for travel expenses only when an individual is "away from home". Hence to establish deductibility of travel expenses, it is necessary to determine the taxpayer's "home" so that expenses incurred while "away" from that home may be identified. The resolution of the issue is essentially a factual one although in very general terms a taxpayer's "tax home" is located at his principal place of business.[26]

9.2.4.3   The foreign earned income component

The "earned income" that may qualify for the exclusion (if from a foreign source as determined under the rules discussed in Chapter 4) is defined in Section 911(d)(2)(A) to include wages, salaries, professional fees or other amounts received as compensation for personal services actually rendered. Certain items are, however, excluded from the definition of "foreign earned income," including pensions, annuities, payments from the US government or any amount received more than one year after the year in which the services were rendered.[27] Thus, assume a US employee in foreign country Y, who otherwise satisfies the conditions of Section 911, enters into a deferred compensation agreement pursuant to which payments are to begin five years after retirement. None of the payments will qualify for the Section 911 exclusion.

The amount excluded under Section 911 may reduce the taxpayer's tax on other nonqualified income; there is no provision for "exemption with progression."

9.2.4.4   The housing cost component

In addition to the exclusion of foreign earned income, a qualifying individual may also exclude a portion of the value of employer-provided housing or housing costs reimbursed by the employer.[28] The "housing cost amount" that may

---

26. Treas. Reg. Sec. 1.911-2(b). The leading case in the area is *Commissioner v. Flowers,* 326 US 465 (1946), in which the Supreme Court articulated a three-part test for deductibility of travel expenses under Section 162(a)(2): (1) The travel expenses must be reasonable and necessary; (2) the expenses must be incurred while away from home; and (3) the expenses must be incurred in pursuit of (i.e. directly connected to) business. The deductibility of travel expenses under Section 162(a)(2) is a frequently litigated issue and, accordingly, reference to that section is in fact a reference to a mass of confusing and often conflicting body of case law and administrative pronouncements. For a summary of the issues under Section 162(a)(2) *see* McDaniel, Ault, McMahon and Simmons, *Federal Income Taxation* (3rd ed., 1994) at pages 551-572. The statute also requires that the taxpayer not have his "abode" in the US although the exact content of this term is unclear. *See* Treas. Reg. Sec. 1.911-2(b) (maintenance of dwelling in US does not "necessarily" establish an "abode" in the US).
27. Sec. 911(b)(1)(B). The rules for determining foreign earned income and the exclusions therefrom are set forth in detail in Treas. Reg. Sec. 1.911-3.
28. Sec. 911(c)(1); Treas. Reg. Sec. 1.911-4.

be excluded is the excess of the individual's housing expenses[29] for the year over sixteen per cent of the salary of a US government employee who is paid at a specified grade level.[30] For example, assume a US citizen employed in a foreign country incurs (and is reimbursed by her employer for) $20,000 of housing expenses in a year. The salary of a statutorily determined US government employee is $50,000. The employee could exclude $12,000 ($20,000 minus $8,000 (16% 3 $50,000)) as a housing cost amount under Section 911.

If an individual's housing cost amount exceeds the amount paid or incurred by her employer,[31] the excess is allowed as a deduction from gross income. The amount of the deduction cannot exceed the individual's foreign earned income less the amount, if any, excluded under the foreign earned income component of the Section 911 exclusion.[32]

9.2.4.5 Election of Section 911 benefits

The taxpayer must make an election to utilize the benefits under Section 911. The election is valid until revoked. If the taxpayer revokes an election without the consent of the Internal Revenue Service, generally no new election can be made until five years have elapsed after the year of revocation.[33]

A taxpayer who makes the Section 911 exclusion is denied any deduction, exclusion or tax credit, including foreign tax credit, to the extent allocable to the amount excluded from gross income.[34] Accordingly, a taxpayer who qualifies for the Section 911 exclusion and is deciding whether to make the election must first determine his US tax liability by including all foreign earned income in gross income, taking all appropriate deductions and reducing US tax liability by the foreign tax credit. Then he must determine his US tax liability by excluding the Section 911 amount from income and reducing deductions and the foreign tax credit to the extent allocable to the income excluded. Since there is a five year waiting period after a Section 911 election is revoked before it can be reelected, careful projections are also required in deciding which of the alternative tax paths to follow.[35]

---

29. Housing expenses must be "reasonable," not "lavish or extravagant." Sec. 911(c)(2)(A).
30. The theory of the provision is that costs in excess of the base amount reflect higher living expenses abroad.
31. Sec. 911(c)(3). Thus, the deduction is available to self-employed individuals.
32. If the deduction exceeds the limit, the excess may be carried over only to the next taxable year.
33. Sec. 911(e); Treas. Reg. Sec. 1.911-7; Rev. Rul. 90-77, 1990-2 Cum. Bull. 183.
34. Sec. 911(d)(6). Treas. Reg. Sec. 1.911-6 details the rules for allocating deductions, exclusions and credits to the income excluded under Sec. 911(a).
35. Additional tax considerations that must be taken into account by a US taxpayer moving abroad include, among others, the special rules on deductible moving expenses where foreign moves are involved (Sec. 217(h)).

9.3   Financial assistance for Puerto Rico and US possessions

For many years, the US provided tax incentives for US corporations to invest in Puerto Rico and US possessions. The form of the incentives was changed with some frequency but the underlying objective was to assist in the economic development of Puerto Rico and the possessions, especially through the location there of job-creating business operations.[36]

In its most recent version, the incentive took the form of a "possessions tax credit" which was available even if no taxes were in fact paid by the corporation to any possessions and thus represented a "tax sparing" credit.

The possessions tax credit was the subject of continual criticism by the US Treasury as an inefficient and highly abusable subsidy. Finally, in 1996, the credit was repealed. Transition rules permit corporations that qualified for the credit at the time of the repeal to continue to use reduced credits for various periods up to 2005.[37]

---

36. The history of the tax incentives prior to 1982 was set forth in the 1981 edition of this book at pages 112–116 and from 1983-1989 in the 1989 edition of this book.
37. Repeal of Sec. 936 is in Sec. 936(j)(i). The transition credit rules for Puerto Rico are in Sec. 30A and for other possessions in Sec. 936(j)(2)-(10).

CHAPTER 10
Foreign currency issues

10.1 Background

International transactions often involve dealings in a foreign currency. Special tax rules are necessary to take into account foreign currency issues in computing the taxpayer's tax liability in his "home" currency. Several different questions are involved. In the first place, there must be some method of translating the income derived in the foreign currency into the currency on which the taxing system is based. In addition, transactions with foreign currency aspects can result in gain or loss because of the change in the relationship of the currencies involved, quite apart from the gain or loss on the underlying transaction. Finally, some taxpayers are actually conducting a business in a foreign currency, while others have only occasional foreign currency transactions, and different rules are necessary for these two classes of taxpayers.

Prior to 1986, the US tax rules applicable to foreign currency transactions were quite undeveloped. Some limited administrative pronouncements dealt with the possible methods of translation for foreign income of branches and a number of court cases had come to conflicting conclusions as to the appropriate treatment of foreign currency gain or loss.[1] In the 1986 Act a comprehensive set of rules dealing with foreign exchange issues was introduced.

10.2 Basic concepts

10.2.1 FUNCTIONAL CURRENCY AND QUALIFIED BUSINESS UNIT

Section 985(a) provides that income determinations are initially to be made in the taxpayer's "functional currency." The functional currency identifies the "base" currency in which the results of the taxpayer's economic activities are

---

1. Rev. Rul. 75-106, 1975-1 Cum. Bull. 31 ("net worth" method); Rev. Rul. 75-107, 1975-1 Cum. Bull. 32 ("profit and loss" method); *see, e.g., National Standard Co. v. Commissioner*, 80 TC 551 (1983), aff'd, 749 F.2d 369 (6th Cir. 1984); *Gillin v. US*, 423 F.2d. 309 (Ct. Cl. 1970).

measured. As a general rule, Section 985 establishes the US dollar as the functional currency and all relevant computations are made in dollars.[2] However, in the case of a "qualified business unit", the functional currency is the currency of the economic environment in which the unit conducts its activities and in which it keeps its books and records. Thus, for example, if a US bank has a branch in France, the functional currency for computing the income of the branch would be the French franc.

The same taxpayer can have several qualified business units, each of which has a different functional currency. Thus if a US corporation has a branch operation in Switzerland and a second branch operation in Sweden, the functional currency of each branch will be the local currency while the functional currency of the head office would be the dollar.[3] Similarly, if a Swiss corporation has a branch operation in the US, the functional currency of the US branch would be the dollar. Detailed Regulations define "qualified business unit" and determine the appropriate functional currency for the unit. In general, the Regulations require that the activities be a "separate and clearly identified unit" of the taxpayer's trade or business, for example, the foreign sales branch of a domestic manufacturing company, for which separate books and records are maintained.[4] The currency which is accepted for US financial accounting purposes generally will be accepted for tax purposes.[5]

10.2.2 TRANSLATION OF FOREIGN CURRENCY INCOME AND FOREIGN TAXES INTO DOLLARS

10.2.2.1 *Translation of branch operations*

If, under the rules discussed in 10.2.1, the taxpayer (or a part of its activities constituting a qualified business unit) has established a foreign currency as its functional currency, as an initial matter it will calculate its income in the functional currency. After that, some method must be provided to translate the income as determined in that currency into dollars to establish its US tax liability. Section 987 requires that the income as determined in the functional currency be translated into dollars at the "appropriate exchange rate." In the case of

---

2. Sec. 985(b)(1)(A). As a result, for most US taxpayers, transactions with foreign currency aspects (except for those specified in Sec. 988 discussed at 10.3.1) do not have any independent foreign exchange implications. The necessary calculations are simply made in dollars and there is no separate treatment of foreign currency gain or loss. See 10.3.3.
3. Treas. Reg. Sec. 1.985-1(f) Ex. 7.
4. Treas. Reg. Sec. 1.989(a)-1(b)(2). An individual's investment activities can constitute a "trade or business" for these purposes. Treas. Reg. Sec. 1.989(a)-1(c).
5. Treas. Reg. Sec. 1.985-1(c)(5).

branch operations, that rate is the "weighted average exchange rate" which has been administratively defined as the simple average of the daily exchange rates for the taxable year.[6]

Thus, for example, if a US corporation has a Swiss branch with the Swiss franc as its functional currency and has SFR4,000 of gross income and SFR1,000 of deductible expenses, the resulting SFR3,000 of taxable income will be translated into dollars by using the average exchange rate for the year and that dollar amount will be the amount includible in income for US tax purposes for the year.

This "profit and loss" method of translating branch income into dollars ignores any unrealized foreign exchange gain or loss on the taxpayer's invested capital. Under pre-1986 Act law, the taxpayer could elect to use a "net worth" or "balance sheet" method (instead of the profit and loss method) which took some portion of unrealized foreign exchange gain or loss into account currently. Since the method of translation under prior law was elective, taxpayers could elect to use the net worth method for operations expected to have unrealized exchange losses and the profit and loss method where unrealized exchange gains were anticipated. Congress viewed this elective treatment as inappropriate and established the profit and loss method as the only acceptable method. In recognition of the special problem of unrealized foreign exchange losses in hyperinflationary economies, however, taxpayers who meet certain requirements can elect to use the dollar as their functional currency, which has the effect of allowing exchange rate losses to be taken into account currently.[7]

Actual remittances of cash or other property have foreign exchange consequences if their value in terms of the functional currency of the head office differs from the functional currency "basis" in the amounts remitted. Assume a US taxpayer has a foreign branch with income of 100 units of foreign currency (FC) translated into dollars at a time when the average weighted dollar: FC exchange rate is 1:1. The FC 100 is later remitted to the US head office when the "spot" (current) exchange rate has changed to FC100=US$120. The US taxpayer must recognize $20 of foreign exchange gain due to the change in the dollar value of its unremitted profits between the time they were taken into account for US tax purposes and the time they were remitted. The gain is ordinary income sourced at the location of the branch activities. The Regulations have detailed rules establishing "pools" of invested capital and unremitted earnings to be used in accounting for remittances.[8]

---

6. Sec. 987(2), 989(b)(4); Treas. Reg. Sec. 1.989(b)-1.
7. Treas. Reg. Sec. 1.985-1(b)(2)(ii)(A); 1.985-3. This "US dollar approximate separate transaction method"("DASTM") option is especially important for banks which have branch operations in countries with high rates of inflation and in which substantial amounts of capital are at risk.
8. Treas. Reg. Sec. 1.987-5(d).

10.2.2.2   Translation of corporate earnings and profits

If a foreign corporation which uses a foreign currency as its functional currency makes a distribution to a US shareholder, the earnings and profits of the corporation are first computed in the corporation's functional currency in order to determine if the distribution will be treated as "out of earnings and profits" and hence a dividend for tax purposes.(See 2.2.6). The amount of the actual foreign currency dividend distribution is then translated to dollars at the exchange rate in effect at the time the dividend is included in income by the shareholder.[9] In effect, exchange rate gain or loss in the period between the time the income is earned and the time it is distributed is treated as an increase or decrease in earnings and profits. The earnings and profits as determined in the functional currency are reduced by the functional currency amount of the dividend distribution.

In the case of the inclusion of the undistributed earnings of a foreign corporation by a US shareholder under subpart F or the foreign personal holding company provisions, the foreign corporation's earnings as calculated in the functional currency are translated into dollars at the weighted average exchange rate. The actual distribution of previously taxed income can give rise to exchange rate gain or loss measured by any change in exchange rates between the date of inclusion and the date of distribution.[10] For example, if a US shareholder is required to include $100 of income under the applicable weighted exchange rate and subsequently the foreign income is distributed at a time when the dollar has weakened so that the foreign currency dividend is worth $125, the additional $25 is includible at the time of distribution as ordinary income with a foreign source.[11]

10.2.2.3   Translation of foreign tax credits

In general, for foreign tax credit purposes, foreign taxes are translated at the exchange rate in effect when the taxes are paid or accrued, depending on the taxpayer's method of accounting. If there is a difference between the dollar amount accrued and the amount actually paid, appropriate adjustments must be made.[12] In the case of dividend distributions which carry with them the deemed paid credit, the amount of the credit is based on the exchange rate at the time

---

9. Sec. 986(a); 989(b)(1).
10. Sec. 986(c).
11. Sec. 986(c)(1). The distributing foreign corporation would not recognize any additional income under Section 311 (see 2.2.6) since it is distributing its functional currency which, in its hands, should not be treated as appreciated property. The US taxpayer would increase its basis in the CFC shares by $100 at the time of the initial income inclusion and reduce it by the same amount at the time of actual distribution. The $25 currency gain does not affect the basis of the CFC shares.
12. Sec. 905(c).

the tax is paid. This means that the dividend inclusion will be calculated at the exchange rate applicable when the distribution is made while the foreign tax credit is translated at the historical rate in effect when payment of the tax was made.[13] Under prior law, both amounts were translated at the current rate.[14] Allowing the amount of the foreign tax credit to change due to fluctuations in exchange rates after the time of payment was viewed by Congress as inappropriate since the taxpayer no longer has any foreign exchange exposure after the foreign tax has been paid.

10.3   Transactions in a nonfunctional currency

In the situations considered so far, the foreign exchange issues have principally involved translating gains and losses when two different functional currencies were involved for one taxpayer or related taxpayers, for example, a US company with a foreign branch or a foreign corporation with a US shareholder. However, if the taxpayer, having one currency as its functional currency, engages in particular transactions which involve another currency (a "nonfunctional currency")a new set of issues arise. In addition to the income or loss on the underlying transaction expressed in terms of the nonfunctional currency, the taxpayer may also have foreign currency gain or loss because of the change in exchange rates between the functional and nonfunctional currency. From the perspective of the functional currency, the nonfunctional currency is a commodity which can independently generate gains and losses. For example, suppose a US taxpayer with the dollar as its functional currency purchases an asset for NF1,000 when $100 = NF100.[15] Later, when the exchange rate has changed to $100 = NF80, it sells the asset for NF1,000. Economically, the taxpayer has engaged in two transactions: the purchase of an asset which did not change in intrinsic value and the sale of which produces no gain or loss and a foreign currency transaction on which, viewed from the perspective of the dollar as the functional currency, the taxpayer has a foreign currency gain of $250.[16] Or suppose the taxpayer borrows NF1,000 when the exchange rate is $100 = NF100

---

13. Sec. 989(c)(4); 986(b). In the case of branch income and income inclusions based on subpart F and the foreign personal holding company rules, there will also be a difference between the weighted average rate on which the inclusion is based and the rate applicable to the taxes paid, but the potential for differences will not be as great as in the case of deemed paid foreign tax credits associated with actual dividends where the date of income inclusion can lag substantially behind the date of payment of the foreign taxes.

14. *Bon Ami v. Commissioner*, 39 BTA 825 (1939).

15. In the text examples, the nonfunctional currency will be indicated as NF, for example NF1,000 = $1,000, and the taxpayer is assumed to have the dollar as its functional currency.

16. That is, the NF1,000 which the taxpayer receives back at the end of the transaction is worth $250 more than the initial dollar investment despite the fact that the value of the investment in terms of NF has not changed.

and repays the loan later when the rate is $100 = NF200. Viewed from the perspective of the dollar, the taxpayer has $500 of gain attributable solely to the change in exchange rates.

Prior to 1986, there was no direct guidance in the statute on the appropriate tax treatment of such transactions and the limited case law authority reached conflicting results. Section 988 provides the framework for dealing with these issues.

10.3.1 "SECTION 988 TRANSACTIONS"

Section 988 defines certain transactions as "section 988 transactions." In general terms, Section 988 covers three types of transactions: (1) borrowing or lending a nonfunctional currency or acquiring a nonfunctional currency obligation; (2) accruing for tax purposes an item of expense or income expressed in a nonfunctional currency; and (3) acquiring and disposing of nonfunctional currency directly.[17]

Where a Section 988 transaction is involved, a portion of the gain or loss may be treated as foreign currency gain or loss. For example, suppose a US taxpayer invests NF250 in a bond when the exchange rate is $100 = NF100 and later sells the bond for NF300 when the exchange rate is $100 = NF125. Economically, the taxpayer has a gain of $40 (NF50 × .8 = $40) on the investment in the bond but an exchange loss of $50 (NF250 invested = $250; NF250 received on disposition = $200) for an overall loss on the Section 988 transaction of $10.

Section 988(b) establishes the source and character of the gain or loss on the Section 988 transaction. The foreign currency gain or loss is treated as ordinary income or loss and sourced at the residence of the taxpayer or the location of the qualified business unit in connection with which the gain or loss is associated. In the above example, the $10 of loss is treated as a foreign currency loss and is an ordinary loss. In effect, the statute nets the investment gain of $40 and the currency loss of $50 and treats the net loss as a currency loss. The $10 loss would be US source unless it arose in a foreign qualified business unit, in which case it would be foreign source.[18]

---

17. Forward contracts and the like involving foreign currency are discussed below at 10.3.2.
18. Sec. 988(a)(1)(a); 988(a)(3). Sourcing foreign currency gain or loss at the residence of the taxpayer in the absence of a foreign qualified business unit means that the gain or loss will not affect the numerator of the foreign tax credit fraction. See 6.6.2. This is the appropriate result since this gain or loss will not be subject to tax by the foreign jurisdiction. From that country's perspective, there has been no gain or loss on the transaction and hence no question of double or undertaxation arises. Allowing any gain to be treated as foreign source (as was arguably possible under pre-1986 law) would artificially inflate the foreign tax credit limitation.

Continuing the example, if the bond had been sold for NF400, the investment gain would have been $120 (NF150 × .8 = $120), the exchange loss would have been $50, and the overall gain $70. In this case, the source and character of the overall gain would be determined under normal rules; no foreign exchange gain or loss is involved after the netting process.

Similar principles apply to accounts payable or receivable denominated in a nonfunctional currency. Suppose a taxpayer with the dollar as its functional currency sends a bill for NF1,000 for services performed abroad when the exchange rate is $100 = NF100. When the bill is later collected, the exchange rate is $100 = NF80. Under Section 988, the taxpayer would have $1000 of foreign source services income and $250 of US source foreign currency gain.

10.3.2 FOREIGN EXCHANGE FUTURES CONTRACTS, HEDGES AND OTHER FINANCIAL TRANSACTIONS

Section 988 and the corresponding Regulations provide extremely complex rules dealing with foreign exchange forward contracts, futures contracts, options and similar financial instruments which are often used by taxpayers both to trade in a foreign currency and to hedge against exposure to fluctuating exchange rates. In general terms, entering into such contracts constitutes a "Section 988 transaction" and thus the gains or losses on the contracts will be subject to the source and character rules of Section 988. Section 988 also applies to "notional principal contracts" if the payments under the contract are determined with reference to a nonfunctional currency.[19] If a currency swap contract is disposed of, the resulting gain or loss is subject to Section 988.[20]

Section 988(d) has a special rule for fully hedged transactions where the taxpayer has in effect completely eliminated the risk of currency fluctuation and ensured itself a cash flow or expense in its functional currency. In such cases, the foreign currency aspects of the transaction are ignored. For example, a fully hedged foreign currency borrowing which locks in a dollar cost is treated as a dollar borrowing with dollar interest payments. Suppose, for example, that a US taxpayer whose functional currency is the dollar borrows French francs but immediately hedges the currency risk of having to make payments with more expensive francs (in dollar terms) by entering into forward contracts to purchase the francs it will need to pay its franc-based obligations. If the taxpayer properly identifies the transaction as a hedge, the hedge transaction will be integrated with the borrowing as a "synthetic debt instrument" denominated in

---

19. Treas. Reg. Sec. 1.988-1(a)(2)(iii)(B)(1). The definition of "notional principal contracts" includes swaps, caps, collars and the like where payments are determined with reference to a notional principal amount calculated with reference to a particular index. Treas. Reg. Sec. 1.988-2(e) deals with currency swaps where the notional amounts are in foreign currencies.
20. Treas. Reg. Sec. 1.988-2(e)(3).

the currency to be paid under the hedge. In this example that approach results in a dollar denominated borrowing and no exchange rate gain or loss is generated since the dollar is the taxpayer's functional currency.[21]

10.3.3 OTHER TRANSACTIONS

Section 988 deals only with certain specifically enumerated transactions. For all other transactions, gain or loss is determined with reference to the taxpayer's functional currency and there is no separate computation of foreign currency gain or loss. Thus with respect to tangible property and financial assets not covered by Section 988, foreign currency gain or loss is treated as part of the gain or loss on the underlying transaction. For example, if a dollar-based US taxpayer invests NF1,000 in the stock of a foreign company when the exchange rate is $100 = NF100 and sells the stock for NF1,000 when the exchange rate is $100 = NF80, the $250 of gain calculated in dollars is treated as attributable to the stock investment and the source and character of the gain are not affected by Section 988. Section 988 also has no application to personal, non-commercial transactions,[22] with the result that gains are taxable but losses are not deductible.[23]

---

21. Treas. Reg. Sec. 1.988-5(a)(9)(ii).
22. Sec. 988(e).
23. *See Quijano v. United States*, 93 F.3d 26 (1st Cir. 1996) where the taxpayer borrowed in a foreign currency to purchase a residence which was later sold at a gain. The taxpayer used the exchange rate at the time the property was purchased to calculate tax basis and the exchange rate at the time of the sale to calculate the amount realized. Due to changes in the exchange rate, the taxpayer realized a loss on the repayment of the mortgage. The exchange loss on the mortgage was not deductible as a Section 988 transaction since it involved a personal transaction and the court refused to integrate the lending and purchasing transactions to net the gain and loss. After 1997, currency gains on personal transactions are excluded from income up to $200 of gain. For these purposes, travel expenses on a business trip are treated as personal expenses. *See* Sec. 988(e).

Chapter 11
Income tax treaties

11.1 Background

The US has entered into numerous bilateral income tax conventions[1] and a few estate and gift tax conventions. The following material will focus on the extent to which the tax treaty provisions modify the otherwise applicable US tax rules discussed in the preceding chapters. Two points must be kept in mind at the outset, however. First, each of the individual treaties represents a separate and independent source of law. Hence a particular question may be resolved one way in Treaty A, another way in Treaty B and not dealt with at all in Treaty C. Second, since the treaties are not uniform, it is sometimes difficult to use the interpretation of one treaty as precedent in a case arising under another treaty. Nonetheless, the treaties show common patterns and are all based, to a greater or lesser degree, on the pioneering Organization for Economic Cooperation and Development Model Convention. There is also a Model US Convention, revised and updated in 1996, which has many features in common with the OECD model.[2] Thus in many areas there is a kind of treaty "common law" which is reflected in the pattern of individual treaties.

11.2 Treaty objectives and techniques

US tax treaties, like those of all countries, deal basically with the problems of double taxation which result when two countries assert taxing jurisdiction over the same persons or transactions. Since this problem is dealt with unilaterally by most countries either in the form of a foreign tax credit or an exemption for foreign source income, the treaties by and large operate to refine and adapt

---

1. While the international agreements here considered are technically conventions, following common usage, they will also be referred to as tax treaties or simply treaties.
2. The 1996 United States Model Convention (the "US Model") superseded the 1981 Model and is accompanied by a very helpful Technical Explanation ("US Technical Explanation") which sets out the US understanding of the positions taken in the US Model. The OECD Model Convention is now issued in a loose-leaf form with periodic supplements, reflecting mostly changes to the Commentary on the Convention.

these methods for avoiding international double taxation to the specifics of the tax relationships between the two countries involved.

Several basic techniques are used in US tax treaties. Most important, a reduction in or exemption from the foreign tax otherwise applicable to US taxpayers is negotiated with the treaty partner on a reciprocal basis. This negotiation usually involves the country of source ceding taxing jurisdiction in whole or in part to the country of residence. In addition, the treaties attempt to clarify and modify the otherwise applicable principles involved in the application of the US foreign tax credit to insure that, to the extent possible, the provision achieves its objective of eliminating tax barriers to foreign investment by US residents. In addition, the treaty partner obligates itself to grant to its residents some form of relief from double taxation (foreign tax credit or exemption) on investment in the US by its taxpayers. This provision removes double tax barriers to investment in the US by treaty country residents. Finally, the treaties attempt to coordinate the administration of the tax laws of the two countries by adopting various procedures for consultation on outstanding tax issues and for the exchange of information.

11.3   Status of treaties

Under Article VI, Section 2 of the United States Constitution, international treaties and legislative enactments are of equal force. As a result, where treaties and legislative provisions conflict, the later in time prevails. This means that, in principle, the United States through subsequently enacted legislation can override an inconsistent treaty provision. In so acting, of course, it is breaching the international law obligation which it undertook to its treaty partner. Historically, there have been very few instances of the legislative override of treaties. Beginning in the 1980's, however, Congress showed a greater inclination to override treaties through legislative enactments, despite the violation of international law which such action entails. In addition, subsequent legislation has attempted to affect the principles pursuant to which the relations between treaties and domestic law are interpreted.

Because the legislative override of treaty obligations has important foreign policy implications, the courts have been reluctant to hold that treaty obligations have been legislatively abrogated in the absence of a clear Congressional statement of that intent.[3] In the context of tax treaties, this principle has tradi-

---

3. *See Cook v. United States*, 288 US 102 (1933). There the Supreme Court stated: "A treaty will not be deemed to be abrogated or modified by a later statute unless such purpose on the part of Congress has clearly been expressed." 288 US at 120. *See also*, Restatement (Third) of Foreign Relations Law of the United States Sec. 114(1).

tionally been interpreted to require that there must be some indication in the legislative history of the overriding statutory enactment that Congress intends that the later legislative pronouncement should control over prior inconsistent treaty obligations.[4]

The question of the relation between treaties and legislation was expressly addressed in 1988 legislation, though the exact effect of the enactment on prior practice is not entirely clear. Section 7852(d)(1) provides: "For purposes of determining the relationship between a provision of a treaty and any law of the United States affecting revenue, neither the treaty nor the law shall have preferential status by reason of its being a treaty or law." In addition, Section 894(a), which previously stated expressly that any income exempted by treaty remained exempt despite any Code provision to the contrary, was amended to state only that Code provisions should be applied with "due regard" to US treaty obligations. The legislative history of these two provisions indicates that their purpose was to give to treaties "[t]hat regard which [they] are due under the ordinary rules of interpreting the interactions of statutes and treaties."[5] The extent to which these legislative changes will in fact affect the relation between treaties and statutes remains for the courts to decide in the context of particular situations of conflict which may arise in the future.

In addition to dealing with the general question of the relation between treaties and the Code, the 1988 legislation expressly provided that some treaty obligations were intended to be overridden by provisions of the Tax Reform Act of 1986. For example, the restriction in the alternative minimum tax foreign tax credit that the credit be allowed only to the extent of 90 per cent of the US taxpayer's US liability is to prevail over treaty obligations which require full double tax relief.[6]

For whatever reason, Congress has seemed to be acting somewhat more responsibly in recent years as regards treaty overrides, perhaps in part because of the reactions of its treaty partners to past overrides.

---

4. *See, e.g.*, Rev. Rul. 80-223, 1980-2 Cum. Bull. 217.

5. H. Rep. 100-1104, 100th Cong., 2d Sess. 16 (1988). The House of Representatives version of the legislation contained a "residual" override provision which would have given the 1986 Act precedence over any conflicting treaty obligation even if the conflict had not been specifically identified. The House Report took the position that *Cook v. US*, note 3 above, did not require as a general matter that Congress specifically advert to treaty conflicts for the subsequent legislation to override treaty obligations. H. Rep. 100-795, 100th Cong., 2d Sess. 305 (1988). The Conference Committee Report reference to the "ordinary rules" of interpretation may be viewed as reaffirming the traditional *Cook* approach.

6. 1988 Act Sec. 1012(aa)(2)(B). *See Robert Lindsey v. Commissioner*, 98 TC 672 (1992), aff'd without opinion, 15 F.3d 1160 (DC Cir. 1994) upholding the override. The other 1986 Act changes in the foreign tax credit are also to prevail over conflicting treaty rules. On the other hand, treaty rules prevail over the changes in the source of income rules in Sec. 865(e)(2)(5.3.5). 1988 Act Sec. 1012(aa)(3)(A)(ii).

11.4 Qualification for treaty benefits

11.4.1 PERSONS COVERED

The various benefits contained in US tax treaties are generally provided to "residents," both natural and juridical, of the countries involved. Residence is typically defined in terms of a person or entity being liable to worldwide taxation on the basis of a personal connection with the taxing jurisdiction.[7] Some treaties provide a more detailed definition of residence for treaty purposes, dealing with special situations such as tax exempt organizations, pension funds and the like. In the absence of a special definition, reference is presumably made to the law of the country involved to determine whether the particular individual or organization claiming treaty benefits qualifies as a resident.[8]

11.4.1.1 "Tie Breaker" clause

The Model Treaty, art. 4.2, also provides for a "tie breaker" which establishes a single residence for treaty purposes if, under the definitional article, the taxpayer would be a resident of both countries. The details of the tie breaker provision, which is contained in most modern treaties, differs from treaty to treaty. The general approach is to select and give priorities to various personal connections between the taxpayer and the two countries in order to establish a single residence.

In the case of corporations, a problem of dual residence often arises where the US determines corporate residence on the basis of the place of incorporation while the other jurisdiction applies a place of management test. The Model Treaty, as would be expected, selects the place of incorporation as controlling. If the treaty partner is not willing to agree to this version of the tie breaker, the treaty may specifically exclude the dual resident corporation from treaty benefits.[9]

---

7. US Model, art.4. The fact that the US imposes worldwide taxation on the basis of citizenship raises some special problems in the definition of residence for treaty purposes. Some countries are reluctant to grant treaty benefits to persons who, while US citizens, have no significant connection with the US even though they are subject to worldwide US taxation and thus are in the same situation as residents generally. Some treaties exclude US citizens from resident status in these circumstances. *See, e.g.*, Sweden, art. 4.1(flush language) [All US treaties are cited by the name of the treaty partner.]
8. For a case involving the question of residence for purposes of the Swiss treaty in which a Swiss administrative determination as to residence was not followed by a US court, *see Johansson v. US*, 336 F.2d 809 (5th Cir. 1964).
9. *See, e.g.*, Australia, art. 3.1.(g).

11.4.1.2 *"Hybrid" entities*

The appropriate treatment of so-called "hybrid" entities has long been a vexing problem in determining qualification for treaty benefits and there is as of yet no international consensus on the issue. The US Model Treaty adopts an innovative approach to the problem. It determines treaty residence (and hence entitlement to benefits) with reference to the person who, under the laws of the treaty partner, is required to include the item in question in income.[10] This determination controls regardless of the treatment of the entity in the jurisdiction of the payor. Thus, for example, if a US corporation pays a dividend to a foreign entity which is treated as fiscally transparent in the other jurisdiction, the participants in that entity who are treaty country residents will be entitled to the benefits of this treaty even if, under US principles, the entity itself would have been the relevant taxpayer. Similarily, if a US payor makes a payment to an entity which the US treats as a partnership but the other jurisdiction treats as a corporation, treaty relief will depend on whether the income is liable to tax in the treaty country in the hands of the entity. Section 894(c); Temp. Treas. Reg. Sec. 1.894-1T.

11.4.1.3 *"Saving clause"*

Most US treaties contain a so-called "saving clause" which in general allows the US to continue to tax its citizens and residents as if the treaty had not come into effect[11] As a result of the saving clause, even though a particular treaty article may, by its terms, appear to assign exclusive taxing jurisdiction of a particular type of income to the country of source, the saving clause would operate to deny that benefit to a US citizen or resident.

On the other hand, the treaties generally provide that they may not operate to the detriment of the taxpayers covered by the treaty. Accordingly, in general the benefits of a provision of the Internal Revenue Code cannot be limited by a more restrictive treaty provision. For example, if a treaty authorizes a withholding tax on interest but interest payments to nonresidents are exempt under the Code, the treaty will not operate to impose a tax. However, there are limi-

---

10. US Model, art. 4.1(d).
11. US Model, art. 1.4. There are usually exceptions in the saving clauses which allow US citizens or residents to claim treaty benefits under the "relief from double taxation" article, the "nondiscrimination" article, the mutual agreement procedure and some other specialized articles. In addition, the article determining residence for treaty purposes is itself generally excepted from the saving clause. Thus, an alien who is a US resident under the Code definition of residence (5.4.2) but a resident only of the treaty country under the treaty tie breaker rule would not be subject to the saving clause.

tations on the taxpayer's ability to select the most favorable of Code or treaty rules. Where a treaty benefit is subject to limitations which are not present in the Code, the taxpayer cannot claim the treaty benefit and at the same time apply the more generous Code limitations.[12]

11.4.2   DISCLOSURE REQUIREMENTS

Section 6614 requires that any taxpayer taking the position that a treaty provision overrides or modifies a Code provision must disclose the position taken on its return or, if no return is required, must otherwise disclose the position in a manner to be determined by the Internal Revenue Service, presumably in Regulations. Section 6712 imposes fines for failure to comply with the disclosure requirements.

11.4.3   LIMITATION ON TREATY BENEFITS

11.4.3.1   Background

All US treaties extend treaty benefits to corporations and other juridical persons which qualify as residents of the treaty partner. As a result, individuals or corporations from third countries could in principle obtain the benefits of a particular treaty by forming a corporation in the treaty country.[13] This course could be advantageous for the third-country investor if there were no treaty between the US and his country or if the third-country treaty had less favorable terms. The US has always had certain restrictions on the ability of third-country residents to "treaty shop" by using a corporation formed in a jurisdiction having a favorable treaty with the US.[14] The scope and importance of such limitations, how-

---

12. US Model, art. 1.2; Rev. Rul. 84-17, 1984-1 Cum. Bull. 308. For a discussion of other aspects of this "cherry picking" problem, see US Technical Explanation, art. 1. para. 1.

13. The treaty benefits involved would typically be the reduction or elimination of US source-based taxation on outbound payments such as dividends, interest, and royalties. In addition, business income could escape US tax if the treaty country corporation was engaged in business in the US but did not have a US permanent establishment.

14. *See, e.g., Aiken Industries, Inc. v. Commissioner*, 56 TC 925 (1971) (interest income was not "received by" a treaty country corporation owned by non-treaty country residents where the corporation was obligated to pay out a corresponding amount in a back-to-back loan transaction; hence the interest did not qualify for treaty benefits). In addition, the so-called "anti-conduit" Regulations issued in 1995 give the IRS the authority to disregard the participation of an intermediate treaty-benefited participant in a financing transaction if the structure is part of a tax avoidance plan. The Regulations would apply to the "classic" back-to-back loan through a treaty conduit as well as to more complex financial schemes. *See* Treas. Reg. Sec. 1.881-3. The US regards these rules as consistent with limitation of benefits principles and with tax treaties generally. Under the anti-conduit rules, the "real" taxpayer is identified; the limitation of benefits rules then determine if the taxpayer so identified is still entitled to treaty benefits. US Technical Explanation, art. 22. para. 2.

ever, have increased dramatically in recent years and the insistence on an extensive limitation on benefits article is a hallmark of current US treaty policy.[15]

Historically, limitations on treaty benefits were usually imposed if the treaty corporation was subject to a special tax regime in its home country and, more generally, if the "principal purpose" of establishing the treaty corporation was to obtain treaty benefits.[16] However, an anti-treaty shopping policy was not actively pursued prior to the 1980's and, indeed, both the Treasury Department and the Internal Revenue Service in effect encouraged treaty shopping in some circumstances.[17]

Beginning with the inclusion of a restrictive limitation on benefits article in the Model Treaty in 1981, the US has shown a much greater concern with treaty shopping issues in recent years. All of its post-1981 treaties have had substantial restrictions on treaty shopping and Congress has indicated that it will not approve a treaty which does not contain such provisions.[18]

11.4.3.2   Structure of limitation on benefits article

While the details of the limitation on benefits provisions vary substantially, they generally provide a "safe haven" test based on share ownership by treaty country residents coupled with restrictions to insure that the corporation has not reduced its tax base in the residence country through deductible payments. If the treaty country corporation has substantial resident share ownership[19] and does not make extensive deductible payments to third country residents who are not entitled to treaty benefits[20] it is fair to assume that the corporation was

---

15. US Technical Explanation, art. 22 sets out the policy rationale for the limitation on benefits approach.
16. *See, e.g.*, Luxembourg, art. 15.
17. Prior to the repeal of the withholding tax on portfolio interest, US corporate borrowers utilized the treaty with the Netherlands Antilles to avoid the US withholding tax on interest payments to nonresident lenders. The Treasury Department indirectly supported these treaty shopping activities because of balance of payments considerations and the Internal Revenue Service issued a number of favorable rulings involving Netherlands Antilles finance companies. The termination of the Netherlands Antilles treaty in 1988 put an end to such transactions.
18. In addition to anti-treaty shopping rules in the treaties, the 1986 Act imposed special statutory rules involving treaty shopping in connection with the branch profits tax. As discussed at 11.10 below, in some cases the nondiscrimination articles of treaties can prohibit the imposition of the branch profits tax. However, Sec. 884(e) provides that the branch profits tax will nonetheless be applicable, despite treaty provisions to the contrary, unless the foreign corporation is a "qualified resident" of the treaty country. "Qualified resident" is defined in terms of share ownership and base erosion safe havens with a more generalized test based on the active conduct of a trade or business in the treaty country. Treas. Reg. Sec. 1.884-5. If a corporation qualifies under a treaty-based limitation on benefits test contained in a treaty entered into after December 31, 1986, it will likewise be treated as a qualified resident under Sec. 884. Treas. Reg. Sec. 1.884-4(b)(8).
19. US Model, art. 22.(2)(f)(i) has a "more than 50%" test.
20. US Model, art. 22.(2)(f)(ii) requires that less than 50% of the gross income be paid out to nonqualified persons. This restriction is focused on "conduit" companies which receive treaty-benefited income and then pay it out in deductible payments which are not subject to treaty country

not established in the treaty jurisdiction simply to obtain treaty benefits and that treaty shopping is not involved.

If the shareholder/base erosion test cannot be met, under most recent treaties the corporation can still qualify for treaty benefits if the corporation is engaged in an active trade or business in the residence country and derives income from the source state connected with that business.[21] The business presence in the source state is deemed to insure that the treaty shopping is not present as long as the income in question arises as part of that business. Similarly, if the stock of the corporation is traded (more than 50%)on a recognized stock exchange, again treaty shopping is assumed to be absent.[22] A number of other specialized rules dealing with headquarters companies, management companies and internationally owned joint ventures are contained in various forms in some treaties.[23] Finally, if none of the explicit tests can be met, competent authority relief may be available.[24]

11.4.4   OVERALL EVALUATION OF LIMITATION ON BENEFITS PROVISIONS

Limitations on treaty benefits raise some difficult issues of tax treaty policy. The developments in the US undoubtedly have been influenced by the existence in the past of tax treaties with tax haven countries. These treaties provided treaty benefits to third country investors having no real economic connection (and making no significant tax payments(!)) to the treaty country. It clearly is undesirable for the US to have a "treaty with the world" through a tax haven. Beyond this generalization, however, the question is how to define a "real" corporation in a treaty jurisdiction which should be entitled to treaty benefits. The present rules, with their various surrogate tests to insure that treaty shopping is not involved, offer one approach to the problem. How well it will work in practice will depend in large part on how the Internal Revenue Service and the foreign tax authorities administer the provisions. It must be noted that the US is something of an "outlier" in this area, especially in its insistence on a detailed limitations articles in all cases, even when a "serious" and high tax country is involved where the possibility of treaty shopping would be highly unlikely.

The limitation on benefits articles also raise a number of practical problems

---

withholding tax. The third country recipients thus indirectly get the benefit of the initial reduction in US source taxation and pay no offsetting tax in the treaty country of residence.

21. US Model, art. 22.3. For example, interest on short-term investment in working capital would qualify under this test, as would interest on trade receivables.
22. US Model, art. 22.2(c).
23. *See, e.g.*, Netherlands, art. 26.3-.5; Switzerland, art. 22.3-4; Austria, 16.1(f)-(h).
24. US Model, art. 22.4.

of enforcement. The withholding agent is not usually in a position to determine if the payee is covered by the treaty shopping provision. The payee's status may change from year-to-year due to changes in share ownership and in income mix. Some type of certification (or refund) system might be possible but only with substantial administrative cost and interruption to international income flows.

11.4.5 TAXES COVERED

The US treaties generally cover Federal income taxes but are not extended to state and municipal levies. Social security taxes are expressly excluded in the Model Treaty.[25]

11.5 Treatment of business income

11.5.1 IN GENERAL

As discussed in Chapter 5, a nonresident alien or foreign corporation is generally taxed on business income from US sources at the usual US tax rates. Technically, the tax is imposed on all income which is effectively connected with the foreign taxpayer's US trade or business. This Code treatment of business income is modified by US treaties. In general, the treaties provide that a foreign taxpayer will not be taxed on business income unless that income is attributable to a permanent establishment located in the US.[26] If no permanent establishment is present, business income which would otherwise be subject to US tax is exempt under the treaty.

Conversely, a US taxpayer who realizes business income in a foreign country with which the US has a treaty will be taxed in that country only if the income is attributable to a permanent establishment located there. While the foreign taxes attributable to the foreign business profits would generally qualify for the

---

25. US Model, art. 2.1(a). The original version of the present treaty with the United Kingdom did not deal directly with state taxation but did have a provision which would have prevented the assertion of state taxing jurisdiction based on the so-called worldwide "unitary" apportionment method. Under the original treaty provision, a state could only tax on the basis of a method that confined its jurisdiction to the particular operation located within the state. The proposed provision proved controversial and led to a reservation on the part of the US Senate with respect to the provision in its consideration of the treaty. The treaty was ultimately ratified without the provision. See also the Exchange of Notes in connection with the 1985 Italian treaty in which the US agreed to reopen discussions with Italy if a provision on unitary tax acceptable to the Senate can be devised. Generally, the "nondiscrimination" articles of US treaties do extend to state taxes. 11.10.
26. US Model, art. 7.1.

foreign tax credit, the exemption is nonetheless important to the US taxpayer. In the first place, it frees the US taxpayer from the burdens of filing and paying foreign taxes which it would then subsequently credit. More important, it allows it to avoid any problems of the possible nonapplication of the foreign tax credit. For example, suppose the foreign country's concept of source of income differed from that of the US. The income could be subject to foreign taxation but not qualify as foreign source income for purposes of the foreign tax credit provisions. The exemption for business income absent a permanent establishment avoids such problems.

11.5.2   PERMANENT ESTABLISHMENT

The definitions of permanent establishment in the various US treaties are similar in outline but differ substantially in detail. In general, a permanent establishment may take the form of an office or other fixed place of business or a resident agent of the taxpayer with authority to enter into contractual relationships or who fills orders from a stock of goods located in the agent's country. On the other hand, an agent of "independent status" will not constitute a permanent establishment.[27] Beyond these general principles, many treaties enumerate in detail the types of activities which will or will not constitute a permanent establishment, reflecting to some extent the special circumstances of the economic relationships between the contracting states. Thus, for example, the Norwegian treaty deals at some length with the treatment of offshore drilling operations.[28]

Most treaties provide that a domestic subsidiary corporation of the foreign taxpayer will not "of itself" be treated as a permanent establishment, though the subsidiary's activities on behalf of the parent could cross the permanent establishment threshold. The permanent establishment of a partnership is attributed to the partners.[29]

An important issue in connection with permanent establishment definition is the treatment of "electronic commerce." For example, is a computer server located in the US a permanent establishment? This and similar questions are under study by national governments and international organizations with no clear answers yet emerging.[30]

---

27. *See Taisei Fire & Marine Ins. Co. v. Commissioner*, 104 TC 535 (1995) (US corporation which did reinsurance business for four unrelated Japanese insurance companies had independent status; the US company was legally and economically independent from the Japanese companies).
28. Norway, art. 4A.
29. *Donroy, Ltd. v. US*, 301 F.2d 200 (9th Cir. 1962).
30. *See, e.g., US Treas. Dep't White Paper on Tax Policy Implications of Global Electronic Commerce* (Nov. 1996). The OECD has under study the international aspects of electronic commerce.

11.5.3   BUSINESS PROFITS

The permanent establishment exemption applies in general only to the business income of the foreign taxpayer. Older US treaties use the expression "industrial or commercial profits" but the US Model and more modern treaties refer to "business profits."[31] The terms are defined with various degrees of specificity in the treaties.

11.5.4   "ATTRIBUTABLE TO"

The business profits which may be taxed because of the presence of a permanent establishment are generally limited to those which are "attributable to" the permanent establishment. The definition includes only profits actually generated by the permanent establishment; the limited force of attraction rule in Section 864(c)(3) (see 5.3.4) is not incorporated into the treaty concept. In general, US treaties by their terms treat the permanent establishment as if it were an independent entity engaged in arm's length dealings with third parties and the home office, rather than allocating the worldwide income of the enterprise on some formula basis.[32] Thus, in general, dealings between the permanent establishment and head office will be based on arm's length principles. See 8.1. However, the fiction of independence of head office and permanent establishment does not extend to "self-charged" expenses. Thus no income would be attributed (and no deduction allowed) for "interest" on a loan between head office and permanent establishment.[33] In addition, the US takes the position that as regards deductions of a permanent establishment, US allocation rules apply for treaty purposes, despite the general acceptance of the "independence" of the permanent establishment. Thus, for example, the deduction for interest expense is determined under Section 882 allocation principles and not on the basis of the interest expense actually booked and paid by the branch.[34] Many treaties contain an article which specifically allows as a deduction a portion of general executive and administrative expenses and other categories of expense incurred with respect to a branch operation.[35] These provisions are in response to the rules of a number of countries which do not allow a deduction for branch expenses not directly incurred in the branch country.

---

31. US Model, art. 7.1.
32. US Model, art. 7.2.
33. *See* US Technical Explanation, art. 7. para. 3.
34. Treas. Reg. Sec. 1.882-5(a)(3).
35. US Model, art.7.3

11.6 Treatment of investment income

11.6.1 IN GENERAL

As discussed in Chapter 5, investment-type income of a foreign taxpayer from US sources is generally taxed at a flat 30 per cent rate on the gross amount of the income. If the income is effectively connected with a US trade or business it is treated as business income and subject to normal rates on a net basis.

US treaties generally modify these rules by providing for a reciprocal reduction of rates (often to zero) for investment-type income. Typically the rates on dividends are reduced to fifteen per cent, with a five per cent rate applicable in the case of dividends paid by a subsidiary to a parent company.[36] The "second level" dividend tax is also usually eliminated for dividends paid by a treaty country corporation. Interest income is generally exempt (in the US Model) or subject to a five per cent rate. Royalties of various types also usually are exempt.

Where investment-type income is attributable to a permanent establishment, it is taxed typically under the business profits article.[37]

11.6.2 CLASSIFICATION ISSUES

The basic "schedular" approach of the treaties in classifying income in categories in order to apply the treaty rules raises some special issues. Thus, for example, while the line between business profits (to which the permanent establishment rule applies) and investment income (taxable at reduced rates) is generally clear, there are some difficult borderline situations. Consider, for example, the case of a commercial bank. Its income consists principally of interest which normally is treated as investment income. On the other hand, interest in the hands of a bank clearly represents business income. A similar problem exists with respect to leasing and rental activities. The banking situation is solved in the US Model by providing a zero rate on interest. Thus if a foreign bank receives interest which is not connected with a US permanent establishment, there is no US tax as would be the case for business profits of a commercial business. If the interest is connected to a US permanent establishment, it would be taxed on a net basis. In the case of the leasing of tangible property, the US Model classifies such income as business profits, not taxable in the absence of a permanent establishment.[38]

An important current classification issue involves the treatment of computer

---

36. The US Model requires a 10% level of shareholding for the reduced 5% rate to apply. Art. 10.2(a).
37. US Model, art. 10.6.
38. US Model, art. 7.7.

software. Depending on the circumstances, a transfer of software can involve a sale of goods (despite the formal structure of the transfer as a license), a royalty or the provision of services. Proposed Regulations offer guidance in the treatment of some commonly recurring fact patterns.[39]

A similar classification issue can arise where the two treaty jurisdictions treat the same payment differently. In Boulez v. Commissioner, 83 TC 584 (1984), the taxpayer received a payment which the US treated as referable to personal services performed in the US which, under the terms of the US-Germany treaty, the US as the source country had the right to tax. Germany classified the payment as a royalty which was exempt from source country taxation but taxable in Germany as the country of residence. The competent authorities of the two countries were unable to agree on the classification issue and the item of income was subject to tax in both jurisdictions with no double tax relief.

11.7   Real property

Income from real property may be taxed without treaty limitation by the source state. An election to have such income taxed on a net basis is provided. Taxation extends to gain on the disposition of directly held real estate and in addition, all modern treaties allow the source country to tax gain on the disposition of the stock of a corporation whose assets consist principally of real property located in the source country.[40]

11.8   Gains from the disposition of property

US treaties generally exempt from source taxation gains on the disposition of assets. However, gains from the disposition of property which are attributable to a permanent establishment or fixed base may be taxed by the source country.[41]

11.9   Treatment of personal services income

11.9.1   EMPLOYEES

Under the Code, a nonresident alien employee of a foreign employer not engaged in a US trade or business is not subject to US tax on compensation for labor or personal services performed in the US if the nonresident is not present

---

39. Prop. Treas. Reg. Sec. 1.861-18 (1996).
40. US Model, art. 6; art. 13.2(b).
41. US Model, art. 13.

within the US for more than 90 days in the taxable year and the compensation does not exceed $3,000. This exemption is liberalized in a number of US treaties. For example, in the US Model the time limit is extended to 183 days and there is no dollar limitation on the compensation which can be received without tax. However, the compensation must be paid by a foreign employer and not "borne by" the employer's permanent establishment within the US. Thus the exempted income will not have figured as a deduction in the accounts of the permanent establishment.[42]

Most treaties also contain special rules dealing with the taxation of students, professors, government service and others in special employment categories.[43]

11.9.2   INDEPENDENT PERSONAL SERVICES

If a nonresident alien individual performs independent personal services in the US, e.g. as a lawyer, under normally applicable Code principles he would be engaged in a US trade or business and would be subject to tax at normal rates. However, a number of treaties exempt such income from US taxation under varying conditions. For example, the US Model exempts income derived from independent personal services if the nonresident alien does not have a "fixed base" in the US for the purposes of performing his services.[44] This exemption does not apply, however, to the services of athletes or entertainers who are taxed if the amount received for performing activities in the source state exceeds $20,000 even though there is no connection to the source jurisdiction other than the preformance of the activity itself.[45]

11.9.3   COMPENSATION FOR PERSONAL SERVICES AS BUSINESS INCOME

As in the situations discussed in 11.6.2, there are some potential overlap problems concerning the treaty articles dealing with business profits and those dealing with personal services. Under the United Kingdom treaty, Article 7.7, the term "business profits" expressly includes "income from the furnishing of services". Thus, such income would be taxed to a foreign corporation only if it had a permanent establishment in the source state. However, the Article specifically excludes personal services performed by an employee or by an individual in an

---

42. US Model, art. 15.
43. US Model, art. 19 (government service).
44. US Model, art. 14. There is an obvious parallel between fixed base and the permanent establishment concept in connection with business profits. The two concepts are said to be "similar but not identical." US Technical Explanation, art. 14. para. 1.
45. US Model, art. 17.

independent capacity. Thus, the taxation of the employee individually would depend, not on the presence of a permanent establishment, but on the length of the stay in the US and satisfaction of the other conditions of Article 15. Similarly, in the case of a professional, taxation would turn on the presence of a fixed base.

A special rule is often provided for entertainers and athletes which prevents them from providing their services through a company (a "rent-a-star" company) which avoids tax because of the absence of a permanent establishment. Where the rule applies, the income can be taxed despite the lack of a permanent establishment.[46]

11.10   Foreign tax credit aspects

In accordance with the overall purpose of tax treaties to reduce international double taxation, the US in its treaties commits itself, with varying degrees of specificity, to grant its citizens and residents a foreign tax credit for the foreign income taxes paid to treaty countries. Correspondingly, the US insists that its treaty partners likewise provide some mechanism to their nationals for the relief of double taxation, by either granting a credit for US taxes or exempting income from US sources.

In addition, some US treaties clarify the operation of the foreign tax credit with respect to the taxes of the treaty partner. For example, Articles 10 and 23 of the United Kingdom treaty set out specific rules for dealing with the United Kingdom's "integrated" corporation tax and its treatment for foreign tax credit purposes.[47] Some treaties expressly give a credit for a foreign tax which arguably would not be creditable under the Code definition of an income tax.[48]

Sometimes the treaties modify source rules which would otherwise prevent the crediting of foreign taxes on items of income because, under normal US concepts, the income would be deemed to be from US sources.[49] Many treaties contain a general rule that any income which may be taxed by the source country under the treaty will be deemed to have its source in that country for purposes of the treaty credit article.[50] In a surprising change in policy, the 1996 US

---

46. US Model Treaty, art. 17.2.
47. For some interpretative difficulties with the article *see, Xerox Corp. v. US*, 41 F.3d 647 (Fed. Cir. 1994).
48. *See, e.g.,* United Kingdom, art. 23(4) (petroleum revenue tax).
49. *See, e.g.,* Japan, art. 6; Rev. Rul. 79-28, 1979-1 Cum. Bull. 457 (for purposes of the direct foreign tax credit, income of a US citizen residing in Japan from services performed within the US as a flight attendant on international flights of a Japanese airline was considered foreign source income by virtue of Article 6(6) of the Japan treaty; the source rules of the Treaty take precedence over the usual source rules of the Internal Revenue Code).
50. *See, e.g.,* 1981 US Model, art. 23.3.(a).

Model in Article 24.1 abandoned this principle and allows the credit "in accordance with the provisions and subject to the limitations" of US law. Thus while the source country may be allowed the right to tax an item of income under the treaty, the US is not obligated to give double tax relief when the item of income consists of US source income under domestic principles. Potential US treaty partners would be well advised to insist on credit relief in these circumstances.

Most modern treaty foreign tax credit articles take into account the fact that the US citizens resident in a treaty country are potentially subject to worldwide taxation in both countries. In effect, the US limits its primary tax claim to the amount it could have collected as a source jurisdiction if the recipient had not been a US citizen and allows the US citizen a foreign tax credit for any foreign tax imposed by the resident country (up to the amount of the US tax) even if the income arises in the US The treaty partner agrees to credit the "notional" US source tax. In effect, source jurisdiction is recognized as primary, residence-based personal jurisdiction as secondary and citizenship-based personal jurisdiction as tertiary.[51]

11.11   Nondiscrimination

US treaties typically contain a "nondiscrimination" article, albeit of varying scope. For example, Article 24.1 of the US Model provides: "Nationals of a Contracting State shall not be subjected in the other Contracting State to any taxation or any requirement connected therewith that is more burdensome than the taxation and connected requirements to which nationals of that other State in the same circumstances, particularly with respect to taxation on worldwide income, are or may be subjected." The qualifying language with respect to the circumstance of worldwide taxation in effect gives the US wide latitude in the taxation of nonresident aliens since they are, by definition, not subject to worldwide tax and thus are not in "similar circumstances" to US nationals who are. In addition, the US permanent establishment of an enterprise of the treaty partner may not be subjected to "less favorable" taxation than a US enterprise engaged in the same activity. Finally, US enterprises which are owned by residents of the treaty partner may not be subject to "more burdensome" taxation than that applicable to similar US-owned enterprises. The nondiscrimination clause applies to state and municipal taxes as well as to Federal taxes.

---

51. *See* US Model, art. 23. For example, suppose a US citizen resident in a treaty country receives 100 of dividend income from US sources. If the US tax rate is 36% and the foreign rate 25%, the US would be entitled to a "notional" 15% withholding tax under the treaty, thus collecting the first 15 of tax. The treaty partner would allow a credit for the notional 15 of tax against its 25 of tax otherwise due. The US would then credit the 10 of additional foreign tax due (despite the fact that it is imposed on US source income) and collect a residual tax of 11, reflecting the fact that the US rate exceeds the foreign rate. US Technical Explanation, art. 23. para. 3.

A number of nondiscrimination issues have been raised by recent US tax legislation. Under the 1980 FIRPTA legislation dealing with the taxation of US real estate investment by foreign persons (see 5.8.2.2), foreign corporations which disposed of US real property interests by means of dividend distributions or pursuant to a redemption or liquidation were subject to tax on the accrued gain in the property. Under the US rules in effect at the time the legislation was passed, US corporations would not have been subject to tax on comparable distributions. In an attempt to avoid treaty nondiscrimination problems, the statute provided that a foreign corporation could in certain circumstances elect to be treated as if it were a US corporation. This election meant that the gain realized by foreign shareholders on the disposition of the corporation's shares could be subject to US tax, but would have allowed the corporation to avoid the special provisions requiring recognition of gain at the corporate level.[52] Thus, arguably no treaty-prohibited discrimination was present since the foreign corporation could put itself in the position of a US corporation if it wished.

Another nondiscrimination issue has arisen in connection with subsidiary liquidations. Under the generally applicable Code rules, a US subsidiary which is liquidated into its parent corporation is not required to recognize gain on the distribution of appreciated assets in the liquidation.[53] However, a special rule requires the recognition of gain where the liquidating distribution is made to a foreign parent corporation.[54] The Internal Revenue Service initially took the position that the special rule requiring gain recognition where a foreign parent corporation was involved violated the treaty nondiscrimination provisions which prohibit "more burdensome" treatment of foreign-owned US corporations. Subsequently, however, the Service reversed itself and held that no treaty violation was involved based on the argument that a foreign-owned US subsidiary was not "similar" to a US-owned US subsidiary. The liquidating distribution to a foreign parent could remove the appreciated assets from the reach of the US taxing jurisdiction while in the US-owned situation the assets in the hands of the US parent would remain potentially subject to US tax. This difference in circumstances justified differing treatment for the two situations without any prohibited discrimination.[55]

A nondiscrimination issue is also involved in the application of the branch profits tax (see 5.5.5.3), which imposes a second "layer" of tax on the profits of the US branch of a foreign corporation. This additional tax can be viewed as "more burdensome" taxation imposed on the permanent establishment of a

---

52. Sec. 897(i).
53. Sec. 337.
54. Sec 367(e)(2).
55. Notice 87-5, 1987-1 Cum. Bull. 416, revoked in part by Notice 87-66, 1987-2 Cum. Bull. 376. This view is confirmed by the US Technical Explanation, art. 24. para. 4.

treaty corporation since a US corporation engaged in similar activity would not be subject to the tax.[56] Section 884(e)(1)(A) specifically recognized that the tax might conflict with treaty obligations and Regulations provided a list of the treaties which prohibit the imposition of the tax.[57] However, treaty protection is only available to foreign corporations which are not treaty shopping. (See 11.4.1.2.)

The US has a number of Treaties of Friendship, Commerce and Navigation ("FCN" treaties) containing nondiscrimination clauses which in the past have had application in the tax area.[58] However, the 1996 US Model in Article 1.3 goes to great length to make it clear that the Model Treaty is the exclusive source of relief for discrimination complaints in the matters which it covers. This would seem to displace FCN treaties as well as trade agreements, at which the provision is presumably aimed, from providing a basis for nondiscrimination claims under subsequent treaties based on the US Model.[59]

11.12 Administrative provisions

11.12.1 COMPETENT AUTHORITY PROVISIONS

US treaties contain a so-called "competent authority" provision which provides a mechanism whereby the taxpayer can insure that his rights under the treaty are respected by the countries involved. In order to invoke the competent authority provision, the taxpayer must in general establish that an action of one or both of the tax authorities of the contracting states has resulted or will result in double taxation contrary to the provisions of the treaty. In such a case, if the state agrees that the claim is worthy of consideration, the competent authority of the state endeavors to reach some agreement with the other country in order to avoid double taxation.

The most important function of the competent authority provision is to deal with the allocation of income between related taxpayers. The Internal Revenue Service has issued detailed guidelines as to how US taxpayers can invoke the competent authority procedure in such cases, including the question of the re-

---

56. The branch profits tax replaced the "second level" withholding tax on dividends distributed by a foreign corporation with US source income to its foreign shareholders. Since that tax was technically imposed on the shareholders, no treaty nondiscrimination issues were involved. Though the branch profits tax is in effect a substitute for the second level dividend tax, it is imposed on the foreign corporation itself and hence arguably involves a nondiscrimination question.
57. Treas. Reg. Sec.1.884-1(g)(3).
58. See Notice 88-1,1988-1 Cum. Bull. 471 dealing with the nondiscrimination clause of the US-Netherlands FCN treaty as it applies to foreign corporations making the election to be treated as US corporations for purposes of Sec. 897.
59. See US Technical Explanation, art. 1. paras. 14-16.

lation between the competent authority process and any ongoing audit or litigation proceedings.[60]

Some of the more recent treaties provide that the taxpayer may obtain relief under the competent authority provisions even where the statute of limitations or other procedural barriers would normally bar relief.[61]

11.12.2 EXCHANGE OF INFORMATION

The US generally obligates itself to exchange information with its treaty partner in order to carry out the provisions of the treaty or of domestic law concerning taxes covered in the treaty. The US routinely supplies its treaty partners with information returns concerning income qualifying for reduced rates of withholding tax in order to assist the treaty country to collect its residence-based tax. In addition, information may be provided at the request of a treaty partner or "spontaneously." The Code authorizes the US to disclose to a competent authority of a foreign government tax return information to the extent provided for in the treaty.[62] The exchange of information procedures can be used to obtain information which is solely necessary to assist the tax authorities of the treaty partner and which has no bearing on US tax liability.[63]

---

60. Rev.Proc. 96-13, 1996-1 Cum. Bull. 616. For a situation in which the taxpayer tried unsuccessfully to force a competent authority procedure prior to litigation of issues involved in the Tax Court, *see Yamaha Motor Corp v. United States*, 779 F. Supp. 610 (D.D.C. 1991).
61. US Model, art. 25.1.
62. Sec. 6103(k)(4).
63. *United States v. A. L. Burbank & Co. Ltd.*, 525 F.2d 9 (2d Cir. 1975).

Chapter 12
Wealth transfer taxation

12.1 The US wealth transfer tax system: general description

12.1.1 BACKGROUND

Prior to the Tax Reform Act of 1976, the US employed a dual wealth transfer tax system. One set of rates, rules, exemptions and exclusions applied to transfers during lifetime and were taxed under the gift tax; a separate set of rates, exemptions, and rules applied to transfers at death, and were taxed under the estate tax.

The Tax Reform Act of 1976 moved the US closer to a unified transfer tax. A single unified rate of tax was adopted to apply to transfers at death and during life. Thus, the rate of tax imposed on a transfer is not affected by whether the transfer is made at death or during life. In addition, a single unified tax credit was adopted in lieu of the prior double set of exemptions (one applicable to the gift tax and one applicable to the estate tax). Under this unified credit, a US individual may transfer wealth in the total amount of $600,000 (increasing to $1,000,000 by 2006 by virtue of the 1997 Act) free of tax. Although the exemption level and rates were thus unified in the 1976 Act, the estate and gift taxes were maintained as separate technical structures. And, in some important instances, the substantive rules do differ depending on whether the transfer is during life or at death.

A third transfer tax, the generation-skipping tax, is designed to insure that property transferred in a form to avoid tax in the next generation will be subject to a transfer tax that is structured to approximate the taxes that would have been paid had the property passed directly from generation to generation in the normal pattern. The generation-skipping tax is, in terms of its technical structure, a third wealth transfer tax.

12.1.2 THE ESTATE TAX

Section 2001 provides that a tax is imposed at progressive rates (from 18 to 55 per cent) on the transfer at death of the taxable estate of every citizen or resident of the US.[1] The taxable estate is equal to the gross estate less certain allowable deductions. The gross estate includes the value of all property interests owned by the decedent at the date of the death. Most typical of these are such items as bank accounts, real estate, and securities. The gross estate is not limited, however, to the value of assets which are physically in the decedent's actual or constructive possession. It includes the value of any interest in property which the decedent had at the time of death, such as a general power of appointment. In addition, there also is included in the gross estate the value of transfers made by the decedent during his lifetime which, under the Code, are treated as substitutes for testamentary dispositions (e.g. a transfer to a revocable trust). The gross estate therefore may exceed greatly the actual wealth which the decedent had in physical possession immediately before death.[2]

The permissible deductions from the gross estate include funeral and administration expenses, claims against the estate, and uncompensated casualty losses arising during the settlement of the estate.[3] A few special deductions from the gross estate are provided for non-tax policy reasons. Among these are deductions for transfers to or for charitable organizations.[4]

Generally, the transfer of property by a decedent to the surviving spouse is not taxed at the time of death by virtue of a "marital deduction." Instead, estate taxation is deferred until the death of the surviving spouse, at which time the then fair market value of all the property of the marital unit is subject to estate tax.[5] In effect, spouses are generally treated as a single tax unit for estate tax purposes.

Until 1988, the marital deduction was available to the estate of any US citizen or resident whether the surviving spouse was a US citizen or resident or a nonresident alien. Legislation in 1988 changed this pattern by denying the marital deduction to a decedent's estate if the surviving spouse is not a *citizen* of the US.[6] Thus, at the outset, no marital deduction is allowed even for transfers to a spouse who is a US *resident.* When the non-US citizen spouse dies and her estate is subject to US estate tax, then the tax paid by the first decedent spouse on property passing to her is allowed as a credit against her estate tax. The credit is not, however, refundable and thus can do no more than reduce her estate tax liabilities to zero. The harshness of the deduction denial is mitigated

---

1. Sec. 2001(c). The benefit of the rate brackets below 50 or 55 per cent (including the zero bracket created by the unified credit) is phased out for estates between $10 million and $21,040,000, so that a flat 55 per cent tax is imposed on estates above that amount. In the phase out range, the marginal tax rate is 60 per cent.
2. Items included in the gross estate are defined in Sec. 2033-2044.
3. Sec. 2053-2054.
4. Sec. 2055.
5. Sec. 2056, 2044.
6. Sec. 2056(d).

somewhat if the property passing to the non-US citizen surviving spouse is placed in a "qualified domestic trust." Where such a trust is employed, the estate of the decedent spouse is allowed a marital deduction under the normal rules. Any distribution of principal from the trust during the life of the surviving spouse triggers an estate tax (unless the distribution is made on account of hardship of the surviving spouse) and the balance in the trust is subject to estate tax upon the death of that spouse. The tax is imposed on the trustee, but is "treated as" a tax paid with respect to the estate of the first decedent spouse. The amount of the tax is that which would have been imposed on the first decedent spouse's estate if the property had been subject to tax therein.[7] The estate of the surviving spouse is entitled to a credit for the taxes paid by the trust.[8]

After the taxable estate has been thus determined, a tentative estate tax is computed by applying the tax rates set forth in Section 2001 to the sum of the taxable estate plus the adjusted taxable gifts of the decedent (that is, taxable gifts made by the decedent after 31 December 1976 minus any gifts which are included in the estate of the decedent) and subtracting from this amount the gift tax payable on account of the decedent's gifts made after 1976. As a result of this computation, the marginal estate tax rate is determined by the amount of lifetime gifts made by the decedent, thus insuring that, in general, lifetime and deathtime transfers are taxed in a unified fashion.

The final estate tax payable is then determined by subtracting from the tentative estate tax the credits against tax which include (1) a unified credit against the estate tax, equal to $192,800, (increasing to the credit necessary to eliminate tax on estates up to $1 million by 2006); (2) a credit for certain state death taxes; (3) a credit for foreign death taxes; (4) a credit for certain transfer taxes paid on prior transfers of property; and (5) a credit for gift taxes paid with respect to property transferred prior to 1977 and included in the gross estate.[9] The subtraction of these tax credits from the tentative estate tax constitutes the final step in the determination of the estate tax payable.

---

7. Sec. 2056A. A qualified domestic trust (a "QDOT" in US tax jargon) is one under which (1) at least one trustee is either a US citizen or domestic corporation (who is *personally liable* for any tax imposed),(2) the trust complies with such Regulations as may be promulgated, and (3) the executor of the estate of the decedent spouse makes an irrevocable election that the trust is to be such a trust.

8. The purpose of the provision is obviously to prevent a US decedent from transferring property to the surviving spouse free of US tax and then have the surviving spouse remove the property from US taxing jurisdiction so that the property can be transferred free of US tax at his or her death. The approach adopted in Section 2056A, however, produces different, and not readily defensible, patterns among spouses whose nationality, residence and reasons for transferring property from the US vary. The US may modify the QDOT rules by treaty. *See, e.g.*, Art. XXIXB of the U.S.-Canada Treaty. Even though Sec. 2107, discussed at 12.6, deals directly with the expatriation situation, Sec. 2056(d) was retained when Congress expanded the reach of Sec. 2107 in 1996.

9. Sec. 2010-2016.

12.1.3   THE GIFT TAX

The tax on any gift made by a donor is determined by adding the amount of the taxable gift to prior taxable gifts and imposing the same progressive tax rates as those applicable to transfers at death under the estate tax.

The tax base for the gift tax is "taxable gifts." This term means the total gifts made during the calendar year minus allowable exclusions and deductions. The allocable exclusions and deductions include (1) a $10,000 per donee annual exclusion (inflation adjusted after 1998); (2) a deduction for charitable contributions; (3) a marital deduction for gifts between spouses (subject to the limitations discussed in 12.1.2 where the donee spouse is not a US citizen but with a $100,000 annual exclusion allowable); and (4) an exclusion for gifts made by married persons to third parties that in effect splits the gifts between the spouses.

The gift tax is then computed by applying the unified transfer tax rates to the taxable gifts. The unified transfer tax credit applicable to the estate tax is applied to the gift tax due. To the extent the unified transfer tax credit is utilized by a donor during lifetime, it is in effect reduced for purposes of computing the estate tax.[10]

12.1.4   THE GENERATION-SKIPPING TAX

A tax is imposed on certain generation-skipping transfers which otherwise are subject neither to estate nor gift tax in the skipped generation.[11] Thus, a transfer in trust from A to B (A's child) for life, remainder to C (A's grandchild) is not subject to estate tax in B's estate upon B's death (because B has no transferable interest at death). However, the generation-skipping tax would apply to impose a tax on the property received by C at B's death. The generation-skipping tax rate is a flat rate equal to the highest marginal estate tax rate (55%). The amount of tax approximates the amount which would have been payable had the property subject to the tax passed outright from A to B to C (with B having the power to transfer the property at death).

In very general terms, the generation-skipping tax is imposed on any generation-skipping transfer, more technically a "taxable distribution", a "taxable termination" or a "direct skip." A generation-skipping transfer is the transfer of property outright or of an interest which gives the transferee a present right to the income or principal of a trust and which is made to a person who is in a generation that is two or more generations below that of the transferor (a "skip per-

---

10. Sec. 2501-2524.
11. The generation-skipping tax rules are contained in Sec. 2601-2663.

son"). A *taxable distribution* results upon the distribution of property from a trust to a skip person. A *taxable termination* occurs at the time a present interest in a trust is held by a skip person and no non-skip person (e.g. a child of the transferor) is a beneficiary. A *direct skip is* a transfer to a skip person.

The following examples illustrate the above situations:

(1) A transfers property in trust to B (his child) for life, with the power in the trustee to make discretionary distributions of income and principal to any of B's children. A taxable distribution occurs upon any distribution of income or principal to a child of B and the generation-skipping tax is imposed. The amount of the distribution is the *taxable amount* and the tax must be paid by the distributee.

(2) Upon the death of B in the Example (1), a taxable termination occurs and a generation-skipping tax is imposed. The taxable amount is the value of the property in the trust and the trustee must pay the tax.

(3) A transfers property either outright or to a trust for the benefit of C (B's child). Either transfer is a direct skip and a generation-skipping tax is imposed. The taxable amount is the value of the property transferred and the tax is payable either by A or by the trustee.

It should be kept in mind that in each of the above examples A incurred a gift or an estate tax at the time of A's transfer; the generation-skipping tax is in addition to those transfer taxes.

A generation-skipping tax exemption of $1 million (inflation adjusted after 1998) is allowed to each individual, which can be allocated among transfers as the transferor determines.

The generation-skipping tax rate is the *maximum* federal estate tax rate in effect at the time of the transfer. This rate, in effect, is applied to the taxable amount less the portion of the $1 million exclusion allocated to the transfer. Thus, if A makes a generation-skipping transfer of $3 million and allocates his entire $1 million exemption to the transfer, a 36 2/3 per cent tax rate is applied to the $3 million transfer, and a tax of $1,099,980 is due.[12] Had none of the $1 million exemption been allocated to the transfer, a generation-skipping tax of $1,650,00 (55% $\times$ $3,000,000) would have been incurred.

Rules are provided which are necessary to integrate the generation-skipping tax with the estate and gift taxes.

---

12. More technically, the maximum Federal estate tax rate is multiplied by the "inclusion ratio," which is equal to one minus a fraction, the numerator of which is the amount of the exemption allocated to the transfer and the denominator of which is the value of the property transferred. In the text example, the fraction is one-third, the inclusion ratio is two-thirds, and a 36 2/3 per cent tax rate (two-thirds of 55%) is thus applied to the $3 million transfer.

12.2 Jurisdictional principles

As in the case of the income tax, the US tax jurisdiction with respect to transfers at death or by gift is likewise global in reach for its citizens and residents.[13] Thus, under Section 2031, the value of the gross estate is determined by including the value of all property owned by the decedent "wherever situated." Likewise, the gift tax applies to all lifetime donative transfers by US citizens or residents regardless of where the property is located. The same is true of the generation-skipping tax. International double taxation is alleviated through the mechanism of the foreign tax credit and/or by death tax conventions.

Special rules are provided for nonresident aliens. As in the case of the income tax, the scope of the US jurisdiction is determined on a geographical basis. Thus, the estate tax, the gift tax, and the generation-skipping tax in general apply to nonresident aliens only with respect to property which is "situated within the United States."[14] The same rates of tax are imposed on transfers by nonresidents as are applied to estates of US decedents.

The US has also entered into a relatively few bilateral tax treaties governing wealth transfer taxation. And, as in the case of the income tax, certain special provisions are included to prevent avoidance of US wealth transfer taxes.

12.3 Estate tax: international aspects

12.3.1 SITUS RULES

The "situs" rules developed to apply the estate tax in an international context perform a function similar to the "source of income" rules in the income tax (discussed in Chapter 4). Whether property is "situated" within the US or in a foreign country determines the amount of the allowable foreign tax credit for US citizens and resident aliens and for non-resident aliens whether the US estate tax will apply at all. The estate tax statutory provisions and Regulations follow the approach of the income tax rules by specifying the circumstances when particular types of property will be situated within or without the US. The level of detail is, however, much less than in the income tax. In each case, the situs rule may be modified by treaty.

---

13. For estate tax purposes, an alien generally is treated as a US resident if his "domicile" is in the US. Treas. Reg. Sec. 20.0-1(b)(1)-(2). The determination of domicile is a factual one, depending in part on whether the decedent had an intention to remain in the US. *See,* e.g. Rev. Rul. 80-209, 1980-2 Cum. Bull. 248. The income tax rules for determining residence, contained in Sec. 7701(b)(5.4.2.) are not applicable for estate tax purposes.
14. Sec. 2106.

12.3.1.1 Property situated within the US

The following property is considered situated within the US
  (1) real estate located in the US;[15]
  (2) tangible personal property located in the US[16] (except for certain works of art as noted in 12.3.1.2);
  (3) shares of stock issued by a corporation organized under the laws of the US;[17]
  (4) transfers of property (a) within three years of death (Section 2035), (b) in which the transferor retained an interest for life (Section 2036), (c) taking effect at death (Section 2037), or (d) which were revocable by the transferor (Section 2038), if the property was situated in the US either at the time of the original transfer or at the decedent's death,[18]
  (5) debt obligations issued by a US "person"[19] or by the US government or a state or local government (except as noted in 12.3.1.2);[20]
  (6) certain deposits with a US branch of a foreign corporation if the branch is engaged in the commercial banking business.[21]

12.3.1.2 Property situated outside the US

The following property is considered situated without the US:
  (1) real estate located outside the US;[22]
  (2) tangible personal property located outside the US;[23]
  (3) works of art owned by a nonresident alien that are at the time of death on loan or exhibition in the US;[24]
  (4) shares of stock in a corporation organized and incorporated under the laws of a foreign country;[25]
  (5) proceeds of insurance on the life of a nonresident alien;[26]

---

15. Treas. Reg. Sec. 20.2104-1(a)(1).
16. Treas. Reg. Sec. 20.2104-1(a)(2).
17. Sec. 2104(a). As a result of this rule, foreign portfolio investors usually employ a foreign corporation as their investment vehicle.
18. Sec. 2104(b). *See Estate of Swan v. Commissioner*, 247 F.2d 144 (2d Cir. 1957) (revocable inter vivos trust property was situated within the US where cash and securities were deposited with New York trust companies).
19. A "person" includes an individual, a trust, estate, partnership, association, company, or corporation. Sec. 7701(a)(1).
20. Sec. 2104(c).
21. Sec. 2104(c).
22. Treas. Reg. Sec. 20.2105-1(a)(1).
23. Treas. Reg. Sec. 20.2105-1(a)(2).
24. Sec. 2105(c).
25. Treas. Reg. Sec. 20.2105-1(f).
26. Sec. 2105(a).

(6) debt obligations issued by a US corporation and deposits with a US bank if the interest thereon would be treated as foreign source income to the nonresident alien holder of the obligation under Section 861(a)(1)(A), (C), or (D) (discussed in 4.2.1) or was exempt from tax under Section 871 (h) or (i) (discussed in 4.2.1 and 5.4.5);[27]
(7) deposits with a foreign branch of a US commercial bank.[28]

12.3.2 US TAXATION OF CITIZENS AND RESIDENT ALIENS: THE FOREIGN TAX CREDIT

US citizens and resident aliens who die owning property situated in another country are subject to full US estate taxation under the rules and at the rates described in 12.3.1 and 12.1.

The estates of US citizens and resident aliens are allowed a foreign tax credit for "estate, inheritance, legacy, or succession" taxes actually paid to a foreign country with respect to property situated within that country.[29] The rules discussed in 12.3.1 are applied to determine the country in which property is situated. Thus, for example, stock of a corporation is situated only in the foreign country in which the corporation is incorporated.[30]

As in the case of the income tax, the allowable foreign tax credit for estate tax purposes is subject to limitations. The maximum credit is the smaller of:
1. The foreign country's death taxes actually imposed on property in the foreign country which is included in the decedent's US computed gross estate (the so-called "first limitation").
2. The portion of the US estate tax attributable to property which is located in the foreign country, subject to death taxes therein, and included in the decedent's US computed gross estate (the so-called "second limitation").[31]

The limitations operate to provide a full credit for foreign death taxes where the effective foreign tax rate is lower than that imposed by the US, but the allowable credit cannot exceed the tax that the US would have imposed on the foreign property.

The "first limitation" is computed by applying a fraction to the foreign coun-

---

27. Sec. 2104(c); 2105(b)(1), (3).
28. Sec. 2105(b)(2).
29. Sec. 2014(a). The foreign tax must be a "transfer tax." Thus, the Canadian tax imposed on transfers of appreciated property at death is part of Canada's income tax and is not creditable under Section 2014 (although a deduction is allowed for the tax as a claim against the estate). *Estate of Ballard v. Commissioner,* 85 TC 300 (1985). Art. XXIXB of the Canada Tax Treaty, however, provides a credit against US wealth transfer taxes for the Canadian income tax.
30. Treas. Reg. Sec. 20.2014-1(a)(3).
31. Sec. 2014(b).

try's death taxes. The numerator of the fraction is the value of the property which is subject to the foreign country's death taxes and which is included in the decedent's US computed gross estate. The denominator of the fraction is the value of all the decedent's property subject to the foreign country's death taxes. "Value" is determined under the foreign country's death tax rules and then converted to US dollars.[32]

The "second limitation" is computed by applying a fraction to the US federal estate tax liability of the decedent. The numerator of the fraction is the "adjusted value" of the decedent's property that is situated within a foreign country, subject to death taxes therein, and included in the decedent's US computed gross estate. The denominator of the fraction is the value of the decedent's entire gross estate minus any allowable charitable contributions deduction and marital deduction. The term "adjusted value" refers to the value of the decedent's gross estate minus any charitable contributions deduction or marital deduction allowable with respect to, and allocated to, the foreign property.[33]

As in the case of the income tax, the foreign tax credit is in general allowed to resident aliens.[34]

12.3.3   US TAXATION OF NONRESIDENT ALIENS

The US estate tax imposed on the transfer of property by a nonresident alien begins with a determination of the value of that part of the decedent's gross estate[35] which, under the rules described in 12.3.1, at the time of death is situated within the US.[36]

From the gross estate situated within the US are subtracted the portion of debts, expenses of administration, claims against the estate, mortgages, funeral expenses, and losses suffered by the estate that is allocable to the US. A deduction for transfers to qualifying charitable organizations is also allowed.[37] The estate of a nonresident alien is allowed a full marital deduction to the extent property situated in the US passes to a surviving spouse *who is a US citi-*

---

32. Treas. Reg. Sec. 20.2014-2.
33. Treas. Reg. Sec. 20.2014-3.
34. *See* Sec. 2014(h).
35. Under Sec. 2031 the gross estate includes the value of "all property, real or personal, tangible or intangible, wherever situated."
36. Sec. 2103.
37. Sec. 2106(a)(1) and (2). In general, the deductions are allowed in the proportion that the US assets bear to the decedent's worldwide assets. The deductions are available only if the US estate tax return discloses that part of the decedent's gross estate which is located outside the US. In general, a deduction is granted only for contributions to charitable organizations that are organized and operated in the US for prescribed charitable purposes such as education, religion, and scientific research.

zen.[38] The result of the subtraction of these items from the gross estate is the taxable estate.

The unified transfer tax rates applicable to US decedents are then applied to the sum of the taxable estate and the "adjusted taxable gifts" (i.e. taxable gifts made by the decedent after 31 December 1976).[39] This "tentative" tax is then reduced by a hypothetical tax calculated on the basis of the unified transfer tax rates applied to the adjusted taxable gifts. In effect, the amounts subject to tax in the estate are treated as coming "on top of" the adjusted taxable gifts for purposes of determining the rate of progression. The tax thus determined is then reduced by three credits against tax:

(1) the credit for death taxes paid to a State government;

(2) the credit for gift taxes paid on gifts made prior to 1977; and

(3) the credit for estate tax paid by another transferor with respect to property included in the decedent's estate where the prior transferor died within ten years before or two years after the decedent.[40]

Finally, the estate is allowed a unified transfer tax credit in the amount of $13,000 (the equivalent of an estate tax exemption of $60,000).[41]

12.4 Gift tax: international aspects

12.4.1 Gift taxation of US citizens and resident aliens

The US gift tax is a cumulative tax imposed annually on all transfers "in trust or otherwise, whether the gift is direct or indirect, and whether the property is real or personal, tangible or intangible." For US citizens and resident aliens, the tax is imposed on all transfers wherever the property is situated under the rules described in 12.3.1. No marital deduction is allowed for a gift to a spouse who is not a US citizen. But a $100,000 annual exclusion for gifts of present interests (rather than $10,000) is available for gifts to such spouses.[42] No statutory foreign tax credit is allowed for transfers of property located abroad even though the transfers are subject to gift tax by a foreign country.

---

38. Sec. 2106(a)(3). Prior to the 1988 legislation, special lower rates had applied to estates of non-resident aliens but no marital deduction was allowed.

39. Sec. 2101(b).

40. Sec. 2101(a) and (b).

41. Sec. 2102(c)(1). When required by treaty, the estate of a nonresident alien is allowed the full US unified credit under Section 2010 multiplied by the proportion of the decedent's worldwide estate that is situated in the US. Sec. 2102(c)(3). *See* Art. XXIXB of the Canada Tax Treaty. In addition, the Treaty with Canada exempts from US transfer taxes, US estates of Canadian residents which have a value of $1.2 million or less.

42. Sec. 2501(a)(1), 2511(a), 2523(i).

12.4.2   GIFT TAXATION OF NONRESIDENT ALIENS

The US imposes a gift tax on transfers by nonresidents who are not US citizens only if the subject of the gift is real property or tangible personal property physically situated in the US; gifts of intangible property are therefore not subject to tax.[43] If a taxable gift is made, the full US unified transfer tax rates apply. Gifts by nonresident aliens qualify for the $10,000 annual per donee exclusion but not for the marital deduction or the unified transfer tax credit.[44] A deduction for charitable contributions is available if, in general, the transfer is to a US organization that will use the gifted funds in the US.[45]

The above rules apply irrespective of whether the donor is engaged in business in the US.

12.5   The generation-skipping tax: international aspects

As discussed in 12.1.4, the US imposes a tax on certain generation-skipping transfers. Treasury Regulations apply the generation-skipping tax to nonresident aliens only if a US gift or estate tax is imposed on the transfer. For example, if a nonresident grandparent makes a gift of US real estate to a nonresident grandchild, the property is subject both to US gift and generation-skipping transfers. But if the property transferred were cash or securities, no US gift tax would be incurred and hence no generation-skipping tax either.[46]

12.6   Expatriation to avoid transfer taxes

12.6.1   ESTATE TAX

If a decedent lost her US citizenship within ten years of death and if avoidance of US estate, gift or income taxes was a principal purpose therefore, the full US estate tax rates apply to the transfer of property situated within the US. Corresponding to the changes made in 1996 to the expatriation income tax rules under Section 2107(a)(2) an expatriate decedent is deemed to have the requisite tax avoidance purpose if the tests of Section 877(a)(2) are met (See 5.4.7).

---

43. Sec. 2501(a)(2); Treas. Reg. Sec. 25.2511-3(a)(1), (b)(1).
44. Sec. 2503(b), 2523(a), 2505.
45. Sec. 2522(b).
46. Sec. 2663(2); Treas. Reg. Sec. 26.2663-2.

A unified transfer tax credit of $13,000 is allowed against the tax so computed (the equivalent of a $60,000 exemption).[47]

The tax is imposed on the taxable estate computed in the manner described in 12.1. However, a special rule requires the inclusion in the gross estate of a portion of the value of the stock owned by the decedent in a foreign corporation if (1) the decedent owned directly ten per cent or more of the voting power of all classes of stock of the foreign corporations and (2) the decedent owned directly and by attribution more than 50 per cent of the voting power of all classes of stock of the foreign corporation. The amount includible in the decedent's US gross estate is determined by applying to the fair market value of the stock owned outright by the decedent a fraction, the numerator of which is the fair market value of the corporation's assets in the US and the denominator of which is the total fair market value of the corporation's entire assets.[48] A proportionate foreign tax credit is then granted if another country also imposes a tax on the property included in the US gross estate by reason of the foregoing rules.[49]

The burden of proving the lack of a principal tax avoidance purpose is on the estate once the Government establishes that it is "reasonable to believe" that the loss of citizenship would result in a substantial reduction in transfer taxes (including the transfer taxes imposed by the US and by other countries).[50]

12.6.2   GIFT TAX

The exemption of intangible property from US gift taxation is removed for nonresident aliens who lost their US citizenship after 8 March 1965 and within ten years of the gift if the loss of citizenship had as one of its principal purposes the avoidance of US gift, estate or income taxes. Again, the requisite tax avoidance purpose is deemed to exist if the tests of Section 877(a)(2) are met(5.4.7). Contrary to the normal US rule, a foreign tax credit is allowed for any foreign taxes imposed on gifts that are subject to US tax under the expatriation rule.[51]

For purposes of this rule, special situs rules are provided for intangible property. The following property is considered situated in the US and hence subject to gift tax:

(1)   shares of stock in a US corporation;

(2)   debt obligations of a US person, including bank deposits;

---

47. Sec. 2107(a), (c)(1).
48. Sec. 2107(b). In determining the value of the stock of the foreign corporation, no reduction is allowed for corporate liabilities. Treas. Reg. Sec. 20.2107-1(b)(1)(ii)(a). The rules of Sec. 957, discussed in 7.2.3, are applied to determine if the requisite "voting power" exists.
49. Sec. 2107(c)(2).
50. Sec. 2107(d).
51. Sec. 2501(a)(3).

(3) debt obligations of the US or a state or local government;

(4) intangible property of any type issued by or enforceable against a US resident or corporation.

These special rules apply regardless of where the stock or written evidence of the property or obligation is located.[52]

12.7   Wealth transfer tax treaties

12.7.1   BACKGROUND

The US network of wealth transfer treaties is substantially smaller than its income tax treaty network. Double taxation in the estate tax area can arise either because both countries claim the decedent as a domiciliary, and thus taxable on his worldwide estate, or because the decedent was domiciled in one country while holding property with a situs in the second country. The US estate tax treaties in general deal with these problems by agreeing on rules to determine a single domicile, by providing rules with respect to which country may tax transfers of particular types of property, and by granting a credit for foreign death taxes paid in certain situations. Since the US unilaterally grants a foreign tax credit for death taxes paid by those estates subject to its worldwide estate tax jurisdiction, the primary function of the estate tax treaties for these taxpayers is to ensure that the credit mechanism functions properly. For other taxpayers, the change in the domiciliary or situs rules may either eliminate assets from the reach of US estate taxation or may qualify the US tax paid on those assets for a credit in the foreign country. In any event, both classes of taxpayers are generally protected by an article which provides that the provisions of the treaty shall not be construed so as to increase the tax imposed by either country.[53]

US treaties generally apply only to the federal estate tax and do not cover state inheritance taxes. The US gift and generation-skipping taxes are covered only by a limited number of treaties.[54]

The estate tax treaties contain provisions for non-discrimination, competent authority procedures and exchange of information which are parallel to those found in the income tax treaties.[55]

---

52. Sec. 2511(b); Treas. Reg. Sec. 25.2511-3(b).
53. *See, e.g.,* the US Model Estate, Gift and Generation-Skipping Tax Convention of 20 November 1980 ("US Model Treaty"), Article 1.1. Since the Model Treaty forms the basis of US tax treaty negotiation, the following discussion is in general based on that Treaty.
54. *See, e.g.,* Sweden Estate Gift and Tax Treaty.
55. *See* US Model Treaty, Articles 10-12.

12.7.2 DOMICILE

Under the US Model Treaty, domicile is determined as an initial matter under the domestic law of each country. An individual is domiciled in the US if he is a citizen or "resident" of the US.[56] The Model Treaty then employs a "tie-breaker" rule to establish a single residence for wealth transfer tax purposes.[57] An overriding proviso is, however, included: A citizen of one country who is domiciled in both by reason of residence is ultimately treated as domiciled in the country of citizenship if he had been resident in the other country for less than seven of the preceding ten years.[58] Under the "saving clause," the US retains the right to tax its citizens on a worldwide basis, although special rules apply to avoid double taxation (see 12.7.5).

12.7.3 RULES FOR TAXATION

In the older US estate and gift tax treaties, specific rules were adopted as to the situs of particular types of property. In the US Model Treaty and newer US tax treaties, situs provisions are replaced by rules for determining which of the treaty countries has primary or exclusive jurisdiction to tax the transfer of particular types of property.

12.7.3.1 Real property

Under Article 5 of the US Model Treaty, the transfer by a domiciliary of one country (for simplicity, hereafter referred to as the US) of real property located in the other country may be taxed in that other country (for simplicity, hereafter referred to as Country X). Thus, Country X may tax the transfer by a US citizen of real property located in Country X. The US will also tax the transfer, but give a credit for the Country X tax.[59]

12.7.3.2 Business property

Under Article 6 of the US Model Treaty, a transfer by a US citizen of assets formerly part of the business property of a permanent establishment situated in Country X may be taxed in Country X. Again, Country X has a primary but not exclusive right to tax the transfer. A similar rule applies to transfers of assets

---

56. US Model Treaty, Article 4.1.
57. US Model Treaty, Article 4.2.
58. *Id.,* Article 4.3. This provision prevents temporary moves by citizens of one country from creating unlimited wealth transfer tax liability in the country of temporary residence.
59. US Model Treaty, Articles 5.1 and 9.

pertaining to a fixed base used for the performance of independent personal services.[60]

12.7.3.3   Other property

Transfer by a US domiciliary of other property may be taxed *only* by the US, regardless of the nature or location of the property. Exclusive taxing jurisdiction is likewise given to Country X as to its domiciliaries.[61] This provision, for example, surrenders the right of the US to tax transfers of stock in US corporations by a domiciliary of Country X. Special rules are provided for transfers of interests in partnerships and trusts.[62]

12.7.4   DEDUCTIONS AND EXEMPTIONS

Article 8 of the US Model Treaty provides a deduction for the "debts"[63] of an estate in a ratio of the value of the property subject to tax in the taxing country to the total value of all property of the decedent wherever situated. Provision is also made for a charitable contributions deduction.[64]

The provisions in the 1980 US Model Treaty regarding the marital deduction and the unified transfer tax credit have been superseded by subsequent legislation.

12.7.5   RELIEF FROM DOUBLE TAXATION

Article 9 of the US Model Treaty establishes reciprocal obligations on the treaty partners to avoid double taxation by means of a foreign tax credit where one of the countries has a primary but not exclusive right to tax a transfer under Article 5 or 6 of the Treaty.

Article 9.6 of the US Model Treaty limits the credit allowed to the portion of the tax imposed on the property with respect to which the credit is allowable. This allocation prevents the credit for one country's tax from offsetting the

---

60. *Id.*, Article 6.1. The term "permanent establishment" is defined in a manner similar to the definition in the US Model Income Tax Treaty, *see* 11.5.2. There is no definition of "fixed base."
61. *Id.*, Article 7.1. The US still retains the right to tax its citizens, although domiciled in another jurisdiction, on a worldwide basis but gives a foreign tax credit for the tax imposed by the treaty partner on all assets except those with respect to which the US retains primary taxing jurisdiction. Article 9.1(b). This provision allows a credit for tax imposed on assets which under the Code rules, would be situated in the US. *See* 12.7.5.
62. *Id.*, Article 7.2.
63. The US interprets the term "debts" to include all items deductible under Sec. 2053-2054 of the Internal Revenue Code. Accordingly, the Treaty provision simply conforms to US domestic law.
64. By virtue of the override provision in US Model Treaty, Article 1.3, the provision is relevant only when the US is taxing on a situs basis.

other country's tax on property as to which the other country has sole taxing jurisdiction under the Treaty. Thus, suppose a US citizen who is a Country X domiciliary transfers US real estate (Article 5) plus other business assets not associated with a US permanent establishment (Article 7). While the US will initially assert jurisdiction to tax all assets on the basis of citizenship, it must allow a credit for the Country X tax on the other business assets; Country X must allow a credit for the portion of its tax attributable to the transfer of the US real estate.

Treasury Regulations specifically state that where the credit for foreign death taxes provided under an estate tax treaty is more favorable than the Code credit under Section 2014, the estate may elect to apply the treaty credit.[65]

---

65. Treas. Reg. Sec. 20.2014-4(a)(1).

Index

215